BOOK OF RAMADOSH
13 Anunnaki-Ulema Mind Power Techniques To Live Longer, Happier, Healthier, Wealthier
Paranormal, alien life, occult, extraterrestrials, UFO, supernatural, PSI, ESP, multiple dimensions
Book 1

Notes from the Publishers and the Editorial Board:

Two new books by Maximillien de Lafayette are published each month. They are reproduced from his writings and work for the past fifty years. To learn about all his current and forthcoming books, please check regularly:

1-www.amazon.com
2-www.anunnakibooks.com
3-www.extraterrestrialsandanunnaki.com
4-www.ufozetareticuli.com
5-www.maximilliendelafayettebibliography.com
6-www.zetareticulibooks.com

The author can be reached through his senior editor Carol Lexter at carollexter@aol.com

⌘ NOTA BENE ⌘

- To avoid all sorts of troubles and psychological confusion (s), all topics discussed in this book were approached from a philosophical-metaphysical-esoteric angle.
- Bear in mind that the Ulema's teachings and/or opinions should not be considered as a professional advice at any level – therapeutic, medical, psychological, mental health, etc. – thus avoiding any conflict with professional licensing bodies and legal practitioners in these fields;
- They are of a purely philosophical-esoteric nature.
- The Kira'ats (Readings) were given by the Ulema in Asia, and the Near/Middle East within a confined milieu of seekers of metaphysical and esoteric knowledge.
- Many of the texts as published in this book are excerpts from their Kira'ats and Rou'ya (Visions) that first appeared centuries ago, and continue to enlighten many of us.
- You enter their world at your own risk.

To Rabbi Mordachai ,
Cheik Al Huseini,
Monsignor Maroun,
and Master Li,
You will always be
In my heart

The Book of Ramadosh (Rama-Dosh) Series:

1-Book One: Book of Ramadosh.13 Anunnaki-Ulema Mind Power Techniques To Live Longer, Happier, Healthier, Wealthier

2-Book Two: The Anunnaki Ulema Forbidden Knowledge. What Your Government and Your Church Didn't Want you to Know.

3-Book Three: The Anunnaki Ulema Extraterrestrial Book of Rama-Dosh. UFOs and the Alien Rapture. The Anunnaki Creation of a New Human Race after 2022

Book I. Date of Publication: November 10, 2008
Book II. Date of Publication: December 10, 2008
Book II. Date of Publication: January 10, 2009

Publishers' Note: The author can be reached at delafayette@internationalnewsagency.org (London)
Senior Editor, Carol Lexter can be reached at carollexter@aol.com

***   ***   ***

BOOK OF RAMADOSH

13 Anunnaki-Ulema Mind Power Techniques To
Live Longer, Happier, Healthier, Wealthier

Book 1

**Paranormal, alien life, occult, extraterrestrials,
UFO, Supernatural, PSI, ESP, multiple dimensions.**

Maximillien de Lafayette

Author of
Anunnaki Encyclopedia.

And

Thesaurus-Dictionary of Sumerian, Anunnaki, Hittite,
Babylonian, Akkadian, Assyrian, Phoenician, Aramaic,
Anatolian, Mesopotamian, Chaldean, Arabic, Syriac,
Hebrew, Ulema, Extraterrestrial languages & civilizations
(11 Volumes)

Translated from de Lafayette's original manuscripts in
German and French by
CAROL LEXTER

A PUBLICATION OF TIMES SQUARE PRESS AND ELITE ASSOCIATES
NEW YORK CALIFORNIA LONDON PARIS TOKYO

PUBLISHED AND DISTRIBUTED BY

AMAZON.COM COMPANY

*** *** ***

2008

Covers Design and Pages Layout-Maquette: Maximillien de Lafayette. Senior Editor: Carol Lexter. Photos' and Graphics' Templates: Robert Howard. Art Production: Solange Berthier and Fabiola Rossi. Pagination: Joy Elliot. Series Editor: Shoshanna Rosenstein. Media: Germaine Poitiers. Series Art Director/Producer: Patrique Dreyfus. Montage and Photoshop: Daniel Iliescu.

Copyright ©2008 by Ilil Arbel and Maximillien de Lafayette. All rights reserved. No part of this book may be used or reproduced by any means, graphic, electronic, or mechanical, including photocopying, recording, taping or by any information storage retrieval system without the written permission of the author except in the case of brief quotations embodied in critical articles and reviews. Date of Publication: November 10, 2008

*** *** ***

Table of Contents

Dedication and gratitude...15
Meet the author...16
Books by Maximillien de Lafayette...17

Introduction...33

Glossary of Anunnaki-Ulema terms...35
Aamala...35
Abgaru...35
Afik-r'-Tanawar...36
Anšekadu-ra abra...37
An-zalubirach...40
Araya...40
Balu-ram-haba...43
Dab'Laa...46
Eido-Rah...47
Ezakarerdi...48
Ezakarfalki...49
Ezbahaiim-erdi...51
Ezeridim...51
Ezrai-il...51
F "ف"...51
Fadi-ya-ashadi...52
Fana.Ri...54
Fik'r...56
Fikrama...60
Ghen-ardi-vardeh...63
Gensi-uzuru...67
Gilgoolim...69
Godumu...69
Goduri...69
Golem...69
Golibu...72
Golim...72

7

Golimu...73
Goirim-dari...73
Goirim-daru...73
Gudinh...73
H...73
Habru...73
Hadiiya...73
Hag-Addar...73
Halida...74
Hama-dar...74

PART 1: TECHNIQUES

- **Technique/Lesson 1:...75**
Godabaari "Gudi-Ha-abri"
Technique/practice aimed at developing a faculty capable of
making objects move at distance by using your mind.
I-Developing the Conduit...77
II-Moving objects by using mental powers...78
III-Preparations...78
IV-Precautions during practice...79
V-The technique...79
VI-Closing the energy...81

- **Technique/Lesson 2:..83**
Gomari "Gumaridu"
I-The exercise...85
II-The equipment...86
III-The technique...86
IV-Closing the energy center...90

- **Technique/Lesson 3:..91**
Gomatirach-minzari "Gomu- minzaar"
The Minzar technique: Known as the "Mirror to Alternate
Realities"
Creating your own world...93
The Minzar technique...96
I-Prerequisites...96

II-Precautions...96
III-Equipment and supplies...97
IV-Building the Minzar...98
V-Contacting the alternate realities...100
VI-Subsequent visits to the alternate realities...103
VII-Benefits and advantages...104
VIII-Returning to your regular reality on earth...105

• **Technique/Lesson 4:..107**
Gubada-Ari
How to find the healthiest spots and luckiest areas on earth, including private places and countries, and take advantage of this.
The Triangle of Life technique...109
I-Synopsis of the theory...109
II-Materials...110
III-The technique...111
Ulema Mordechai and Germain Lumiere dialogue...114

• **Technique/Lesson 5:..119**
Cadari-Rou'yaa
The technique that develop the faculty of reading others' thoughts, intentions, and feelings. Cadari-Rou'yaa is also a method to diagnose health, and prevent health problems from occurring in the present, and in the future.
The technique...121

• **Technique/Lesson 6...127**
Chabariduri
Technique/exercise to develop the faculty of remote viewing.
Stage one...129
Stage two...130
Stage three...130

• **Technique/Lesson 7...133**
Daemat-Afnah

Technique/exercise for how to stay and look 37
permanently...135
Understanding human life-span and our body longevity...135
A-The brain motor...138
B-Vibrations, frequencies, and luck in life...139
C-The Conduit: Health/youth/longevity...140
Some of the Ulema's guidelines and techniques...142
Introduction...122

• Technique/Lesson 8...147
Da-Irat
This technique eliminates stress, through one's self-energy. In
other words, it is an Ulema technique used to energize one's
mind and body, and to eliminate worries that are preventing a
person from functioning properly everywhere, including office,
school, home, hospital, social gatherings, etc.
Application and use...149

• Technique/Lesson 9...155
Dudurisar
The ability to rethink and examine past events in your life,
change them, and in doing so, you create for yourself a new life
and new opportunities. To a certain degree, and in a sense, it is
like revisiting your past, and changing unpleasant events,
decisions, choices, and related matters that put you where you
are today.
The concept...157
The technique: It works like this...159
How real is the holographic/parallel dimension you are
visiting?...166
Some of the benefits...168
Closing the technique...168

• Technique/Lesson 10...169
Arawadi
Technique to develop a supernatural power or faculty that allows
initiated ones to halt or send away difficulties, problems and

mishaps into another time and another place, thus freeing themselves from worries, anxiety and fear.
The Arawadi technique...171

• **Technique/Lesson 11...175**
Baaniradu
The healing touch technique...177
I-Prerequisites and preparation...177
II-The technique...181
Stage one...181
Preparation for stage two...183
Stage two...183
Stage three...186
Introduction...187
The technique...179

• **Technique/Lesson 12...191**
Bari-du
The technique that allows you to zoom into an astral body or a Double.
Bari-du: The concept...193
Anunnaki-Ulema explained Bari-du as follows...193
Excerpts from their Kira'ats "Reading"...195

• **Technique/Lesson 13...201**
Bisho-barkadari "Bukadari"
The Ulema technique to block negative vibes and bad thoughts aimed at you, your business, and your health...203
Excerpts from their Kira'at, verbatim...203
Case study...207
Excerpts from the Ulema's Kira'at (Verbatim)...208
The Ulema technique: How to block negative vibes...209

***   ***   ***

PART 2: TECHNIQUES Q&A, AND DISCUSSIONS

Introduction...213

Question 1: Why the Conduit is not catching your messages? ...215
Answer to question 1...216

Question 2: The opening of the Conduit...219
Answer to question 2...220

Question 3: The Godabaari technique, moving objects at distance...221
Answer to question 3...222

Question 4: The Gomari "Gumaridu" technique...224
Answer to question 4...225

Question 5: Godabaari's projected mental lines toward the coaster...226
Answer to question 5...227

Question 6: Anunnaki's Miraya and Akashic Records ...229
Answer to question 6...230

Question 7: Gubada-Ari: How to find the healthiest spots and luckiest areas on earth...242
Answer to question 7... 243

Question 8: Gubada-Ari: On the bad and unlucky areas/spots on Earth...245
Answer to question 8...246

Question 9: The Double and the Baridu technique...247
Answer to question 9...248

Question 10:...251
Answer to question 10...252

Question 11: Bukadari technique and people's bad vibes...254
Answer to question 11...255

Question 12: Arawadi Technique and the afterlife...257
Answer to question 12...258

*** *** ***

PART 3: SUBJECTS OF INTEREST Q&A, AND DISCUSSIONS

Introduction...263
Anunnaki in the Western and Eastern hemispheres...265
Betraying the ancient texts...266
False and outrageous interpretations...267
Lack of authoritative sources...267
The Anunnaki-Sumeria-Phoenicia-Ulema-Book of Ramadosh connection...270
Chronology, etymology, human astro-genetics/DNA...270
The real meaning of the word Anunnaki...272
Possibly a wrong translation of the word Anunnaki on the part of authors...272
How the word Anunnaki was used...272
The different meanings of the word Anunnaki...273
The Anunnaki were known to many neighboring countries in the Near East, Middle East, by and under different names...273
Various attributes or definitions were given to the Anunnaki...274
Epistemology and historical terminology of the word Anunnaki...275
Linguistic examples...275

*** *** ***

Chronology: Anunnaki and their time on Earth ...277
450,000-460,000 B.C. ...278
449,000 B.C. ...279

13

446,000-445,000 B.C. ...280
440.000-430.000 B.C. ...281
415,000-416,000 B.C. ...281
400,000 B.C. ...282
380,000 B.C. ...282
350,000 B.C. ...282
340,000 B.C. ...283
300,000 B.C. ...283
272,000 B.C. ...284
200,000-195,000 B.C. ...284
160,000 B.C. ...285
125,000-100,000 B.C. ...285
75,000 B.C. ...286
70,000 B.C. ...287
65,000 B.C. ...287
49,000-45,000 B.C. ...287
49,000 B.C. ...288
13,000 B.C. ...288
12,000-10,500 B.C. ...288
7,000 B.C. ...288
4,750 B.C. ...290
4,000 B.C. ...290
3,800 -3,550 B.C. ...290
3,450 B.C. ...291
3,100 B.C. ...291
3,000 B.C.- 2,123 B.C. ...292
2,100 B.C. ...293
2,096 B.C.-1,363 B.C. ...293
1,362-64 B.C. ...295
1,260 B.C.: -1,080 B.C. ...296
1,000 B.C. ...296

Index...298-312

*** *** ***

Dedication and Gratitude

To the honorable teachers, masters and Ulema
Who showed us the way...
Opened our eyes...
And filled our essence with wisdom, knowledge
And goodness.

Ulema Sijo Win Li
Ulema Dr. Farid Tayarah
Ulema Swami G. Gupta
Ulema Cardinal Bertolli
Ulema Monsignor J. Maroun
Ulema Rabbi Mordachai
Ulema Rabbi Sorenztein
Ulema Marash Anu Sherma
Ulema Cheik Al Bakri Bin Ani Sufian
Ulema Cheik Al Huseini
Ulema Govinda
Ulema Saddik Ghandar Ranpour
Ulema Jean-Robert Sabalat
Ulema Dr. J. Chen
Ulema Amir N. Nejad
Ulema Cheik Imad Turqi Al Bakr Al Rifai
Ulema Imam Salah Al Badri Al Na'amani
Ulema Dr. K. Openheimer
Ulema Rabbi Naphtali Ben Yacob

Without their guidance, inspiration, and blessing, this book would have remained words, phrases, and shadows in my drawer.
Thank you!

The author

*** *** ***

Meet The Author: Maximillien de Lafayette

International best-selling author, Maximillien de Lafayette wrote 150 books, 11 encyclopedias, 41 books on UFOs, 12 books on the paranormal/occult, 27 volumes/dictionaries of ancient and modern languages, and several world premiere musicals (One play was produced at the John F. Kennedy Center for the Performing Arts in Washington, D.C., USA.) De Lafayette is an expert linguist-historian of modern and ancient Middle/Near East languages, tribal dialects, and comparative history. He was commissioned by Yale University- School of Law to translate the New Constitution of Iraq from English to Arabic. This was the draft proposed by The White House and submitted to the Iraqi Council, then the governing body of Iraq. He authored numerous authoritative books and encyclopedias such as, the 4 volume-"The 10 Language Universal Dictionary", the 10 volume- "Anthology and History of French Literature", "Encyclopedia of the 21st Century: Biographies and Profiles of the First Decade", "Biographical Encyclopedia of People in Ufology and Scientific Extraterrestrial Research", the 20 volume "World Who's Who in Jazz, Cabaret, Music and Entertainment", and "The Book of Nations". For 25 years, De Lafayette has been researching subjects pertaining to space, time, gravity, multiple universes and "Space civilizations", and exchanging dialogues and rapports with scientists, and authorities in the field, from around the globe.

A multi-lingual, a syndicated columnist, a world traveler who has visited 46 countries, studied and taught comparative civilizations, international law and social systems for two decades; de Lafayette is in a privileged position to write this book. His columns, articles and books are read by more than 20 million readers in 135 countries. At 13, he published his first book; a collection of poems in French, hailed by members of the L'Academie Française as a masterpiece. Said book was translated in English by Dr. John Chen, Laureate of the United Nations/UNESCO, and former member of The White House Presidential Convention on Library Science and Information Services. His latest international best-sellers were (a) "Entertainment: Divas, Cabaret, Jazz Then and Now". It hits the top chart, the world's 25 most popular items on the international market of Amazon. Uk.com on November 17, 2006; (b) "Anunnaki Enclopedia" which was listed on amazon.com as one of their 100 best-selling encyclopedias. In addition, he has 3 international bestsellers, and two #1 bestsellers in Europe. Lawyer by trade, de Lafayette practiced international law for 20 years and served as legal advisor and counsel to several world organizations and governments in Europe and the Middle East.

Books by Maximillien de Lafayette

Read more about these books, description and reviews at your local library, Amazon.com, Barnes & Noble and other booksellers, and distributors websites worldwide.

Read more at
1-ufozetareticuli.com
2-anunnakibooks.com
3-maximilliendelafayettebibliography.com
4-extraterrestrialsandanunnaki.com

Books on UFOs and Extraterrestrial Civilizations:

- **1**-From Zeta Reticuli to Earth: Time, Space and the UFO Technology. (400 Pages)
- **2**-The Biggest Controversies, Conspiracies, Theories and Cover ups of our Time: From the Secret Files of Science, Politics, The Occult and Religion. (400 Pages)
- **3**-Inside A UFO: Alien Abduction, Hypnosis, Psychiatry, Quantum Physics and Religions Face to Face. (400 Pages)
- **4**-UFOs and the Alien Agenda. The Complete Book of UFOs, Encounters, Abduction And Aliens Bases On Earth. (400 Pages)
- **5**-Extraterrestrials Agenda: Aliens' Origin, Species, Societies, Intentions and Plan for Humanity. (400 Pages)
- **6**-The Anunnaki's Genetic Creation of the Human Race: UFOs, Aliens and Gods, Then and Now. (400 Pages)
- **7**-Extraterrestrials-US Government Treaty and Agreements: Alien Technology, Abduction, and Military Alliance. (400 Pages)
- **8**-Biographical Encyclopedia of People in Ufology and Scientific Extraterrestrial Research: People Who Matter. (740 Pages)
- **9**-Zeta Reticuli and Anunnaki Descendants Among Us: Who Are They? (400 Pages)
- **10**-UFO-USO and Extraterrestrials of the Sea: Flying Saucers and Aliens Civilizations, Life and Bases Underwater (400 Pages)

- **11-**What Extraterrestrials and Anunnaki Want You To Know: Their True Identities, Origins, Nibiru, Zeta Reticuli, Plans, Abductions and Humanity's Future (300 Pages)
- **12-**UFOs and Extraterrestrials Day By Day From 1900 To The Present: Flying Saucers and Aliens Civilizations, Life and Bases Underwater (400 Pages)
- **13-**Hybrid Humans and Abductions: Aliens-Government Experiments (400 Pages)
- **14-**UFOs, Aliens Impregnated Women, Extraterrestrials And God: Sex with Reptilians, Alien Motherhood, The Bible, Abductions and Hybrids (300 Pages)
- **15-**460,000 Years of UFO-Extraterrestrials Biggest Events and Secrets from Phoenicia to The White House: From Nibiru, Zetas, Anunnaki, Sumer To Eisenhower, MJ12, CIA, Military Abductees, Mind Control (400 Pages)
- **16-** Extraterrestrials, UFO, NASA-CIA-Aliens Mind Boggling Theories, Stories And Reports: Anunnaki, Zeta Reticuli, Area 51, Abductees, Whistleblowers, Conspirators. The Real & The Fake (400 Pages)
- **17-**Anunnaki Encyclopedia: History, Nibiru life, world, families, secret powers, how they created us, UFO , extraterrestrials. Volume I (400 Pages)
- **18-**Anunnaki Encyclopedia: History, Nibiru life, world, families, secret powers, how they created us, UFO , extraterrestrials. Volume II (400 Pages)
- **19-**Anunnaki Encyclopedia: History, Nibiru life, world, families, secret powers, how they created us, UFO, extraterrestrials. (Condensed Edition, 740 Pages)
- **20-**Revelation of an Anunnaki's Wife. (310 Pages) Co-authored with Ilil Arbel.
- **21-**2022 Anunnaki Code: End of The World Or Their Return To Earth? Ulema Book of Parallel Dimension, Extraterrestrials and Akashic Records (400 Pages)
- **22-**Anunnaki Greatest Secrets Revealed By The Phoenicians And Ulema. Are We Worshiping A Fake God? Extraterrestrials Who Created Us. The Anunnaki who became the God of Jews, Christians and Muslims (310 Pages)

- **23**-2022: The Anunnaki Return to Earth, and the End of Religions, God and the Human Race. The Day The Earth Will Not Stand Still (500 Pages)
- **24**-Ulema-Anunnaki Matrix: Map of the Afterlife and Road to Immortality (312 Pages)
- **25**-The Annotated Ulema-Anunnaki Matrix: Map of the Afterlife and Road to Immortality, Second Edition (550 Pages)
- **26**-Thesaurus Dictionary of Sumerian, Anunnaki-Anakh, Assyrian, Chaldean, Phoenician, Babylonian, Mesopotamian, Akkadian, Aramaic, Hittite.
- World's first languages and civilizations: Terminology & relation to history, Ulema and extraterrestrials (10 volumes: 3,750 Pages).
- **27**-Ulema Code and Language of the World Beyond. Secret Doctrine of the Anunnaki and Extraterrestrials. (400 Pages)
- **28**-Anunnaki Ultimatum: End of Time (312 Pages). Co-authored with Dr. Ilil Arbel.
- **29**-On the Road to Ultimate Knowledge: Extraterrestrial Tao of the Anunnaki and Ulema (312 Pages). Co-authored with Dr. Ilil Arbel.
- **30**-The Book of Ramadosh (312 Pages)
- **31**-The Anunnaki Face on Mars on the Shroud of Turin: Leonardo da Vinci, Jesus and the Extraterrestrial Link.(312 Pages)
- **32**-Anunnaki and the Real God Face to Face (400 Pages)
- **33**-The Anunnaki Ulema Forbidden Knowledge. What Your Government and Your Church Didn't Want you to Know. (312 pages)
- **34**-The Anunnaki Ulema Extraterrestrial Book of Rama-Dosh. The Anunnaki Creation of a New Human Race after 2022. (312 pages)
- **35**-Nibiru Manual of Style: Guide to the Anunnaki Language, Grammar and Conversion. (312 pages)
- **36**-The Best of Maximillien de Lafayette on Ulema, Anunnaki, Extraterrestrials, UFOs, Nibiru, Zeta Reticuli. (400 pages. V.1)

- **37**-The Best of Maximillien de Lafayette from 1958 to the Present: UFOs, Anunnaki, Extraterrestrials. (400 pages. V.2)

In other fields:

1-Washington Does Not Believe in Tears: Play Their Game Or Eat The Blame!
2-What Foreigners Should Know About Liberal American Women
3-The Nine Language Universal Dictionary. (New Edition: The Ten Language Universal Dictionary
4-Anthologie De La Literature Française (Anthology & History of French Literature)
5-The Dating Phenomenon In The United States: Great Expectations or Justified Deceptions
6-Marmara the Gypsy: Biography of Baroness Myriam de Roszka (The script of the original play at   the John F. Kennedy Center for the Performing Arts.)
7-One Hundred Reasons Why You Should And Should Not Marry An American Woman: Take Him to the Cleaners, Madame!
8-The United States Today: People, Society, Life from A to Z
9-Causes Celebres from 2,000 BC to Modern Times
10-The World's Best and Worst People
11-How Psychologists, Therapists and Psychiatrists Can Ruin Your Life in Court of Law in America
12-International Encyclopedia of Comparative Slang and Folkloric Expressions
13-Encyclopedia of Science of Mind: Religion, Science, and Parapsychology
14-Essay on Psychocosmoly of Man, Universe and Metalogics
15-The Social Register of the Most Prominent and Influential People in the United States
16-How to Use Easy, Fancy French & Latin to Your Advantage and Impress Others
17-How People Rule People with Words: From speechwriters and tele-evangelists to lawmakers and politicians
18-How to Protect Yourself from Your Ex-Wife Lawsuits
19-Divorces for the Highest Bidders
20-The International Book of World Etiquette, Protocol and Refined Manners

21-Bona Fide Divas & Femmes Fatales: The 700 Official Divas of the World

22-How Not To Fail In America: Are You Looking For Happiness Or Financial Success?

23-How to Understand People's Personality and Character Just by Looking at Them

24-The Art and Science of Understanding and Discovering Friends and Enemies

25-New Concise Dictionary of Law for Beginners

26-Comparative Study of Penal Codes As Applied In France and Great Britain

27-How to Understand International Law

28-La Pensee Arabe Face Au Continent Europeen

29-Beyond Mind & Body: The Passive Indo-Chinese School of Philosophy & Way of Life

30-New Approach to the Metaphysical Concept of Human Salvation in the Anthropological Psychology of Indian Religions

31-Worldwide Encyclopedia of Study and Learning Opportunities Abroad.

32-World Who's Who In Contemporary Art

33-World Who's Who in Jazz, Cabaret, Music and Entertainment

34-Thematic Encyclopedia of Cabaret Jazz

35-United States and the World Face to Face

36-Music, Showbiz and Entertainment

37-Entertainment: Divas, Cabaret, Jazz Then and Now

38-Showbiz, Pioneers, Best Singers, Entertainers & Musicians from 1606 to the Present

39-Best Musicians, Singers, Albums, and Entertainment Personalities of the 19th, 20th and 21st Centuries

40-Entertainment Greats From the 1800's to the Present: Cinema, Music, Divas, Legends

41-You, the World, and Everything Around You

42-World of Contemporary Jazz: Biographies of the Legends, the Pioneers, the Divas

43-Living Legends and Ultimate Singers, Musicians and Entertainers

44-People Who Shaped Our World

45-International Register of Events and People Who Shaped Our World

46-United States Cultural and Social Impact on Foreign Intelligentsia

47-Directory of United States Adult and Continuing Postsecondary Education
48-Comprehensive Guide to the Best Colleges and Universities in the United States
49-The Best of Washington: Its People, Society, and Establishments
50-Credentials Academic Equivalency and New Trends in Higher Education Worldwide
51-How Foreign Students Can Earn an American University Degree Without Leaving Their Country
52-Comprehensive Guide to the Best Academic Programs and Best Buys In College Education In The United States
53-How to Learn Seven Thousand French Words in Less Than Thirty Minutes
54-Comprehensive Guide to the Best Colleges and Universities in the U.S.
55-World's Best and Worst Countries: A comparative Study of Communities, Societies, Lifestyles and Their People
56-World Encyclopedia of Learning and Higher Education
57-How Much Your Degree Is Worth Today In America?
58-Worldwide Comparative Study and Evaluation of Postsecondary Education
59-Thematic Encyclopedia of Hospitality and Culinary Arts
60-Five Stars Hospitality: La Crème de la Crème in Hotel Guest Service, Food and Beverage
61-Hospitality Best & Worst: How to Succeed in the Food and Hotel Business
62-Encyclopedia of American Contemporary Art
63-Encyclopedia of Jazz: Life & Times of the 3.000 Most Prominent Singers & Musicians
64-Encyclopedia of Jazz: Life and Times of the 3.000 Most Prominent Singers and Musicians (V.2)
65-Concise Encyclopedia of American Music and Showbiz
66-The World Today: Headliners, Leaders, Lifestyles and Relationships
67-Evaluation of Personal and Professional Experiences: How to convert your knowledge and life experiences into academic degrees.
68-Contemporary Art, Culture, Politics and Modern Thought
69- Maximillien de La Croix « Mistral », Life and Times of Maximillien de La Croix de Lafayette

70-International Rating Of Countries in Higher Education And Comparative Study of Curricula, Degrees And Qualifications Worldwide

71-Alternative Higher Education

72-Dictionary of Academic Terminology Worldwide

73-Fake Titles Fake People

74-How to Use Greek, Latin and Hieroglyphic Expressions and Quotations to Your Advantage and Impress Others.

75-The Best and Worst Non-Traditional and Alternative Colleges and Universities in the United States

76-Directory of United States Traditional and Alternative Colleges and Universities

77-The Non Traditional Postsecondary Education in the United States: Its Merits, Advantages and Disastrous Consequences

78-Lafayette's Encyclopedic Dictionary of Higher Education Worldwide

79-Academic Degrees, Titles and Credentials

80-Independent Study Programs

81-America's Best Education at a Low Cost

82-Fictitious Credentials on Your Resume

83-Distance Learning

84-New Trends in American Higher Education

85-Directory of United States Postsecondary Education

86-Directory of United States Traditional and Alternative Colleges and Universities

87-National Register of Social Prestige and Academic Ratings of American Colleges and Universities

88-The Book of Nations

89-The World's Lists of Best and Worst

90-The Ultimate Book of World's Lists, Volume I

91-The Ultimate Book of World's Lists, Volume 2

92-Biographical Encyclopedia of the Greatest Minds, Talents, Personalities of our Time

93-Encyclopedia of the 21st Century. Biographies and Profile of the First Decade

94-Hospitality and Food Best and Worst: How to Succeed in the Food and Hotel Business

95-The Biggest Controversies, Conspiracies, Theories & Cover ups of our Time, Vol. I

96-The Biggest Controversies, Conspiracies, Theories, & Cover ups of our Time, Vol. II

97-Ulema: Code and Language of the World Beyond

98-The 1,000 Divas and Femmes Fatales of the World
99-140 Years of Cinema
100-Ulema: Code and Language of the World Beyond
101-Anunnaki Map of the After Life: Where And How You
Continue Your Life After Death

Encyclopedias:

1-International Encyclopedia of Comparative Slang and Folkloric
Expressions
2-Encyclopedia of Science of Mind: Religion, Science, and
Parapsychology
3-World Encyclopedia of Learning and Higher Education
4-Worldwide Comparative Study and Evaluation of
Postsecondary Education
5-Thematic Encyclopedia of Hospitality and Culinary Arts
6-Encyclopedia of American Contemporary Art
7-Encyclopedia of Jazz: Life & Times of 3.000 Most Prominent
Singers and Musicians
8-Concise Encyclopedia of American Music and Showbiz (2
Volumes)
9-Encyclopedia of the 21st Century. Biographies and Profile of the
First Decade
10-Biographical Encyclopedia of the Greatest Minds, Talents and
Personalities of our time
11-Biographical Encyclopedia of People in Ufology and Scientific
Extraterrestrial Research: People Who Matter and Most
Important Figures
12-Thematic Encyclopedia of Ufology and Extraterrestrial
Sciences (En route)
13-Anunnaki Encyclopedia (A set of 2 Volumes)
14-Maximillien de Lafayette Anunnaki Encyclopedia (1 Volume.
Condensed Edition)

Dictionaries

1-The Nine Language Universal Dictionary: How to Write It and
Say It in Arabic, English, French, German, Italian, Japanese,
Portuguese, Russian, Spanish (4 Volumes). Out of print
2-How to Learn 7,000 French Words in Less than Thirty
Minutes. Out of print

3-Lafayette's Encyclopedic Dictionary of Higher Education
Worldwide. Out of print
4-Dictionary of Academic Terminology Worldwide. Out of print
5-How to Use Easy, Fancy French & Latin to Your Advantage and
Impress Others. Out of print
5-Thesaurus-Dictionary Of Sumerian, Anunnaki, Babylonian,
Mesopotamian, Assyrian, Akkadian, Aramaic, Hittite, Arabic,
Hebrew, Phoenician: World's first languages & civilizations:
Terminology & relation to history, Ulema & extraterrestrials (10
volumes).
6-De Lafayette Encyclopedic Dictionary-Lexicon of Sumerian
Language and Civilizations (4 Volumes)
7-De Lafayette Encyclopedic Dictionary-Lexicon of Akkadian
Language and Civilizations (3 Volumes)
8-De Lafayette Encyclopedic Dictionary-Lexicon of Assyrian
Language and Civilizations (4 Volumes)
9-De Lafayette Encyclopedic Dictionary-Lexicon of Hittite
Language and Civilizations (3 Volumes)-
10-De Lafayette Encyclopedic Dictionary-Lexicon of Aramaic
Language and Civilizations (1 Volume)
11-De Lafayette Encyclopedic Dictionary-Lexicon of Hebrew
Language and Civilizations (1 Volume)
12-De Lafayette Encyclopedic Dictionary-Lexicon of Phoenician
Language and Civilizations (1 Volume)

Anunnaki Language Series (2 Volumes):
13-Anunnaki Dictionary Thesaurus. Ana'kh; Language of the
Extraterrestrial Gods and Goddesses (Volume 1)
14-Anunnaki Language and Vocabulary. Ana'kh Dictionary
Thesaurus (Volume 2)

*** *** ***

Enrich Your Mind

Highly recommended books, dictionaries and encyclopedias by the international best-selling author Maximillien de Lafayette, available worldwide and directly from amazon.com

Explosive Book
The Anunnaki's Genetic Creation of the Human Race
UFOs, Aliens and Gods, Then and Now

The most comprehensive published work on the Anunnaki and their impact on the human race. Wealth of information and in-depth articles on so many topics, including, but not limited to:

1-ETs' role in human development
2-God and the extraterrestrials
3-The mystery surrounding Jesus and the Sons of God
4-The extraterrestrials are responsible for genetic intervention in the modern era
5-The 'God' of the Old Testament, Yahweh/Jehovah, is in fact an "intermediary god" or extraterrestrial
6-How the Anunnaki created us genetically
7-The real story of Nibiru (Planet X)
8-We created you. We came from space
9-The truth behind human origins
10-The alien gods were genetic engineers
11-The Nephilim an ancient race of half-breed humans... And much much more...

*** *** ***

NEW BOOK

WHAT EXTRATERRESTRIALS AND ANUNNAKI WANT YOU TO KNOW

Their true identities, origins, Nibiru, Zeta Reticuli, Plans,
Abductions and humanity future

**This is the book that will turn the world of ufology,
extraterrestrials and paranormal upside down.**

The most powerful, revealing and unique book ever written in the field.
New information, secrets and ultimate knowledge revealed for the first
time in history directly by Victoria, A Human-Hybrid Annunaki Wife,
her Husband, Sinharmarduchk, An Anunnaki Leader, and The Ulema
Masters. Among the topics: the 7 different genetic human races, the
habitat and life on Nibiru, Zeta Reticuli and dozens of other planets,
how they live, what they do, the origin of humanity, predictions about
our future and all the military cooperations with governments
worldwide.

Partial listings of discussed topics:

On Religions:
1-The Immaculate Conception: An Anunnaki pattern
2-The Exodus as we know it, never happened
3-The Origin of the Ten Commandments
4-The real Moses
5-Ufology's major theories about the Anunnaki, extraterrestrials, Greys
and how they fit in the scenario of the creation and the origin of the
human race

**Communicating with extraterrestrials via channeling and
telepathically:**
1-Communication with aliens is done through artificial spatial structures
in fifth or higher dimension
2-What is the best way to communicate with extraterrestrials?

Real physiognomy, faculties and senses of extraterrestrials:
1-Description of all the extraterrestrial races

From metaphysical to bio-electro-plasma and to physical:
1-Some aliens are from our future
2-What is an "Alien's Manifestation"? What is an "Alien's Apparition"?
3-You can interpret it as "Metaphysical Energy" before it fully
materializes
What is an "Alien's teleportation"?

JUST PUBLISHED
460,000 Years of UFO-Extraterrestrials Biggest Events and Secrets

Contacts, Anunnaki Language, Cover-Ups, Discoveries From Phoenicia to Area 51

Partial listing of discussed topics:

1-From 460,000 to the Present

2-Man was created from the clay which is found in abundance in the region and, so that he would look like the Igigi

3-The DNA imprint is carried over after death

4-Sixteen males and sixteen females who comprised a married family traveled to Earth from Sirius

5- All lifeforms generate their own bioenergetic grids

6- The theory of the ORME (The Tree of Life and Ha Qabala). From levitation to zero point energy

7-The traditions of the Anunnaki in raising their own from the dead

8-The Alphabet: Phoenicians take letters and words from the Anunnaki's language

9-Secret extraterrestrial words that can create wealth, fortune and power

10-Ulema: God is Not the creator of the universe. The universe per se is the logical reason of its very self-existence

11-The Nephilim, Anakim, Elohim, Baalshalimroot, and the Shtaroout-Hxall Ain

12-Anunnaki live on three planets: Ashtari (Nibiru), Zeta 1 and Ashartartun- ra

13-Birth of the explosive theory of the direct link of Phoenicia, extraterrestrials, Roswell's UFOs, the Illuminati, and the Freemasons to the government of the United States

14-Phoenicia was the land of descent of the "Sons of God" described in Genesis 6

15-The amazing story of Helen and Betty Mitchell and their encounters with aliens

16-Dancing and playing games with aliens inside a UFO

17-The birth of explosive theories, claims and allegations

MOST INFORMATIVE BOOK ON EXTRATERRESTRIALS:

EXTRATERRESTRIALS, UFO, NASA-CIA-ALIENS MIND BOGGLING THEORIES, STORIES AND REPORTS

Anunnaki, Zeta Reticuli, Area 51, Abductees, Whistleblowers, Conspirators. The Real & The Fake

The world's most mind-boggling theories about UFOs, extraterrestrials, contacts with the human race, revelations by alien-hybrid-human people living among us, United States astronauts encounters with UFO on the moon and around the earth orbit, messages from aliens received by NASA, SETI and the United States Air Force, MJ12 documents, accounts by abductees taken to military bases...in brief all the theories from the most realistic ones to the strangest and most explosive as publicly stated by Ufology's leading figures, scientists, channelers and contactees.

Some of the discussed topics:

1-Theory of "Null Hypothesis"
2-Theory of "Subjective/Psychological"
3-Theory of "Subjective Projections"
4-Theory of "Psychosocial/Folklore"
5-Theory of "Natural/Fortean Phenomenon"
6-Theory of "Human Origin"
7-Theory of "Extraterrestrial Origin"
8-Theory of "Ultraterrestrial Origin"
9-Theory of "Ultraterrestrials, Fairies and UFOs"
10-Theory of "Deception"
11-Theory of" Occult/Magical/Supernatural"
12-Theory of "USO (Water UFO; Unidentified Submerged Objects)
13-Theory of "UFO's Underground Bases and Origin"
14-Theory of "UFO/USO Underground Bases and Origin"
15-Theory of "UFOs are time travelers from future human and alien civilizations"
16-Theory of "UFOs come from Wormholes and Hyperspace"
17-Theory of "UFOs Come from a Parallel Universe of Anti-Matter"
18-Theory of Dr. Carl Jung
19-Theory of "Demoniac Origin"
20-Theory of "UFOs are a Nazi Technology"
21. Theory of the Asian Vimanas (Tibetan and Indian Origin)

22-Theory of "UFOs are the Technology of an Advanced Subterranean Civilization"
23-Theory of "Erroneous observations, mass hysteria and some outright charlatanism"
24-The "Synthetic Theory"
25-The Theory of "UFOs are paraphysical phenomena"
26-The Theory of "UFOs are an affair of the mind"
27-The Theory of the "UFO phenomenon is a psychological aberration as much as it is an observable phenomenon."
28-The Theory of "UFOs are quantum manifestations"
29-Theory of the "UFOS do not exist"

*** *** ***

The World's First, Largest And Most Comprehensive And Authoritative Published Work On The Anunnaki "A MASTERPIECE...A TREASURE!"

ANUNNAKI ENCYCLOPEDIA

ORIGIN, HISTORY, AND SOCIETY OF THE ANUNNAKI NIBIRU, THEIR SUPERNATURAL POWERS, HOW THEY CREATED US, EXTRATERRESTRIAL UFOs

**In Two Formats
Two Volumes Set; Each 400 Pages
One Volume, Condensed Edition Of 740 Pages**

This encyclopedia is unique, much needed, and "genetically correct" for various reasons, including but not limited to:

1-This is the world's first massive encyclopedic work on the Anunnaki.
2-The book is a rarity in that it uses the authentic ancient languages, such as Aramaic, Hebrew, Arabic, Greek, Latin, Sumerian, Phoenician, Babylonian, Mesopotamian, Syriac, and even Anak'h, the Anunnaki language.
3-The Anunnaki civilization is rich in literature, poetry, ethics, and rules governing societies.
The author, therefore, included the Epic of Gilgamesh, and the Code of Hammurabi, as examples of this rich heritage.

30

4-New light is shed on the proven direct links of the Phoenicians to the Anunnaki, substantiated by the author's visits to their historical sites and ancient cities on the Island of Arwad, Tire, Sidon, Baalbeck, Amrit, and Byblos, to name a few.
5The encyclopedia includes breakthrough theories, studies, and essays on unknown, major discoveries by leading authorities in the field.

*** *** ***

ULTIMATUM: END OF TIME
REVELATIONS OF AN ANUNNAKI'S WIFE

Co authored by Maximillien de Lafayette and Ilil Arbel, Ph.D.

THE WORLD'S FIRST AUTO-BIOGRAPHY OF AN EXTRATERRESTRIAL

The amazing autobiography of Victoria, an Anunnaki wife in her own words...no channeling, no trances, no séances.
Direct data by and rapport with Victoria in person. Including explosive revelations about:

- Major UFOs-Extraterrestrials incidents and threats inside secret military bases,
- Governments' involvement with 2 particular alien races,
- Description of the world of extraterrestrials,
- The Anunnaki's community, societies and families,
- Description of life on Zeta Reticuli,
- Description of the habitat on Planet X,
- Victoria-Alien husband love story, and wedding ceremony,
- Victoria's voyage to Zeta Reticuli,
- Victoria's personal involvement with her alien in-laws, and the leader of the Anunnaki,
- Victoria's hybrid congressman son and the major role he will be playing on the arena of world politics,
- Dwight Eisenhower's direct contact with extraterrestrials,
- The Vatican's secret files on UFOS, extraterrestrials, Christianity-Alien entities connection,
- Jesus Christ's life after the crucifixion; his trip to Marseille, his family, children and their bloodlines, and his wife Mary Magdalene,

- Victoria's take on channelers, contactees, abductees, ufologists, and charlatans,
- Earth's future, multiple universes, interdimensional beings,
- Anunnaki's existence and civilization on earth: Past, present and future.

*** *** ***

Introduction

This book reveals knowledge that is thousands of years old. Generally, such a statement would bring to mind images of the occult, hidden mysteries, perhaps ancient religious manuscripts. However, the *Book of Ramadosh* is different.

It is based on the science of the "Transmission of Mind", which even though it was used eons ago by the Anunnaki and their remnants on Earth, is more fresh and new than much of the technology and inventions of our modern laboratories.

This is not a replica of the ancient *Book of Ramadosh*. There is no need to be familiar with the Ana'kh language, which may be difficult for the modern reader who had not been exposed to it before and has no time to learn it.

Rather, the author selected parts of the book that he thought were the most useful to the modern reader, consisting of the most useful techniques, and translated them into clear and concise English.

Read the book with an open mind. It does not require spiritual exercises or faith. It does not interfere with anyone's philosophy or religion.

It is based on the power of the mind alone.

The word "occult" means "hidden," but this book gives such a clear view of ourselves and the universe we live in, that it is the exact opposite of anything hidden or mysterious. On the contrary, it sheds light on many of our most perplexing problems and helps us resolve them in a simple and intelligent manner.

The book not only gives you techniques that could bring you health, happiness, and prosperity, but goes deeply into the why and how these techniques do so.

For that purpose, the author divided the book into three sections.

a-The first is an overview and the techniques themselves.

b-The second is a question and answer sequence that is meant to clarify any question remaining in the readers' minds.

c-The third is a brief chronology of the Anunnaki and their time on Earth.

The author will be grateful for readers' suggestions and for their sharing experiences in that arena. Understanding the readers' views and needs will be a great help as the series evolves. Please contact me using this e-mail: carollexter@aol.com

Carol Lexter
Senior Editor
Times Square Press

*** *** ***

Glossary of Anunnaki-Ulema Terms

Sources: Three books by Maximillien de Lafayette
1-Anunnaki Dictionary Thesaurus. Ana'kh, Language of the Extraterrestrial Gods and Goddesses. Book 1.
2-Anunnaki Language and Vocabulary. Ana'kh Dictionary Thesaurus. Book 2.
3-Anunnaki Encyclopedia.

*** *** ***

Aamala: Anunnaki's registry of future events.
It is used as a calendar to show important events that will occur on other planets.
According to Ulema Rajani, time is not linear. And because space bends on itself, therefore, events don't have a chronology or time-sequences.
"Things and events happen on the net of the cosmos. When your mind perceives them, they happen before your eyes. But in fact, they have already happened before your have noticed them. This applies to all future and forthcoming events, because also they have occurred on another cosmos net parallel to the one that have contained separate events. It is a matter of perception, rather than observation or taking notice..." said Ulema Govinda.

Abgaru: Balance; equilibrium.
Balance does not mean a physical balance, but a position or a situation where and when a person maintains a perfect vision, assimilation and understanding of the limits, dimensions and length of objects surrounding him/her.
In other words, it is sensing and remembering the exact position of objects that can expand within the area where we are standing or walking, even in the dark.
Objects are not limited by their physical dimension, and/or the physical place they occupy. "Almost all objects extend and expand outside what it defines their measurement, shape, and size, because they have inertia "Energy" rays or vibrations that

Glossary of terms

constantly emanate from them, thus occupying an extra physical place. Not to bump into the vibes area is maintaining balance," said Ulema W. Li.

Afik-r'-Tanawar: Enlightenment through the development of the mind. Composed of two words;
a-Afik-r, which means mind.
b-Tanawar, which means the act of enlightenment.

Excerpt for a Kira'at (Reading) by Ulema, verbatim:
The Anunnaki have created us on earth to serve their needs.
Their intentions were to create a race that could carry heavy physical load and do intense physical labor.
This was their initial and prime objective. Thus, the "Naphsiya" (DNA) they put in us had limited lifespan, and mental faculties.
Later on, they discovered that they had to prolong the human lifespan and add more developed mental faculties, so they added the Hara-Kiya (Internal energy or physical strength).
Few generations later, the early human beings stock evolves considerably, because the Anunnaki geneticists added a fully operational mind in the human body.
To do so, they installed a Conduit with limited capabilities. In the same time, this Conduit was also installed into the prototype of the human body.
Thus, through the mind, the physical body of the humans got linked to the Double. This non-physical link created a Fourth dimension for all of us.
In fact, it did not create a Fourth dimension per se, rather it activated it.
So now, at that stage, humans had a physical dimension (Life on earth), and not-a-totally separated non-physical dimension called Nafis-Ra. So, the Bashar (Humans) became destined to acquire two dimensions, as exactly the Anunnaki decided. Later on, centuries upon centuries, the human mind began to evolve, because the other mind, call it now the Double or prototype began to evolve simultaneously and in sync.
The more the prototype is advanced the more the "Physical Mind" becomes alert, creative and multidimensional.

Glossary of terms

But we are not trapped, and our mind is no longer conditioned by the Anunnaki.

The Anunnaki gave us all the choices, opportunities, freewill and freedom to learn on our own and progress.

This is why we are accountable and responsible for everything we do and think about.

Because of the evolution of our mind, and realization of an inner knowledge of our surroundings, and understanding what is right and what is wrong, a major mental faculty emerged in all of us: Conscience.

Anšekadu-ra abra "Anshekadoora-abra":
Learning by traveling or traversing other dimensions.
Composed of four words:
a-Anše, which means magnificent.
b-Kadu, which means ability, or to be able.
c-Ra, which means heavenly; godly.
d-Abra, which means to cross over; to traverse.

Ulema Shimon Naphtali Ben Yacob explained that the Anunnaki have acquired an enormous amount of knowledge by entering different dimensions, and visiting multiple universes.

These dimensions are sometimes called parallel universes, future universes, and vibrational spheres.

He said: "Some are physical/organic, others are purely mental.

There are billions and billions of universes.

Some are inhabited by beings, super-beings, multi-vibrational beings, and even negative entities known to mankind as demons and evils.

Planet earth is considered the lowest organic and human life-form in the universe. The human beings are the less developed living entities, both mentally and spiritually." Anšekadu-ra abra also means Anunnaki's branching out and changing individuality in multiple universes. To understand the concept, consider this scenario said Ulema Mordachai Ben Zvi: "Let say, you wish if you could do something differently in your life, something like changing the past, changing a major life decision you have made

Glossary of terms

some years ago, like perhaps, going back in time to a point before you have made a bad decision.

Or for instance, you wish if you could do something really good by changing an entire event that has happened in your past. In the Anunnaki's case, they have the solutions for these dilemmas. They can go back and forth in time and space, including the past, the future, and meta-future.

An Anunnaki can split himself/herself in two, three, or more if necessary, and move on to a universe that is very much like the one they live on (Nibiru), or totally different.

There are so many universes, and some of them do not resemble Nibiru at all. If an Anunnaki wishes to branch out and move on, he/she must study the matter very carefully and make the right selection. And the branching, or splitting, results in exact copies of the person of the Anunnaki, both physically and mentally.

At the moment of separation, each separate individual copy of an Anunnaki grows, mentally, in a different direction, follows his or her own free will and decisions, and eventually the two are not exactly alike."

So what do they do, first of all?

Ulema Ben Zvi said verbatim: "The old one stays where he/she is and follows his/her old patterns as he/she wishes. The new one might land one minute, or a month, or a year, somewhere, some place, right before the decision he/she wants to change or avoid.

Let's take this scenario for instance; Some 30,000 years ago in his life-span; an Anunnaki male was living a nice life with his wife and family. But he felt that he did not accomplish much, and suddenly he wanted to be more active in the development of the universe; a change caused by witnessing a horrendous event such as a certain group of beings in his galaxy destroying an entire civilization, and killing millions of the inhabitants, in order to take over their planet for various purposes.

It happened while an Anunnaki was on a trip, and he actually saw the destruction and actions of war while he was traveling. It was quite traumatic, and he thought, at that moment, that he must be active in preventing such events from occurring again, ever. So, he went back in time to be in a spot to prevent these fateful events from happening again.

Glossary of terms

There, in that new dimension, the Anunnaki leaves his former self (A copy of himself) as a guardian and a protector.
The other copy (Perhaps one of the original ones) is still on Nibiru. The branching out phenomenon occurred in one of the designated locals of the Anunnaki Hall of Records, also called in terrestrial term Akashic Records Hall."
Ulema Openheimer said: "For the Anunnaki fellow there is no problem or any difficulty in doing that. He/she will go back in time and space and change the whole event. This means that this particular event no longer exists in a chronological order. This also means that the event has been erased, because the Anunnaki can de-fragment the molecules, the substance, the vibrations and the fabric of time, but necessarily space.
In other words, that event never happened in one dimension, but it is very possible, that it might still exist in another world.

You could consider the cosmos as an assemblage of several layers of universes, each one on the top of the other, and sometimes parallel to each other. When the Anunnaki traverses more than two layers, we call this Anšekadu-ra abra."
Can a human being traverse multiple layers of time and space?
Yes, said Ulema Ben Zvi. He added: "However, the human being will be facing a series of problems. For instance:
1-Case one: Although, he/she may cross over and enters another dimension, and succeeds in altering, changing or even erasing a past event, the human being might get stuck in that dimension, and remains there for ever.
In this condition, he/she is transformed into a new person without an identity or a past.
A brand new person who is out-placed, without a job, without a residence, without credentials, and without social or professional context. It would become very difficult for that person to make a living.
How the others would look upon him? A person from the past? A person from the future? It is not an easy situation.
2-Case two: Because everything in the world is duplicated ad infinitum in many universes, only one copy of the past event has been altered.

39

Glossary of terms

3-Case three: What would happen to that person, should he/she decides to return back to his/her original world?

The real problem here is not how to go back to his/her world and relive an ordinary life, the life he/she had before, but what is going to happen to him/her when that person leaves the new dimension he/she has entered?

Every time a person enters another dimension, he/she creates a new copy of himself/herself, and occupies a new spot on the cosmos net. In our case here, that human being by entering another dimension, he/she has duplicated himself/herself in that new dimension, and returning to Earth, he/she will be facing another copy of himself/herself. "

Is this possible? Quantum physic theorists say yes. And they add that humans can enter and live in multiple universes and acquire new identities, and new copies of themselves.

An-zalubirach: Collecting and sorting thoughts and multiple mental images; using mental energy to move or teleport things. This is one of the phases and practices of Tarkiz.

Tarkiz means deep mental or intellectual concentration that produces telekinesis and teleportation phenomena. Anunnaki's young students, apprentices, and novices learn this technique in Anunnaki schools in Ashtari.

Usually, they use their Conduit (Which is located in the brain's cells), and deep concentration on an object hidden behind a screen or a divider made from thin paper.

Synchronizing the frequency of their Conduit and an absolute state of introspection, the Anunnaki student attempts to move the hidden object from one place to another without even touching it.

In a more advanced stage, the Anunnaki student attempts to alter the properties of the object by lowering or increasing the frequencies and vibrations of the object.

Araya: Prediction; code.

According to the Ulema, the Anunnaki's Araya is an effective tool to foresee forthcoming events in the immediate and long term future.

Glossary of terms

The expression or term "foreseeing" is never used in the Ana'kh language and by extraterrestrials because they don't foresee and predict. They just calculate and formulate.

In spatial terms, they don't even measure things and distances, because time and space do not exist as two separate "presences" in their dimensions.

However, on Nibiru, Anunnaki are fully aware of all these variations, and the human concept of time and space, and have the capability of separating time and space, and/or combining them into one single dimension, or one single frame of existence.

Anunnaki understand time differently from us, said the Ulema. For instance, on Nibiru, there are no clocks and no watches. They are useless. Then you might ask: So, how do they measure time? How do they know what time it is...now or 10 minutes later, or in one hour from now?

The answer is simple: If you don't need time, you don't need to measure it.

However, on Nibiru, Anunnaki experience time and space as we do on earth. And they do measure objects, substances, distances and locations as we do on earth. But they rarely do.

"The Anunnaki (In addition to the Nordics and Lyrans) are the only known extraterrestrials in the universe to look like humans, and in many instances, they share several similarities with the human race..." said Ulema Ghandar.

This physiognomic resemblance explains to a certain degree, the reason for Anunnaki to use time.

To calculate and formulate information and to acquire data, Anunnaki consult the Code Screen.

Consulting the screen means pragmatically, the reading of events sequences, explained the Ulema.

Every single event in the cosmos in any dimension has a code; call it for now Nimera, a "number", added the Ulema. Nothing happens in the universe without a reason.

The universe has its own logic that the human mind cannot understand. In many instances, the logic of numbers dictates and creates events. And not all created events are understood by the extraterrestrials.

Glossary of terms

This is why they resort to the Araya Code Screen. Activating the Araya Code requires four actions or procedures:

1-Taharim:

This demands clearing all the previous data stored in the "pockets" of the Net.

A net resembles space net as usually used by quantum physics scientists. They do in fact compare space to a net. According to their theories, the net as the landscape of time and space bends under the weight of a ball rotating at a maximum speed.

The centrifugal effect produced by the ball alters the shape of the net, and consequently the fabric of space. And by altering space, time changes automatically.

As time changes, speed and distances change simultaneously. Same principle applies to stretching and cleaning up the net of the screen containing a multitude of codes of the Anunnaki.

2-Location of the Spatial Pockets:

The word pockets means the exact dimension and exact space an object occupies on the universe's net or landscape. No more than one object or one substance occupies one single pocket; this is by earth standard and human level of knowledge. In other parallel worlds, more than one object or one substance can be infused in one single pocket. But this could lead to loss of memory.

Objects and substances have memory too, just like human beings; some are called:

a-Space memory,
b-Time memory,
c-String memory,
d-Astral memory,
e-Bio-organic memory,
etc...

The list is endless.

Thus, all pockets containing previous data are cleared.

3-Feeding the Pockets, also called Retrieving Data: All sorts and sizes of data are retrieved and stored through the Conduit.

The Conduit is an electroplasmic substance implanted into the cells of the brain.

42

4-Viewing the data: Retrieved data and information are viewed through the Miraya, also called Cosmic Mirror.

Some refer to it as Akashic Records.

Can the Anunnaki go forward in time and meet with the future? Yes, they can! One Ulema said that future events have already happened at some level and in some spheres.

It is just a matter of a waiting period for the mind to see it.

Balu-ram-haba: Composed of three words:

a-Balu, which means power; transition; contact.

b-Ram, which means people. In this case, entities; other life-forms.

c-Haba, which means beyond; other dimension.

Possibly, from Balu-ram-haba, derived the Hebrew word Olam ha-ba. This Ana'kh term or expression pertains to circumstances in the world beyond, and/or experiences, the departed humans might encounter in the next dimension, following their death. On this subject, the Anunnaki-Ulema have said (Excerpts from their Kira'at, verbatim):

Afterlife does not necessarily begin after we die, because death does not exist; it is simply a transitory stage.

Within our physical world exist so many other worlds.

And far away, and deep in the fabric of the universe, distances are reduced, even eliminated, if we zoom into our Double. Matter and anti-matter are de-fragmented in the parallel dimension.

The initiated and enlightened ones can transport themselves to the other world, and visit the far distant corners of the universe through their Double.

Those who are noble in their thoughts, intentions and deeds can accomplish this after an Ulema initiation.

- The righteous people will be reunited with their loved ones including their pets in the afterlife.
- This reunion will take place in the 1st level of the ethereal 4th dimension.

Glossary of terms

- The reunion is not of a physical nature, but mental.
- This means, that the mind of the deceased will project and recreate holographic images of people, animals and places.
- All projected holographic images are identical to the original ones, but they are multidimensional.
- Multidimensional means, that people, animals and physical objects are real in essence, in molecules, in DNA, and in origin, but not necessarily in physical properties. In other words, what you see in the afterlife is real to the mind, but not to your physical senses, because in the after life (In all the seven levels/dimensions of life after death), physical objects, including humans' and animals' bodies acquire different substances, molecular compositions, and new forms.
- The physical rewards and punishments are mental, not physical in nature, but they are as real as the physical ones.
- The deceased will suffer through the mind.
- The pain sensations are real, but are produced by the mind, instead of a physical body. So in concept and essence, the Ulema and Hebraic scholars share similar beliefs; the good person will be rewarded, and the bad person will be punished.
- For the Jews, it is physical, while for the Ulema it is mental, but both reward and punishment are identical in their intensity and application.
- The wicked will not be indefinitely excluded from a reunion with loved ones.
- The wicked will remain in a state of loneliness, chaos, confusion and mental anguish for as long it takes to rehabilitate him/her.
- This state of punishment and rehabilitation can last for a very long period of time in an uncomfortable sphere of

existence inhabited by images of frightening entities created by the mind as a form of punishment.

- Eventually, all wicked persons will reunite with their loved ones after a long period of purification and severe punishment.

Note: Some scholars believe that the projection of these macabre and scary entities are created by the subconscience of the wicked person. Other scholars believe that the holographic imageries are produced by the Double housing the mind.

The Torah speaks of several noteworthy people being "gathered to their people." See, for example, Gen. 25:8 (Abraham), 25:17 (Ishmael), 35:29 (Isaac), 49:33 (Jacob), Deut. 32:50 (Moses and Aaron) II Kings 22:20 (King Josiah).

This gathering is described as a separate event from the physical death of the body or the burial.

Certain sins are punished by the sinner being "cut off from his people." See, for example, Gen. 17:14 and Ex. 31:14.

This punishment is referred to as Kareit (Kah-Rehyt) (literally, "cutting off," but usually translated as "spiritual excision"), and it means that the soul loses its portion in the world to come.

Later portions of the Tanakh speak more clearly of life after death and the world to come. See Dan. 12:2, Neh. 9:5.

Here are the views of the Anunnaki-Ulema:
- Soul is a metaphysical concept created by Man.
- Soul is a religious idea created by humans to explain and/or to believe in what they don't understand.
- It is more accurate to use the word Mind instead.
- The mind thinks and understands. The soul does not, perhaps it feels, if it is to be considered as a vital force and source of feelings in your physical body.
- In the afterlife, such source of feelings is nonexistent, and in the dimensions of the world beyond, such source is useless.

Glossary of terms

Dab'Laa: Term for the Anunnaki's branching out and changing individuality in multiple universes.

This is a very complex topic, and a phenomenon difficult to comprehend or to explain in terrestrial terms. To understand the concept, the closest metaphor in human terminology would be going back in time by bending space and time. In this case, time and space are no longer influenced or regulated by the laws of physics as we understand them on Earth.

Distances became shorter and time acts strangely, according to speed. Through the Dab'Laa, an Anunnaki can duplicate himself or herself, and transpose one of the copies of himself/herself to a new dimension. This dimension is real, because it has always physically existed in the cosmos, but at a different vibrational level.

Vibrational level does not mean that all substances and life forms in that new dimension exist and appear as frequencies, rays and vibrations. They have physical properties and dimensions, but are structured differently.

They are made from the same molecules, and particles, but their vibrational intensity varies. This variation allows the substances to take on different forms, i.e. water can be solidified as ice cubes, and ice cubes can melt to become liquid water.

The Anunnaki's branching, or splitting results in duplicate copies for 2 dimensions, or multiple copies to use in multiple universes.

But these copies are not exactly alike, for the original remains the primordial center of knowledge, while the duplicates traverse the universe as a mirrored spatial memory.

However, the physical structure and molecular substance of all copies are identical.

Note: More information on pages: 37, 38, 39.

Ulema can duplicate themselves, copy themselves, but cannot clone themselves. These faculties allow them to materialize and dematerialize in parallel spheres. The Ulema are also capable of elevating the vibrations of their body and mind to a higher level. This act allows them to penetrate solid substances, such as walls.

Glossary of terms

In the new dimension, the Anunnaki uses a vivid copy of himself or herself, while the primordial composition of his/her persona remains unaltered on Nibiru.

Eido-Rah: Term for the non-physical substance of a human being's body. In other words, the mental or astral projection of the body leaving earth.
Eido-Rah manifests to human beings, and particularly to the parents of the deceased person during a period of less than 40 days, following the death of a relative. From Eido-Rah, derived the Greek word Eidolon (A phantom).

According to the scribes of the Book of Rama-Dosh: "After we die, the primordial source of energy in our body leaves our body.
This energy is a substance made out of Fik'r closely connected and attached to a copy of ourselves preserved in the Fourth dimension, which is not very far away from us, and from Earth.
As soon as this energy leaves the physical body, the mind of the deceased becomes confused instantly.
The mind does not realize that the body is dead.
At this particular stage, the mind is unable to realize right away that it has entered a new dimension.

Although this new dimension is identical to the one we live in and what we call Earth, it is also very different because time, space and distance no longer exist. And also because, it exists at a different vibrational level.
Everything becomes meta-linear.
Because the mind is confused, it tries to return to Earth. The first places, the mind (Or the new form-substance of the deceased one) searches for, and/or tries to return to, are always the familiar places on Earth, such as home, office, recreation center, church, mosque, synagogue, temple, etc...but the most sought place is usually home. So, the deceased person returns home for a very short period. This does not happen all the time. Only when the deceased person is totally confused and disoriented.
First, the deceased tries to contact relatives and close parents.

Glossary of terms

When the deceased begins to realize that parents and relatives are not responding, the deceased tries again to send messages telepathically.

Some messages if intensified can take on ectoplasmic forms, or appear as a shadow usually on smooth substances such as mirror and glass.

Some deceased people will keep on trying to contact their beloved ones left behind for a period of 39 days and 11 hours. After this time, the deceased dissipates, and no further attempts to establish contact with the living are made."

In another passage of the Book of Rama-dosh, we read (Verbatim): "Although, it is impossible to reach the deceased one as soon as he/she leaves the body, and/or during the 39 days and 11 hours period following his death, sometimes, if we are lucky, and/or were extremely attached to the person we lost, a short contact with him or with her is still possible if we pay attention to unusual things happening around us...those unusual things are difficult to notice, unless we pay a great attention....they happen only once, sometimes twice, but this is very rare..."

The book provides techniques and methods pertaining to all forms and means of such contact.

Ezakarerdi, "E-zakar-erdi "Azakar.Ki":
Term for the "Inhabitants of Earth" as named by the Anunnaki, and mentioned in the Ulemite language in the "Book of Rama-Dosh."

Per contra, extraterrestrials are called Ezakarfalki.

"Inhabitants of Heaven or Sky". The term or phrase "Inhabitants of Earth" refers only to humans, because animals and sea creatures are called Ezbahaiim-erdi. Ezakarerdi is composed of three words:

1-E (Pronounced Eeh or Ea) means first.

2-Zakar: This is the Akkadian/Sumerian name given to Adam by Enki. The same word is still in use today in Arabic, and it means male. In Arabic, the female is called: Ountha (Oonsa).

The word "Zakar" means:

a-A male, and sometime a stud.

b-To remember.

48

In Hebrew, "Zakar" also means:
a-To remember (Qal in Hebrew).
b-Be thought of (Niphal in Hebrew).
c-Make remembrance (Hiphil in Hebrew).

There is a very colorful linguistic jurisprudence in the Arabic literature that explains the hidden meaning of the word "Zakar"; Arabs in general believe that man (Male) remembers things, while women generally tend to forget almost everything, thus was born the Arabic name for a woman "Outha or Oonsa", which means literally "To forget!"
Outha (Oonsa) either derives from or coincides with the words "Natha", "Nasa", "Al Natha", "Nis-Yan", which all mean the very same thing: Forgetting; to forget, or not to remember.
On a theological level, Islamic scholars explain that the faculty of remembering is a sacred duty for the Muslim, because it geared him toward remembering that Allah (God) is the creator.
Coincidently or not, Zakar in Ana'kh (Anunnaki language) and ancient Babylonian-Sumerian means also to remember. Could it be a hint or an indication for Adam's duty of remembering Enki, his creator?
3-Erdi means planet Earth. Erdi was transformed by scribes into Ki in the Akkadian, Sumerian and Babylonian epics.
From Erd, derived:
a-The Sumerian Ersetu and Erdsetu,
b-The Arabic Ard,
c-The Hebrew Eretz.
All sharing the same meaning: Earth; land.
Thus the word Ezakarerdi means verbatim: The first man (Or Created one) of Earth or the first man on Earth, or simply, the Earth-Man. In other word, the terrestrial human.

Ezakarfalki "E-zakar-falki":
Term for extraterrestrials as mentioned in the "Book of Rama-Dosh."
Per contra, inhabitants of planet Earth are called Ezakarerdi or Ezakar.Ki.

Glossary of terms

In terrestrial vocabulary, extraterrestrial(s) is a term applied to any entity(ies), object(s), substance(s), life-form(s), intelligence, and presence that have originated from beyond planet Earth. Also referred to as alien(s).

Contemporary ufology etymology added extraterrestrial origins coming from outer-space, other planets, stars, galaxies, and dimensions.

The word extraterrestrial is composed from three words:

A-Extra, which is derived from the Latin word Extra, which means outside; additional; beyond.

b-Terrestri, derived from the Latin Terrestris, which means pertaining to earth; belonging to earth; earthly; made out of earth, itself derived from the Latin words Terranum and Terrenum, which are derived from the word Terra, which means earth; ground; piece of land; soil.

(Note: From the Latin word Terrenum, derived the French word Terrain; and from the French word derived the English word terrain.)

c-Al, an English addition.

(Note: The Latin word Terra originally derived from the Arabic word "Tourab" (Terrab), which means dirt; dust; earth, itself derived from the Arabic word Tourba (Terrba), which means a piece of land, originally derived from the Ana'kh word Turbah, pronounced Toorbaah, which means dirt from planet Earth.

In the Sumerian/Akkadian epics and mythologies, the words dirt and earth refer to clay; the very clay found in abundance in ancient Iraq that was used by the Anunnaki to genetically create the human race.

Evolution of the extraterrestrials and the human races:
The evolution of aliens, and the extraterrestrial races on many galaxies evolved inter-dimensionally by copying, duplicating, and cloning themselves and fertilizing their own genes.

On other planets, more advanced extraterrestrial civilizations multiply and prosper through the development of brain's waves and thoughts frequencies.

They did not need to immigrate to other planets in order to survive, and/or to recreate (Reshape) themselves, as mistakenly

Glossary of terms

claimed by some ufologists, extraterrestrialogists, mediums, and channelers, for they did not encounter insurmountable ecological or bio-organic catastrophes on their own planets or stars.
Zetas and Anunnaki did alter their genetics but, not for survival purposes or for intra-planetary immigration. The alteration came as cause and effect, much needed to reach a higher level of awareness and scientific advancement.

Ezbahaiim-erdi:
Term for the animals, and sea creatures living, and/or created on planet Earth. It is composed of three words:
a-Ez means first creatures of a second level. (In comparison to humans.)
b-Bahaiim means animals. The same word exists in Arabic, and means the very same thing (Animals).
c-Erdi means planet Earth.

Ezeridim:
Term for entities or super-beings from the future. In Ufology and paranormal terminologies, they are called chrononauts, a word derived from the Greek Khrono, which means time, and "nauts" referring to space travelers, or simply voyagers.

Ezrai-il:
Name of super-beings, who can transcend space and time, and appear to humans as angels, in terrestrial term.
The Ana'kh literature refers to them as ethereal manifestation of the matter. But, our religions and Holy Scriptures depict them as the fallen angels. Ezrai-il or Ezrail is composed of two words:
a-Ezra, which means message or manifestation.
b-Il, which means divine; god; creator(s).

F "ف": One of the esoteric letters in the Anunnaki, Ulemite and Arabic alphabets. Typical with ancient Semitic names, there are none that begin with an 'F'.
The Ulema called "F" the forbidden letter, or more precisely, the letter that was never allowed to be included in the Phoenician Aramaic, and Hebrew alphabets.

Glossary of terms

"Thus all secret sounds and meanings associated with F would not be pronounced or heard, or known to the un-enlightened ones..." said Ulema Hanafi.

"There are 12 secret words starting with the letter F that are hidden in the Torah, and the Book of Rama-Dosh...", explained Ulema Sadiq Al Qaysi. And accordingly, each word produces a powerful sound capable of changing the fabric of time.

The letter F was substituted by Ph, pronounced Pveh in several Semitic languages, except Arabic; the proto-Semitic "P" became the Arabic "F".

Fadi-ya-ashadi:
Term for non-terrestrial shape-shifting entities.
The Ulema have explained this phenomenon.
Herewith, an excerpt from their Kira'at (Taken verbatim):

- For extraterrestrials, shape-shifting is necessary.
- Shape-shifting includes skin color change, organs size, general physical appearances, but not the functionality of the body.
- The fingers become longer; thin and beneath the skin, there are millions of microscopic hair filaments and pores (orifices) that help them hold on slippery surfaces like glass and wet areas.
- Many of the extraterrestrial races wear tight outfits, almost glued to their skin. Anunnaki don't.
- The "Greys" are notorious for shape-shifting.
- They can appear like a reptile, an insect and even like humans.
- Aliens of lower dimensions need to manipulate their bodies to enter different spheres, the atmosphere of other planets, particularly underwater and underground environments and habitats.
- This is exactly what happens all the time with the "Greys" who live on earth and work with scientists in restricted/confined areas, such as underground genetic labs, and military research centers and bases.

Glossary of terms

- One of their striking characteristics is claustrophobia.
- Once confined for a long time in a limited space, the "Greys" go through intense crises. And almost all their supernatural powers weaken considerably.
- For instance, they loose the ability to go through walls and rigid substances, and teleport themselves.
- Even though, some of them, like their head scientists for instance retain the ability to resize their bodies, lower the density of their bodies' molecules and penetrate dense layers, the confined condition diminishes many of their faculties, and limits the possibilities of body's manipulations.

Anunnaki vis-à-vis other alien races:

Anunnaki look very different from the Zetas and the numerous alien races that have visited the Earth. In this context, they never appear or manifest like reptilians or short "Greys".

Sinhar Ambar Anati said:

- "It is easy to recognize an Anunnaki, because he usually appears like a tall warrior.
- An Anunnaki's vest is made from thin layers of metal called "Handar".
- His wears a long robe "Arbiya" of dark colors.
- Underneath the Arbiya, he wears a sort of pans with wide contour.
- On his wrist, you always notice his navigation tool."

(Sources: 1-Ambar Anati's statements in the books: 2002: The Anunnaki Return to Earth and the End of Religions, God, and the Human Race"; 2-"What Extraterrestrials and Anunnaki Want You to Know", both by Maximillien de Lafayette.)

Anunnaki's characteristics:

- The Anunnaki can transmute and manipulate their bodies if needed. This happens very rarely.
- In many instances, they don't need to do so, because they are already known to so many galactic and outer-galactic civilizations, and are seen by inhabitants of millions and millions of stars, planets and moons.

Glossary of terms

- They are superstars in their own rights.
- The Anunnaki can easily shape-shift themselves. This is necessary for climatic and atmospheric reasons.
- Each planet, star and dimension has its own climate, temperature and atmosphere.
- Consequently the organic-galactic body must adapt to these environment's conditions in order to remain functional.
- When they visit earth or a similar sphere, the Anunnaki slightly change their physical appearances, not so much, because in general, they look like us, except their eyes are much bigger, and they are much taller than us.
- Some Anunnaki are 9 foot tall.
- Even their women are extremely tall by human standard. Some women are 8 foot tall.
- When they travel to other planets, minor changes are required. For instance, when they get out of their galaxy and visit the planets Niftar, Marshan-Haloum and Ibra-Anu, they change the color of their skin, and the shape of their hands.
- On Niftar, inhabitants have grey-blue color skin and 3 fingers in each hand. (Source: The Book of Rama-Dosh.)

Fana.Ri "Fanna-Ri":
Name for a beam, or a sort of light used in the fertilization and genetic reproduction process of the Anunnaki.
According to Ulema Albaydani, "Anunnaki reproduction is done by technology, involving the light passing through the woman's body until it reaches her ovaries and fertilizes her eggs.
The eggs go into a tube. The woman is lying on a white table for this procedure, surrounded by female medical personnel.
No discomfort is caused by this operation, because it resembles a scanning process." If performed by uncaring aliens (such as the Greys and Reptilians) it is unpleasant and even can be painful, which has given rise to abductee's stories of suffering. However, not all aliens are created equal, and have similar agenda.

Glossary of terms

The Anunnaki, which are a very compassionate race, are very gentle and the procedure is harmless. Apparently, the Anunnaki version of sex is much more enjoyable for both genders.
It involves an emanation of light from both participants.
The light mingles and the result is a joy that is at the same time physical and spiritual.
The Anunnaki do not have genitals the way we do.
As an Anunnaki hybrid becomes more and more Anunnaki, he/she loses the sexual organs.
The hybrid welcomes the changes and feels that he/she has gained a lot through the transformation.
The Anunnaki mate for life, like ducks.
They don't even understand the concept of infidelity, and don't have a word for cheating, mistress, extramarital affairs, etc. in their language.
Like many extraterrestrials, the Anunnaki do not have genital organs, but a lower level of aliens who inhabit the lowest interdimensional zone and aliens-hybrids living on earth do.
The stories of the abductees who claim to have had sex with Anunnaki are to be disregarded. Those stories are pure fiction.

Summary of fertilization and reproduction:
1-Aliens reproduce in laboratories.
2-Aliens do not practice sex at all.
3-Aliens fertilize "each other" and keep the molecules (not eggs or sperms, or mixed liquids from males and females) in containers at a very specific temperature and following well-defined fertilization-reproduction specs.
4-Alien babies are retrieved from the containers after 6 months.
5-The following month, the mother begins to assume her duty as a mother.
6-Alien mothers do not breast-feed their babies, because they do not have breast, nor do they produce milk to feed their babies.
7-Alien babies are nourished by a "light conduit."

Glossary of terms

8-Human sperm or eggs are useless to extraterrestrials of the higher dimension.

9-Extraterrestrials are extremely advanced in technology and medicine. Consequently, they do not need any part, organ, liquid or cell from the human body to create their own babies.

10--However, there are several aliens who live in lower dimensions and zones who did operate on abductees for other reasons – multiple reasons and purposes – some are genetic, others pure experimental.

Fik'r: The ability of reading others' thoughts.
Derived from the Anakh Fik-R'r, and Fik.Ra.Sa.
The esoteric Arabic word "Firasa" is derived from Fik.Ra.Sa. It means in Arabic the ability to read thoughts, to understand the psyche of a person just by looking at him/her.
The Ulema uses Fik'r to read the mind, to learn about the intentions of others, and assess the level of intelligence of people.
As defined in the "Anunnaki Encyclopedia" (Authored by M. de Lafayette), and according to the doctrine and Kira'at of the Ulema, the soul is an invention of early humans who needed to believe in a next life. It was through the soul that mortals could and would hope to continue to live after death.
Soul as an element or a substance does not exist anywhere inside the human body.
Instead, there is a non-physical substance called "Fik'r" that makes the brain function, and it is the brain that keeps the body working, not the soul.
The "Fik'r" was the primordial element used by the Anunnaki at the time they created the final form of the human race.
Fik'r was not used in the early seven prototypes of the creation of mankind according to the Sumerian texts.
Although The "Fik'r", is the primordial source of life for our physical body, it is not to be considered as DNA, because DNA is a part of "Fik'r"; DNA is the physical description of our genes, a sort of a series of formulas, numbers and sequences of what there in our body, the data and history of our genes, genetic origin, ethnicity, race, so on. Thus Fik'r includes DNA.

Glossary of terms

Ulema said: "Consider Fik'r as a cosmic-sub-atomic-intellectual-extraterrestrial (Meaning non-physical, non-earthly) depot of all what it constituted, constitutes and shall continue to constitute everything about you.

And it is infinitesimally small.

However, it can expand to an imaginable dimension, size and proportions. It stays alive and continues to grow after we pass away if it is still linked to the origin of its creation, in our case the Anunnaki.

The Fik'r is linked to the Anunnaki our creators through a "Conduit" found in the cells of the brain.

For now, consider Fik'r as a small molecule, a bubble.

After death, this bubble leaves the body. In fact, the body dies as soon as the bubble leaves the body.

The body dies because the bubble leaves the body. Immediately, with one tenth of one million of a second, the molecule or the bubble frees itself from any and everything physical, including the atmosphere, the air, and the light; absolutely everything we can measure, and everything related to earth, including its orbit.

The molecule does not go before St. Paul, St. Peter or God to stand judgment and await the decision of God -whether you have to go to heaven or hell— because there is no hell and there is no heaven the way we understand hell and heaven.

So it does not matter whether you are a Muslim, a Christian, a Jew, a Buddhist or a believer in any other religion.

The molecule (Bubble) enters the original blueprint of "YOU"; meaning the first copy, the first sketch, the first formula that created you. Humans came from a blueprint.

Every human being has a Double.

Your double is a copy stored in the "Rouh-Plasma"; an enormous compartment under the control of the Anunnaki on Nibiru and can be transported to another star, if Nibiru ceases to exist. And this double is immortal. In this context, human is immortal, because its Double never dies. Once the molecule re-enters your original copy (Which is the original You), you come back to life with all your faculties, including your memory, but without physical, emotional and sensorial properties (The properties you had on earth), because they are not perfect."

57

Glossary of terms

Ulema Sadiq said: "At that time, and only at that time, you will decide whether you want to stay in your Double or go somewhere else...the universe is yours. If your past life on earth accumulated enough good deeds such as charity, generosity, compassion, forgiveness, goodness, mercy, love for animals, respect for nature, gratitude, fairness, honesty, loyalty...then your Double will have all the wonderful opportunities and reasons to decide and select what shape, format, condition you will be in, and where you will continue to live."

In other words, you will have everything, absolutely everything and you can have any shape you want including a brand new corporal form. You will be able to visit the whole universe and live for ever, as a mind, as an indestructible presence, and also as a non-physical, non- earthly body, but you can still re-manifest yourself in any physical body you wish to choose.

Worth mentioning here, that the molecule, (So-called soul in terrestrial term) enters a mew dimension by shooting itself into space and passing through the "Baab", a sort of a celestial star-gate or entrance.

If misguided, your molecule (So-called your soul) will be lost for ever in the infinity of time and space and what there is between., until reconnected to your prototype via the "Miraya".

Is the afterlife a physical world?

According to the Anunnaki Ulema: "No and yes. Because life after death unites time and space and everything that it constitutes space and time.

It means extending to, and encompassing everything in the universe, and everything you saw, knew, felt, liked and disliked.

Everything you have experienced on earth exists in other dimensions, and there are lots of them. Everything you saw on Earth has its duplicate in another dimension.

Even your past, present and future on Earth have another past, another present and another future in other worlds and other dimensions. And if you are lucky and alert, you can create more pasts, more presents and more futures, and continue to live in new wonderful worlds and dimensions; this happens after you die. Anunnaki and some of their messengers and remnants on Earth can do that.

Glossary of terms

The physical aspect of the afterlife can be recreated the way you want it by using your Fik'r. Yes, you can return to Earth as a visitor, and see all the shows and musicals on Broadway or hang out on Les Champs-Elysées.

You can also talk to many people who died if you can find their Double in the afterlife.

You can also enjoy the presence of your pets (Dead or alive), and continue to read a book you didn't finish while still alive on earth. What you currently see on Earth is a replica of what there is beyond Earth and beyond death.

The afterlife is also non physical, because it has different properties, density and ways of life."

Anunnaki Ulema Wang Lin said: "Through Fik'r, a person can enter higher dimensions. It is of a major importance to train your Fik'r. "Transmission of the mind" training sessions can develop extra-sensorial faculties and open your "inner eye" commonly referred to as the Third Eye..." (Source: The Book of Rama-Dosh.)

Metaphysical-religious context:

"Although the Anunnaki do not believe in the same God we worship, revere and fear, understanding their concept of Khalek, the creator of our universe (Our galaxy), and other galaxies, the whole universe and especially life after death (The afterlife) could change the way we understand "God", the universe, the reason for our existence on earth, the principle of immortality, because it opens up a new way to comprehend the place of Man in the universe in this life and all the ones beyond the frontiers of time and space...", said Ulema Ghandar.

"The Anunnaki-Ulema's view of the afterlife gives a great hope and an immense relief to human beings...to all of us...", added Ulema Stambouli.

According to the "Book of Rama-Dosh", the only Anunnaki's manuscript left on earth in the custody of the Ul'ma (Ulema), humans should not be afraid to die, nor fear what is going to happen to them after they die. SinharMarduck, an Anunnaki leader and scholar said human life continues after death in the form of "Intelligence" stronger than any form of energy known to mankind.

59

Glossary of terms

And because it is mental, the deceased human will never suffer again; there are no more pain, financial worries, punishment, hunger, violence or any of the anxiety, stress, poverty and serious daily concerns that have created confusion and unhappiness for the human beings.

After death, the human body never leaves earth, nor comes back to life by an act of God, Jesus, or any Biblical prophet. This body is from dirt, and to dirt it shall return. That's the end of the story. Inside our body, there is not what we call "Soul".

Soul is an invention of mankind. It does not exist anywhere inside us. Instead, there is a non-physical substance called Fik'r that makes the brain function, and it is the brain that keeps the body working, not the soul.

The Fik'r was created by the Anunnaki at the time they designed us. The Fik'r is the primordial source of energy for our body. "However, the Fik'r despite its close tie to the human body, it does not belong to our physical properties...our mind has its own sphere, and quite often, it works independently from the body, this is how imagination and mental creativity are produced..." said Ulema Ghandar.

The Fik'r contains the DNA and all its genetic data.

Fikrama "Fikr-Rama": The "Fik'r" (Brain cell-Conduit) sixth wave, unknown yet to science.

It is related to An-zalubirach, also known as Tarkiz; a mental training that develops a supernatural power.

To fully understand what Fikrama "Fikr-Rama" means, we must first comprehend what An-zalubirach is, and how it works.

An-zalubirach is an Ana'kh/Ulemite term meaning the following:

A-Collecting thoughts, receiving and sending multiple mental images via brain wave synchronization, to improve mental and physical health;

B-Using mental energy to move or teleport things.

This is one of the phases and practices of Tarkiz.

Tarkiz means deep mental or intellectual concentration that produces telekinesis and teleportation phenomena.

Ulema's students learn this technique in various forms.

60

Glossary of terms

Basically it works like this:

a-The students use their Conduit (Which is located in the brain's cells) to control the waves of their brains (First level of learning)
b-The students concentrate on an object hidden behind a screen or a divider made from thin rice paper. (Second level of learning)
By synchronizing the frequency of their Conduit and an absolute state of introspection, the students attempt to move the hidden object from one place to another without even touching it.
In a more advanced stage, the students attempt to alter the properties of the object by lowering or increasing the frequencies and vibrations of the object itself.

I. Scientifically speaking:

The brain is constantly producing different types of frequencies and transmitting various messages based on our mental activity and state of consciousness.
A frequency is also known as the number of repetitive waves that occur in a unit of time. Brain frequencies are measured in Hertz or cycles per second and can be scientifically calculated by an electroencephalograph (EEG) machine.
Brain waves are divided in four states or categories called:

1-Beta:
It corresponds to 14 to 40 cycles per second and is associated with a fully awake and conscious state of mind. That is the frequency/state in which we spend most of our awaken time.

2-Alpha:
It corresponds to 8 to 13 cycles per second and is associated with relaxation, concentration, daydreaming and a calm state of mind. We usually experience this state when engaged in daydreaming, enjoying some music or natural scenery, or in the first stages of falling asleep.

3-Theta:
It corresponds to 4 to 7 cycles per second and is generally associated with deep meditation, hypnosis, or altered states of consciousness.
This state allows us (All of us) to have deeper insights, access our higher self (At ethical & mental level), enhance the body's healing

Glossary of terms

potential, and even multiply the power of thought for creative purposes.
This state can be accessed during deep meditation, or during the intermediate stages of falling asleep.

4-Delta:
It corresponds to 0 to 3.9 cycles per second and is generally associated with a state of deep dreamless sleep, anesthesia, or unconsciousness.
 Because of the complexity of our brains there are often several brainwave types interacting at the same time.
The particular brainwave frequency which dominates at any given time determines our state of mind.
Scientists have found that when people meditate, they reach a state of deep awareness and an internal mental serenity, allowing the two hemispheres of their brain to become synchronized, and both hemispheres commence to generate the same unified brain waves.
Brainwaves can be either conditioned, regulated, or guided to synchronize certain frequency, and in doing so, achieve the mental state associated with that frequency.
Synchronized brain waves have been associated with positive change. Audio embedded with binaural beats is one technique used to synchronize the hemispheres of the brain.
For example, when working with weight loss, a CD with specific affirmations can be created and played along with music that is designed with special software at both the alpha range, for rapid retention and motivation, and theta, for healing.
Many individuals have reported that inducing the brain to a specific frequency also produces states of expanded awareness.
(Sources: Anya; Psychospiritual Trip; Dr. Bruce Lipton.)

II. The Ulema brain's waves:
In addition to Beta, Alpha, Theta, and Delta, the Anunnaki Ulema developed a sixth wave called Fikr-Rama. It is neither measurable nor detectable, because it does not emanate from the physical brain.

It is triggered by the Conduit situated in the brain's cells. No science on earth can direct us to the exact position of the Conduit.

The Ulema said:

1-Through the mechanism of the Conduit, the enlightened ones regulate mind's waves and frequencies.

2-The Fikr-Rama allows them to enter other dimensions, solid substances and matter.

3-The Fikr-Rama is a sort of a beam much lighter than laser. It does not have particles.

4-It has no substance per se, yet, it contains energy.

5-Extraterrestrials in general, and Anunnaki in particular have a multitude of similar brain's waves.

6-The Fikr-Rama is one single tone in the rainbow of their mental vibrations.

7-Highly advanced extraterrestrial beings can project thoughts and holographic images using any of their mental vibrations waves.

Ghen-ardi-vardeh "Gen-adi-warkah":
Aagerdi-deh for short.
The act or process of talking to others without using words, and in a total silence.
Composed from three words:

a-Gen, which means people; others.

b-Ardi, which means earthly; land; location. Ertz in Hebrew, and Ard in Arabic. Ersetu "Erdsetu" in Assyrian and Sumerian. All derived from the Ana'kh Erd and Ard.

c-Vardeh, which means rose; flower; aroma; chalice; quest.
Vardeh in Hebrew and Arabic, and it means a rose in both languages.
Warkah is a substitute for Vardeh, and it means a paper; a page.
Ulema Seif Eddine Chawkat told a great story about Gen-ardi-vardeh, and briefly explained how it works in the Book of Rama-Dosh.
He said (Verbatim, unedited): "During World War One, my father worked as a military superintendent for the Turkish army.

Glossary of terms

In prisoners of war camps, some medical visits and check-ups were scheduled once a month.

It did not happen in all the concentration camps and centers of detention, but it did happen at one particular place, and my father worked there.

Some British officers (Prisoners of war) were treated properly, while others were not so lucky.

Malaria, dysentery, and other health problems among prisoners were frequent.

The Turkish army ran out of medicine and quinine pills, and the prisoners' health condition began to deteriorate. In brief, not all prisoners received medical treatment. One of those unfortunate British officers was Major V. H.

He was in serious trouble. And because he fell so ill, he could not talk anymore, and succumbed to a threatening fever.

Yet, no medical attention was given to him, until, and probably by pure coincidence or luck, a military doctor entered the tent and saw him there agonizing in his bed. The doctor noticed his serious condition and approached him.

Unfortunately, nothing could be done; medicine and pills were no longer available, and the only thing one could have done in similar situations was to wipe out the sweat of the sick prisoners. But something very unusual happened there.

The doctor briefly examined the major who was agonizing, but could not utter not one word. He placed his hand on his forehead and throat, and all of a sudden, as my father recalls, "the whole situation changed immediately.

The doctor ordered one of his adjutants to fetch a certain box; we did not know what it was. When the adjutant returned carrying the box, we saw what was in it...bandages, medicine, pills, everything you needed...syringes...etc. the major was lucky; the doctor took care of him, he gave him a few pills, told the adjutant to watch over him, and asked him to bring the major new clean pillows and blankets. We were stunned.

All of a sudden, the doctor and the major became friends.

Glossary of terms

Two years later, when the war ended, and by a pure coincidence, my father met the military doctor in Budapest, and they start to talk about the war and so many other things. One of those things was Major V. H. story.

My father asked the doctor why he cared so much for the major, and not the others. And the doctor replied that the major was one of the "Brothers". In other words, a novice-Ulema just like himself. How did he find out?

Smiling, the doctor told my father: "I touched his forehead and his throat...and by touching his throat I could read his silent message to me.

He told me that he was an Ulema."

In other words, the British major used the technique of Aagerdi-deh to talk to the doctor without opening his mouth, and of course to let him know that he was an Ulema. The British major hoped that the Turkish doctor might be an Ulema himself, and if so, he would be able to get his "silent message."

And he was!

Both were Ulema, and this is why the Turkish physician cared so much for the British prisoner.

"Of course nobody believed this", said my father. In fact, every time my father told this story, people laughed at him."

Amazingly, ninety years later, NASA began to explore Aagerdi-deh. They call it now the "Subvocal Speech."

Most recently, NASA issued a press release to that effect; it is self-explanatory. Herewith an excerpt from the release, and update on NASA's most fascinating project.

"NASA develops system to computerize silent, "Subvocal Speech": NASA scientists have begun to computerize human, silent reading using nerve signals in the throat that control speech.

In preliminary experiments, NASA scientists found that small, button-sized sensors, stuck under the chin and on either side of the "Adam's apple," could gather nerve signals, and send them to a processor and then to a computer program that translates them into words.

Glossary of terms

Eventually, such "subvocal speech" systems could be used in spacesuits, in noisy places like airport towers to capture air-traffic controller commands, or even in traditional voice-recognition programs to increase accuracy, according to NASA scientists.

"What is analyzed is silent, or subauditory, speech, such as when a person silently reads or talks to himself," said Jorgensen, a scientist whose team is developing silent, subvocal speech recognition at NASA's Ames Research Center, Moffett Field, Calif.

"Biological signals arise when reading or speaking to oneself with or without actual lip or facial movement," Jorgensen explained.

"A person using the subvocal system thinks of phrases and talks to himself so quietly, it cannot be heard, but the tongue and vocal chords do receive speech signals from the brain," Jorgensen said.

In their first experiment, scientists "trained" special software to recognize six words and 10 digits that the researchers repeated subvocally. Initial word recognition results were an average of 92 percent accurate. The first sub-vocal words the system "learned" were "stop," "go," "left," "right," "alpha" and "omega," and the digits "zero" through "nine." Silently speaking these words, scientists conducted simple searches on the Internet by using a number chart representing the alphabet to control a Web browser program.

"We took the alphabet and put it into a matrix -- like a calendar. We numbered the columns and rows, and we could identify each letter with a pair of single-digit numbers," Jorgensen said. "So we silently spelled out 'NASA' and then submitted it to a well-known Web search engine.

We electronically numbered the Web pages that came up as search results. We used the numbers again to choose Web pages to examine.

This proved we could browse the Web without touching a keyboard," Jorgensen explained.

Scientists are testing new, "noncontact" sensors that can read muscle signals even through a layer of clothing.

Glossary of terms

A second demonstration will be to control a mechanical device using a simple set of commands, according to Jorgensen. His team is planning tests with a simulated Mars rover.

"We can have the model rover go left or right using silently 'spoken' words," Jorgensen said.

People in noisy conditions could use the system when privacy is needed, such as during telephone conversations on buses or trains, according to scientists. "An expanded muscle-control system could help injured astronauts control machines.

If an astronaut is suffering from muscle weakness due to a long stint in microgravity, the astronaut could send signals to software that would assist with landings on Mars or the Earth, for example," Jorgensen explained.

"A logical spin-off would be that handicapped persons could use this system for a lot of things."

To learn more about what is in the patterns of the nerve signals that control vocal chords, muscles and tongue position, Ames scientists are studying the complex nerve-signal patterns. "We use an amplifier to strengthen the electrical nerve signals. These are processed to remove noise, and then we process them to see useful parts of the signals to show one word from another," Jorgensen said. After the signals are amplified, computer software "reads" the signals to recognize each word and sound.

"The keys to this system are the sensors, the signal processing and the pattern recognition, and that's where the scientific meat of what we're doing resides," Jorgensen explained.

"We will continue to expand the vocabulary with sets of English sounds, usable by a full speech-recognition computer program."

The Computing, Information and Communications Technology Program, part of NASA's Office of Exploration Systems, funds the subvocal word-recognition research. There is a patent pending for the new technology. (Source: NASA).

Gensi-uzuru: Apparition of deceased pets.
The Ulema are very fond of animals. Extensive passages in the Book of Rama-Dosh speak about the important role animals play in the life of humans, especially at emotional and therapeutic levels.

Glossary of terms

The Ulema believe that pets understand very well their human-friends (Instead of using the word "owners"). And also, pets communicate with those who show them love and affection.
This loving relationship between pets and their human-friends does not end when pets die.
Although the Anunnaki-Ulema do not believe in any possibility of contacting deceased people or animals, they have explained to us that contacting our departed ones is possible for a very short time, and only during the 40 days period following their death.
In other words, we can contact our deceased parents and dear ones, or more accurately enter in contact with them if:
a-They contact us short after their death;
b-They must initiate the contact;
c-This should happen during a 40 days period following their departure;
d-Their contact (Physical or non-physical) must be noticed by us. This means that we should and must pay an extra attention to "something" quite irregular or unusual happening around us. Because our departed pets will try to send us messages, and in many instances, they do.
e-We must expect their messages, and strongly believe in those messages.

The Ulema said that humans cannot contact their dead pets.
But pets can contact us via different ways we can sense and feel, if we have developed a strong bond with them.
Pets know who love them and those who don't, because pets feel, understand, sense and see our aura.
All our feelings and thoughts are imprinted in our aura, and the aura is easily visible to pets, particularly, cats, dogs, parrots, lionesses, pigs, and horses.
This belief is shared by authors, people of science and therapists in the West, despite major difference between Westerners and Ulema in defining the nature and limits of pets-humans after death contact. Ulema in defining the nature and limits of pets-humans after death contact. For instance, in the United States, pets lovers and several groups of therapists and psychics think that "a pet can reappear as a ghost.

Glossary of terms

And a ghost could be luminous or even appear as it did in life. You don't necessarily know when you see an animal if it's a ghost or not, said Warren, a researcher in the field. "It's much easier to identify a loved one who's passed and come back."
"Don't forget them because they're gone," said Jungles, who owns three cats. "Keep their toys and blankets around.
They (ghosts) will go where they're happiest." Warren agrees. "Recreate an environment conducive to the pet's life," he said. "Use your imagination and treat it like it's alive.
In other words, you should create or re-create conditions ideal for their re-appearance, even though, for a very short moment.

Gilgoolim: The non-physical state of a deceased person, at the end of the 40 days period. At that time, the deceased person must decide whether to stay in the lower level of the Fourth dimension, or head toward a higher level of knowledge, following an extensive orientation program/guidance.
From Gilgoolim, derived the Kabalistic/Hebrew word Gilgoolem referring to the cycle of rebirths, meaning the revolution of souls; the whirling of the soul after death, which finds-no rest until it reaches its final destination.

Godumu "Godumari":
The lines that appear on a Miraya, in order to register codes for galactic communications.

Goduri "Goduri-mara":
The process that prints pages or symbols from the Ulemite's Book of Rama-Dosh, using electro-magnetic beams, projected on the Minzar box.

Golem: Boor; dummy; an artificially created man.

I. Golem in Tehillim:
The word Golem in the sense of an unformed substance is to be found in Tehillim 139:16.

Glossary of terms

II. Golem in the Mishnah:
In the Mishnah (Avot 5:9), Golem is used in the sense of a stupid person, whose habit is to interrupt the speech of his fellow man and be hasty to answer, without acknowledging the truth or admitting that he does not know what he does not know.
The Mishnah uses Golem as the opposite of a wise person when it says: There are seven characteristics of a Golem, and seven of a wise man. The wise man does not speak in the presence of one who is greater than he in wisdom.
The opposite is to be found in a stupid person.

III. In medieval Jewish legends:
In medieval Jewish legends, the word signified an automaton, an artificial man, created by Kabalistic methods, such as placing in its mouth a piece of paper inscribed with the divine name. When thus created, the automaton became the servant of its creator carrying out his orders, and at times turned into a monster of destruction. It turned into an inert mass when the divine name was removed. These legends always describe the Golem as serving for the protection of the persecuted Jews of that period. (Source: Deborah.)

IV. Golem in the Kabalah:
The Golem of Prague:
Of all the Golem legends, none is as famous as the story cycle of the Golem of Prague. There had been books, plays, and even films depicting it, and often they included the creator of the Golem of Prague, Rabbi Loeb.
Prague was home to many Jewish scholars and mystics; Rabbi Loeb was probably the most famous. He lived a long life, 1513-1609, and defended his people valiantly against their enemies. His followers loved him so much they called him "The Exalted One."
Even to a holy man, or a great mystic, creating life is forbidden. It can only be justified if many lives would be saved by doing so, and not always even then. But Rabbi Loeb was instructed to try the horrifying task.

Glossary of terms

He created his Golem with divine help, using Kabalistic formulas communicated to him in dreams. Acquiring this God-given knowledge was neither simple nor easy.

The formulas were given, but deciphering them had to be done by the person himself.

Worse, he had to use the Shem Hameforash; the true name of God, which was known only to a few holy men in each generation, and was very dangerous to pronounce.

The power it unleashed could turn against the man who uttered it. This myth is unusual in that it is supposed to have happened in a specific year -- 1580.

There was a new danger brewing in Prague; a notorious priest, Taddeush, planned to accuse the Jews of a new "ritual murder." Rabbi Loeb heard about it, and to avert the horrible danger, directed a dream question to heaven to help him save his people.

He received his answer in an order that is alphabetical in Hebrew: Ata Bra Golem Devuk Hakhomer VeTigzar Zedim Chevel Torfe Yisroel .

The simple meaning was: Make a Golem of clay and you will destroy the entire Jew-baiting company. But this was only part of the message. The inner meaning had to be understood to be effective.

Rabbi Loeb extracted the real message by using Zirufim, special Kabbalistic formulas. And when he was done, he knew he could accomplish the creation of a Golem. He called two people to assist him. His son-in-law, a Kohen (a Jew descended from the ancient order of priests) and his pupil, a Levite (a Jew descended from the servants of the Temple).

He explained that they needed four elements -- fire, water, air and earth. The two assistants represented the fire and water, Rabbi Loeb, air, and the Golem, earth. He explained how they had to purify themselves, because unless they were completely ready, the Shem Hameforash would destroy them. After a day of purification, they read various chapters from a particularly holy book, Sefer Yezira (The Book of Creation) and then went to the River Moldau.

By torchlight, they sculpted a giant body out of river clay.

The Golem lay before them, facing the heaven.

Glossary of terms

They placed themselves at his feet, looking at the quiet face.

The Kohen walked seven times around the body, from right to left, reciting special Zirufim. The clay turned bright red, like fire. Then the Levite walked another seven times around the body, from left to right, reciting some more Zirufim.

The fire-like redness disappeared, and water flowed through the body. He grew hair and nails. Then Rabbi Loeb walked once around the body, and placed a piece of parchment in his mouth, on which was written Shem Hameforash.

He bowed to the East, West, South and North, and all three of them recited together: "And He breathed into his nostrils the breath of life; and man became a living soul." The Golem opened his eyes and looked at his creator.

They dressed him and took him to the synagogue, where he could get ready to start his mission. Eventually, when the Golem was no longer necessary (and some claim he went mad and became a danger to everyone) Rabbi Loeb decided to return him to the void from which he came.

He did that by recalling the Shem Hameforash, and with it the life principle, and thus restored the Golem into lifeless clay. The clay figure had to be hidden in the attic of the synagogue, and no one was permitted to enter it again until many years later.

Some writers during the nineteenth century claimed that the outlines of a giant body could still be seen there. (Sources: Dr. Ilil Arbel; Encyc. Mythica; World Jewish News Agency.)

Golibu "Golibri":
Term for the passage or transition from a physical existence to a mental or non-physical sphere, usually associated with the first dimension of the Anunnaki's Shama, meaning sky; outer space; a parallel dimension.

Golim:
A prototype of a created presence or entity, usually associated with the mixture of a terrestrial element and the thought of a Golimu who creates a non-human creature. From Golim, derived the Kabbalistic/Hebrew word Golem. See Golem and Golimu.

Glossary of terms

Golimu: The enlightened Ulema who creates a Golem look-like. See Golem.

Goirim-dari: A mental catalyst.

Goirim-daru: The vibes produced by one's double, according to the Book of Rama-Dosh; a sort of bio-plasmic rays that project the non-physical properties of an object or a thought.

Gudinh: To move around; the act or the attempt of bringing things (even thoughts) together and creating a virtual three dimensional reality from assembling collected thoughts, desires and ideas, and projecting them over a mirror serving as a catalyst. This mirror is called Miraya in Ana'kh language.

H: A symbol. It represents the two parallel lines emanated from the "Conduit" during a telekinesis training exercise, called Haabaari "Ha-abri".

Habru: Term for the mental powers of the Anunnaki-Ulema students implanted and programmed in the "Conduit".

Hadiiya: Successful completion of a study, usually referring to the initiation of the "Eight Degree".
This initiation leads to the opening or activation of the Conduit; a cell in the brains that contains supernatural powers.

Hag-Addar: Literally, the right to enter a palace; a metaphoric expression for an Ulemite adept spiritual initiation, sometimes referred to as the 18th degree ritual ceremony.
According to Ulema Govinda, during this ceremony, the adept is taught the secrets of the origin of the creation, and the invisible dimensions that co-exist with the physical world.
In addition, a multitude of techniques are revealed to the initiated, that allow him/her to acquire extraordinary powers, such as teleportation, Tay Al Ard, Firasa, dematerialization, and psychotelemetry.

Glossary of terms

Halida: Invisibility.

Hama-dar: A library. Composed of two words:
a-Hama, which means information; data; knowledge.
b-Dar, which means a place; a home, a center.

*** *** ***

Technique/Lesson 1

Godabaari "Gudi-Ha-abri"

Term for an Ulema's technique/practice aimed at developing a faculty capable of making objects move at distance, by using vibes emanated by the "Conduit" implanted in the brain. It is composed of three words:

a-Goda or Gudi, which means great; influential; powerful,

b-Ha, which means first; the first vibration,

c-Abaari or Abri, which means to cross over or to displace.

*** *** ***

Technique/Lesson 1
Godabaari "Gudi-Ha-abri"

Excerpts from a Kira'at "Reading/Training" by Rabbi Mordechai, a contemporary Anunnaki-Ulema, reproduced from the Books "On the Road to Ultimate Knowledge: Extraterrestrial Tao of the Anunnaki and Ulema" co-autored by Ilil Arbel and M. de Lafayette.

I-Developing the Conduit:

There are techniques which are partially physical and partially mental. You could refer to them as psychosomatic. As a beginner, even though your Conduit is now open, you cannot tap directly into it, because consciously, you don't even know where it is located in your brain. By adopting some postures and positions, you will send sensations to your brain.

These positions will create internal muscular vibrations, and your mind will read them. You will be sending mental visionary lines, and these will activate the cell which is responsible for imagination.

By the power of concentration and introspection, you will start to get intensified activity in the brain. This causes a buzz vibration in the brain the Conduit begins to detect.

Then, the Conduit will absorb the vibrations and organize them, and from that moment on, the Conduit will take over.

To summarize, by attempting certain activities, you are sending a message to your Conduit.

It will take some time, because at the beginning, your Conduit may not catch the messages, or if it does catch them, may not interpret the messages correctly, because the Conduit is not one hundred percent awake.

With practice, the Conduit becomes familiar with these type of messages, and it begins to give them codes.

Godabaari

Each activity would have its own code.
One thing must be understood. You cannot do these techniques
to amuse yourself, since they simply will not work unless there is
a purpose to the activity, and it must be a beneficial, positive
purpose.

***   ***   ***

II. Moving objects by using mental powers:

As mentioned earlier, you cannot do any of these techniques to
amuse yourself, it simply will not work unless there is a purpose
to the activity, and it must be a beneficial and positive purpose. It
does not have to be a great undertaking, a simple positive intent
will be just fine.
Put a lightweight coaster on the table. You wish to manipulate it
with the beneficial intent of preventing a cup of coffee or tea
from spilling on the table. Before starting, sit in a comfortable
position next to the table.
Never attempt to do this technique standing up – you may very
easily lose your balance and fall. You should not try to start with
a heavy object, but once you learned how to work with this
techniques, and your powers become stronger, you could
increase the weight of the objects.

***   ***   ***

III. Preparations:

In preparation, certain changes in lifestyle are needed during two
weeks before you start your exercises:
- 1-Avoid all alcoholic beverages.
- 2-Avoid smoking, or tobacco in any form
- 3-Abstain from sexual activity.
- 4-Do not eat meat.
- 5-Do not use any animal fat, such as lard, bacon
drippings, or butter, in your cooking.

Godabaari

IV. Precautions during practice:

During your practice, certain precautions must be taken:
- **1-**Take off your shoes, and make sure your feet touch the ground, to anchor yourself
- **2-**Do not wear anything made of metal.
- **3-**Do not allow either people or pets in the same room with you. You must have complete privacy.
- **4-**Do not have any crystal glass in the room with you.

*** *** ***

V. The technique:

- **1-**Extend your hands in front of you from the elbow up and shake them in the air for four or five seconds. This cleanses the hands from superfluous energy that might have accumulated on them.
- **2-**With your arms in the same position, spread your fingers and hold for three seconds.
- **3-**Put your thumbs right on the temples, with the fingers still spread in front of your face.
  Make sure the thumbs are located in the small indentation that is close to your eyes. People who practice acupressure will recognize this spot – pressing it is used to cure headaches. Hold the position for three seconds.
- **4-**Rotate your thumbs, taking your fingers to the back of your head, and put your forefingers in the indentation at the back of your head, where it meets the neck. Again, people who practice acupressure will recognize this spot; it is used to cure headaches.
- **5-**Push your forefingers into the indentation, and hold the position for ten seconds.

Godabaari

- **6-**Close your eyes.
- **7-**While still sitting with your back straight, bring your chin as close to your solar plexus as possible. Remain in this position for ten seconds. At this point, you will feel a slight dizziness. This is perfectly fine, it is part of the procedure.
- **8-**Keeping your thumbs in their position, release the forefingers, and rotate your hands forward until you can put your forefingers in the small indentations by the sides of the bridge of your nose. In acupressure, this is the site for one of the techniques that release pressure in the sinuses, so practitioners would be able to recognize the sensation.
- **9-**The rest of your fingers should be kept in a horizontal position, the fingers of one hand resting over the fingers of the other hand, the thumbs pointing down.
- **10-**Move your thumbs toward each other and have them touch. Your hands will form a triangle. Your arms will be in a position of ninety degrees, relative to your body.
- **11-**Say to yourself, mentally, I will now make the coaster move.
- **12-**In your mind, draw one line from the middle of your left wrist, and another line from the middle of your right wrist, toward the coaster. Visualize the coaster between the two lines.
- **13-**Keeping your hands in the same position, raise your head and sit straight.
- **14-**Drop your hands down slowly. In your mind's eye, keep on visualizing the coaster.
- **15-**Bring your arms close to your body so the arms touch the ribs.
- **16-**Move your hands up to a position in which they are horizontal to the floor.
- **17-**The left hand should serves as a rod, moving the left line further to the left. The same should be done with the right hand, moving the line further to the right.

- **18-**Keep concentrating on the coaster, with your eyes still closed, for at least another minute.
- **19-**With your eyes still closed, you will notice blue lines and bubbles moving in front of your eyes.
- **20-**At this point, decide which side of your body you are about to employ. You may use either side, but not both at the same time.
- **21-**Let's assume you chose the left side. Open your eyes, and concentrating on the left line, look intently at the coaster. Move your left hand a little to the side, and the coaster will move with it. You have accomplished your mission.

*** *** ***

VI. Closing the energy:

This is the end of the exercise, but like any other mental technique, you cannot just leave and go about your business. You have created a center of energy, which should never be left open. The energy you have created with this exercise is linear.
To create an all-around center of energy needs a higher training, and closing it is more difficult, but closing the linear energy is relatively easy.

- **1-**Extend both hands, straight in front of you.
- **2-**Make the hands stay in the direction of the lines.
- **3-**Bring the hands close together, with a very little distance between them.
- **4-**Visualize a very thin thread entering the space between the hands. Close your hands around the thread.
- **5-**Bring your closed hands toward your solar plexus.
- **6-**Open your hands, and shake them as you have done in the beginning. You have closed the center of energy.

*** *** ***

82

Technique/Lesson 2

Gomari "Gumaridu"

A term referring to an Anunnaki Ulema technique capable of manipulating time. It is also called the "Net Technique".

Ulema Rabbi Mordachai said: "Human beings treat time as if it were linear. Day follows day, year follows year, and task follows task. The Anunnaki Ulema, however, have long ago learned how to treat time nonlinearly, and thus be able to accomplish more in their lives."

84

Technique/Lesson 2
Gomari "Gumaridu"

Note: Ulema Rabbi Mordechai is talking to his student Germain Lumiere, who visited with him in Budapest, where he resided for some years. (Excerpts from the books "On the Road to Ultimate Knowledge", and "The Book of Rama-Dosh, both co-authored by Ilil Arbel and M. de Lafayette.)

"It would be beneficial if you could manipulate time in such a way as to be faster than normal people, and this is what we are going to do in the forthcoming exercise..." said Rabbi Ulema Mordechai.

I. The Exercise:

For the purpose of this exercise, one must have complete privacy, and in addition, one's consciousness changes under the influence of the exercise to such an extent that a mother, for instance, would not hear her children if they need her. So the exercise cannot be done while young children are at home.

Also, if you are taking care of an ill or elderly relative, you should not pursue it either.

If parts of the tasks you wish to accomplish are to be done at work, again, you cannot accomplish that because almost all jobs involve the presence of other people. Therefore, for the purpose of this exercise, we will choose a simple frame and an acceptable set of tasks.

Let's choose a Saturday, and you have to accomplish a few tasks. All of them must be done on Saturday, because on Sunday you are expecting to be busy with other things. You have, in short, seven hours. Let's assume you have chosen these tasks:

Gomari "Gumaridu"

- You have to drive your spouse to the airport.

- You have committed yourself to your boss, promising that you will write a report of a hundred pages or so for Monday.
- You want to shop for food for the week.

This is quite a lot to do in the seven hours that we will assume are available to you during that day. The trip to the airport would take about an hour.

The shopping will take about an hour and a half. As for the report, it looks like it should take at least ten hours. So obviously some of the things you wanted to do will not get done.

But the Anunnaki-Ulema say that all these things can be done if you learn to break the mold of the linear time, and they have a technique one can learn to do so.

II. The Equipment:

For this technique, you will need a few props:
- A round net. It can be anything – a fishing net, a crochet tablecloth, anything made of thread or yarn with perforations. It should be around four feet in diameter.
- Paper
- Pencil
- Scissors.

III. The Technique:

- **1-**Since one of the tasks involves taking your spouse to the airport, work on the preliminary preparations behind a closed door.
- **2-**Look intently at the net, and memorize the way it looks, so that you can easily visualize it.
- **3-**Close your eyes and visualize the net.

- **4-**In your mind, draw a large circle on the net.
- **5-**In your mind, let the net float in the air, making sure it is not flat and horizontal, but moving, bending, waving, and being in a vertical position most of the time.
- **6-**In your mind, concentrate on the tasks you wish to accomplish.
- **7-**In your mind, represent each task as a hole that you mentally perforate in the net. Since you have three tasks, you visualize three holes.
- **8-**Open your eyes, take the physical net, and toss it lightly on a chair or a couch nearby. Do not make it flat and horizontal, just let it land on the piece of furniture like a casual throw.
- **9-**Close your eyes again, and visualize the holes in the mental net. Look at the holes you made, visualizing their shape, their edges, and their exact position on the mental net.
- **10-**In your mind, throw the mental net on the physical net.
- **11-**Take the paper and pencil, and draw three circles that would match, by their shape and size, the mental holes you have visualized.
- **12-**Cut the circles with the scissors.
- **13-**Write the descriptions of the tasks you wish to perform on the back of the paper, a single task for each circle. If possible, break the task into segments. For example, if you are working on the circle that represents the trip to the airport, write:
- **A-**Take car out of the garage – five minutes.
- **B-**Drive to airport and drop spouse at the terminal – twenty five minutes.
- **C-**Return home – twenty five minutes.
- **D-**Return car to the garage – five minutes. Do the same for all the tasks.

Gomari "Gumaridu"

- **14-**Put the circles on the physical net and fold it around them. Tie the top with a ribbon, so the papers will not fall out, and suspend it on a hook or a door.

  It must remain suspended until the tasks are done, or until the seven hours are over.

- **15-**Start with a linear task, which will anchor you. The best one will be the trip to the airport, and for this task no Anunnaki-Ulema powers are used at all. Even though your Conduit is not open, since you have not been trained by a master, it is still there and it can calculate what it needs to do, and how to partially and gradually squeeze the other tasks into the frame of seven hours.

- **16-**When you come back home, you should start the second task, the shopping. While you are shopping, the Conduit will employ a system that will be like two old-fashioned tape recorders working at the same time.

  One tape recorder is working slowly, about 30 turns per second.

  The other tape recorder does 1000 turns a second. They do not interfere with each other.

  While you are shopping, which is represented by the slow tape recorder, the time you are using is slower than the time the Conduit is squeezing in.

  The Conduit knows how quickly to "spin" because you have outlined the tasks and the time they take on the circles of paper. This is, therefore, the way the faster tape recorder works.

- **17-**When you come back from your shopping trip, you decide to go to your computer to work on your report. You have to make sure all the physical parts are working properly: The computer is connected to the printer, the paper in the printer is sufficient for printing the entire report, your ink cartridge is fresh, and everything on your desk is in order.

- **18-**Before you start working on your report, unplug the telephone, turn off the TV, make sure nothing is on the stove, and your room's door is locked.

- **19-**Start typing the report.
- **20-**What will happen now will not be entirely clear and understandable to you, because you will be existing, for the duration, on different levels of vibrations.
- **21-**Everything will seem, and actually be, faster than you are accustomed to, including your typing speed.
- **22-**Your body will function normally, but you will not be entirely aware of it, and you will lose your awareness of your physical surrounding.
- **23-**After working for a while, you will feel extremely tired, and without much thinking you will lie down and fall asleep. This is important, because at this time, it is not your normal physical faculties that are in control, but copies of yourself, your doubles, are handling the job. Unless you are a master, it is best to sleep during such occurrences.
- **24-**After a while, and the time for that varies greatly, you will wake up. Naturally, you will return to the computer, feeling again like yourself, and ready to resume your typing.
- **25-**You may be stunned to see that the report of a hundred pages, which you expected to spend hours upon hours preparing, will be neatly stacked by your printer, completely done.
- **26-**When you read it, it will be perfectly clear that it was written by yourself, entirely your work and your style, including your regular mistakes and typos, since the doubles do not edit your work.
- **27-**The only difference is that it was done with supernatural speed.
- **28-**This is a proof positive that you have done the work personally and did not hallucinate these occurrences.

*** *** ***

Gomari "Gumaridu"

IV. Closing the Energy Center:

You have created a strong field of energy, which now must be closed.

- 1-Take the net you have suspended, and open it up.
- 2-Take out the paper circles, and cross out the tasks that have been accomplished.
- 3-Fold the net and put it in its accustomed place.
- 4-Throw out the circles.
- 5-You have closed the energy center. Tour tasks are done.

*** *** ***

Technique/Lesson 3

Gomatirach-Minzari
"Gomu-Minzaar"

Known also as the "Mirror to Alternate Realities."
Rabbi Mordechai said: "Building and using the Minzar is risky. However, if the student reads the instructions carefully and does not deviate from them, it should be a reasonably safe procedure. If you choose to try it, this may be one of the most important lessons you will ever learn, since the benefits, both physical and spiritual, are without equal.

Technique/Lesson 3
Gomatirach-Minzari
"Gomu-Minzaar"

Note: From Ulema Rabbi Mordechai's Kira'at (Reading). (Published in part in the books "On the Road to Ultimate Knowledge", and "The Book of Rama-Dosh, both co-authored by Ilil Arbel and M. de Lafayette.)

Those who are familiar with the concept of the Anunnaki's Miraya would notice a resemblance in the way these tools are used.

However, one should realize that we are not pretending to use the kind of cosmic monitor that is connected, through the Akashic Libraries on Nibiru, to the Akashic Record itself.

It is beyond our scope to even conceive how such a tool had ever been created. Nor are we attempting to recreate the kind of Minzar that is used by the Anunnaki-Ulema, who are enlightened beings whose Conduit has been opened.

Most of us possess a Conduit that has not been opened, and the Minzar we recommend is fitted to our level of advancement. Nevertheless, working with the Minzar will open doors that will astound and amaze any student. You will be using the techniques to create an alternate reality that will allow you to do things you have never imagined are possible.

***   ***   ***

CREATING YOUR OWN WORLD

What you are aiming for is a place to which you can retreat at will, a place where you can have many options. It will be a place of beauty and comfort, and it should allow you opportunities to learn, to create, to invent, to meet compatible people, to connect with animals, to heal, or to simply take a vacation.

Gomatirach-Minzari "Gomu-Minzar"

The place is designed and planned entirely by you, and is brand new. You cannot say "My new alternate reality is exactly like Rome, Italy," because there is a good possibility that the Conduit, confused by this mixed message, will actually take you to Rome, Italy, in our own world.

If this happens, no real harm is done, but no benefit will occur either. You will simply be wandering the streets of another city, not benefiting from the advantages of an alternate reality at all. However, you should certainly take certain elements from places you like, Rome included if that is what you wish, since you are not required to build your new reality in a vacuum.

However, don't limit yourself to one place. You may want to copy a particular art museum from Rome, where you can always indulge in looking at your favorite sculptures and paintings. Then, you might want to add the gorgeous rose garden from the Brooklyn Botanic Gardens in New York City.

A charming old-world train station from somewhere in Eastern Europe might make the place more interesting, with perhaps a touch of the Orient Express, and a sunny Mediterranean beach would not hurt, either.

How about a café you liked in Paris, and the cozy little library from your home town, where you used to have so much fun during your childhood and you knew you could find every book that was ever written?

Design the house you would want to live in. It may be an opulent mansion, or on the other hand, some of us would prefer a small, simple, rural-type house with a restful cottage garden.

It's all entirely up to you.

Create your new world carefully and don't worry if you change things around as you go along, there is always room for change and development. Did you suddenly remember your trip to China and a wonderful Pagoda you liked? Put it in. Did you enjoy your snorkeling in Australia? Add a barrier reef. One thing should be made entirely clear. Any place you want is allowed, except a place where others are hurt in any way whatsoever, and that includes not only humans, but animals as well. Do not imagine a steak dinner, do not imagine fishing, do not imagine hunting.

Gomatirach-Minzari "Gomu-Minzar"

Don't waste your time imagining the "glories" of wars. Do not imagine a place where you demean your spouse and yourself by having multiple partners. Do not imagine pornography. Do not imagine a place where you revenge the ills brought on you by people you hate.

Your Conduit will not accept any action that can cause pain or even discomfort to any living creatures.

Therefore, if you have any negative intention, you are wasting your time. You can build twenty Minzaars, but none of them will take you to such a place.

Rather, if you wish to heal from hurts imposed by others, or painful addictions, imagine yourself getting away from all and entering a fresh new world where nothing of this sort exists.

Rest assured that you will never meet anyone who had ever hurt you in your new reality.

Do this for a few weeks before you build the Minzaar, so the new place is well established in your mind and you can imagine it in seconds.

This is essential because contacting the new reality during the building of the Minzaar requires speed, and no one can create a new world for themselves in a few minutes! And most important, don't do it as a chore.

This should be a fun, rewarding mental exercise.

There is no doubt that you will meet pleasant people in your new reality, but there are those who would also wish to have a guide, or a friend, to introduce them to the new world.

This is also possible, and the directions are given below.

If this is part of your plan, by all means do the same and imagine the person you wish to contact with.

Don't limit yourself to the kind of person you think you should choose. The friend does not have to be a conventional "spiritual guide" which is often described by people who channel entities, such as a Native American guide, an Asian guru, or a guardian angel. The guide can be just about anyone you would like to have as a friend.

95

Gomatirach-Minzari "Gomu-Minzar"

The Minzaar Technique

I. Prerequisites:

- For seventy-two hours before building the Minzaar, and before any subsequent visit to the alternate reality, you must abstain from:
    o Drinking alcohol
    o Using any addictive substance
    o Eating meat.
    o Wearing nail polish
- Do not wear clothes made of polyester.
- Wear white or light colored clothes.
- Imagine only positive conditions (see above for details).

II. Precautions:

- Before starting, remember the full instructions carefully.
- These procedures are for novices, and involve mental transportation only.
- If, however, you become extremely adept, there is a possibility of future physical teleportation. In such event, please exercise some logical restrictions on your activities.
- For example, people who had heart problems, pregnant women, and individuals with severe arthritis, asthma, diabetes, should not take the chance of moving physically between realities without consulting first with an Enlightened Master who would advise them on the best way to proceed.
- The Minzaar, during building or using, may explode. The explosion is small, and the glass that is used does not shatter or fly around, so you will not be hurt by it.

- However, if it is built inside your home, or in any confined area, such an occurrence may cause damage to children, pets, furniture, or decorative objects.
- The Minzaar must be built in an outdoor location, where the energy that will be released during such an explosion will not cause damage.
- You can build it in your back yard, but if you live in an apartment in the city, you must find an appropriate location where you will be outside, but still have some privacy.
- A woman should not wear loose skirts, flowing dresses, or scarves. For everyone, close-fitting clothes, though not too tight for comfort, are highly recommended.
- Never wear clothes made of polyester.
- Remove any jewelry or metal objects you may be wearing.
- You will be using dry ice. When you handle it, make sure to wear gloves, since direct contact with dry ice will burn your skin.
- You will be using two bowls. Make sure they are not made of metal.
- When you cut the dry ice, be sure to place it in the dry bowl. Never mix dry ice and water, this can cause serious injury.

*** *** ***

III. Equipment and Supplies:

The supplies required to build the Minzaar are readily available. You will need:
- Laminated glass, two feet by two feet, with rounded, smooth edges. Laminated glass is made of two layers of glass, and it does not shatter into sharp-edged slivers when it breaks. It is the safest glass you can use. Have the store cut it for you to the right dimensions.

Gomatirach-Minzari "Gomu-Minzar"

- A few pieces of charcoal.
- A role of aluminum foil.
- A very small quantity of dry ice. You will only need a small cube, approximately the size of a dice.
- Two very thin pieces of wire, each three feet in length.
- Two iron nails.
- A Magnet.
- Two plastic or glass bowls that would contain sixteen ounces of liquid each. Never use metal.
- Lumber, enough to build a two feet by two feet base, two inches height.
- Wood glue.
- Adhesive spray.
- Fabric glue.
- Small finishing nails.
- A small hammer.
- Water.
- A sheet of white linen, large enough to create four panels that you will use to surround yourself as you work with the Minzaar.
- This sheet should be made of flame-retardant fabric, or if you cannot find such a sheet, spray your linen with flame-retardant spray.
- Four Pieces of cardboard, six feet by two feet.

IV. Building the Minzaar:

- Magnetize the iron nails by placing them next to the magnet for a few hours.
- Build a wooden base. It should be a simple box, two feet by two feet, and two inches tall.
- Use the wood glue and the finishing nails to make it steady.

- Fold each piece of cardboard vertically, ending with a small pyramid measuring three feet by two feet.
- Make all four can stand up steadily.
- With the fabric glue, attach four panels from the white linen sheet to the cardboard pyramids.
- Rub the coal on one side of the glass, until it covers the surface with a thin black film.
- Use the adhesive glue spray to stabilize the film. Allow to dry thoroughly.
- From the aluminum foil, cut seven ribbons.
- Each should be a little less than one inch in width.
- Six of the ribbons should be exactly two feet long, and the seventh should be two inches longer.
- Take four ribbons, not including the longer one, and glue them to the coal covered side of the glass.
- They should be placed with equal distance between them and from the edges, creating five equal sized spaces where the coal dust will be visible.
- Take the remaining three ribbons.
- They should be glued on top of the four ribbons, but in ninety degrees to them, creating a grid.
- The longer ribbon should be glued in the middle of the box, with an inch extending on each side.
- The others should be glued with equal distance between the middle ribbon and the edges, creating four spaces. The grid will thus be made of a square spaces between the ribbons.
- Use the extra ribbon that is extending from both sides to attach the wires. Each wire will be extending vertically from the box.
- Place the glass on the wooden base, coal and ribbon side down, and clean side up.
- Make sure the glass and the base are squared and the edges are perfectly aligned.
- To each wire, attach one of the magnetized nails you have prepared in advance.

Gomatirach-Minzari "Gomu-Minzar"

- Arrange the panels around the box.
- There should be one on three sides, and the fourth one will be placed behind you.
- Pour the water into one of the bowls, and place one of the nails into it. The wire that is attached to this nail must be fully stretched.
- Cut the dry ice, wearing gloves, into a dice-sized cube. Place it in the dry, empty bowl. Remember never to mix dry ice and water!
- That wire should be closer to the glass than the one that is touching the water, so bend it slightly.
- The dry ice will produce some smoke. That is normal, it is an effect that is often used for theatrical production, and it will not hurt you.
- Sit in front of the glass box, put the fourth panel behind you, and close your eyes.

V. Contacting the Alternate Realities:

- Close your eyes and visualize a green, virgin land, a place no one has ever seen before.
- Imagine, dream, and think about the land you have been visualizing for the past few weeks.
- You are bringing the things you love and want most, the good things that you wish to see in your life, to the green land. You are creating a new earth, the way you want it.
- There are people in the new place.
- You must build places for them, streets, houses, a wonderful city or countryside, exactly the way you want it.
- Working as fast as you can, and with your eyes still closed, in a few minutes you will sense smoke coming from your left side. It will not rise high, but remain rather low, and it will creep close to the glass.

Gomatirach-Minzari "Gomu-Minzar"

- Realize that even though your eyes are closed, you will actually see the smoke.
- When you are sure you are seeing the smoke, open your eyes.
- Put both your hands on the glass, with your fingers spread out.
- Concentrate your gaze on the spaces between the fingers. Bring to mind all the beautiful things you imagined in the new land, and place them in the spaces between the fingers.
- Start alternating your concentration between the tips of your fingers and the spaces between the fingers.
- Continue for about five minutes.
- You will notice that the tips of your fingers will produce light, in the form of sparks. There will be no physical sensation caused by these sparks.
- Slide your hands closer to your body until they are about an inch or two from your body.
- Put your hands on the edges of the glass, each on one side.
- Look down into the bottom of the Minzaar. You will notice that the color of the aluminum ribbons has changed, and that the charcoal film looks as smooth as a marble. The glass has turned into a black mirror, and a line of light will vibrate on the black surface.
- You will begin to see the things you have imagined as miniatures in the black mirror.
- Some will look proportional and organized. Others will be out of proportion. They will be moving and shifting.
- You may have created a person to function as a friend and a guide.
- If you did so, look for that person in the Minzaar.
- You will soon find him or her, so try to increase the size of the person. In a few seconds, the person will acquire dimension, proportion, and personality, and will appear as real, in or out of the Minzaar.

Gomatirach-Minzari "Gomu-Minzar"

- You will establish a true rapport with him or her, though you may not quite understand the nature of the rapport.
- If what you imagined is a country, or a place, or a house rather than a person, you will develop the connection to it so that you will be able to escape to this place at will. Many students prefer creating such a place, since, as it will most likely to have people in it, will combine the advantages of both.
- In the future, you will not need to build a second Minzaar, or even use the many steps of preparations to envision the person or the place you have created.
- They will be stored in your brain. The act of building the Minzaar was meant to trigger one of the Conduit faculties in the brain. A rudimentary one by comparison to what the Anunnaki-Ulema can do, but of great benefit none the less.
- You could not, for example, simply buy a ready-made black mirror, and work with it.
- You must follow the step-by-step the creation of the Minzaar to achieve the effect.
- It will be a good idea to throw out the unnecessary equipment, such as the nails, the bowls, etc., but keep the Minzaar, which has turned into a beautiful black mirror, as a stimulus for the activity.
- You can go into the new country anytime you wish. It is a physical place, located in a different dimension, but just as real as this one.
- When you go there, you can spend months in that time frame, while here on earth only a few minutes will pass. That is because the Conduit allows you to duplicate yourself, to create a double, and time is different in other dimensions.
- What you can do there is limitless. You can simply rest and enjoy a place that will never hurt you, a vacation from the trials and tribulations in the here and now. Or, perhaps, you wish to create something.

- Let's say you want to write a screenplay, and can never find the time or the leisure to do it here. Well, you can go to your special place for the duration of the time you need for writing this screenplay, and come back to your present existence after a few seconds of leaving it.
- The advantage will be that you have written the play and it is all there in your memory, one hundred percent of it. All you will need is the short time needed to type it. Or perhaps you are not well, and you would like to see the doctors and the hospitals you have created at this new environment.
- It is quite likely that they may have a cure to at least some ailments – it won't hurt to try. Possibly you wanted to build a magnificent library, containing an enormous number of books. By all means, this is a wonderful experiment, with one added bonus.
- When you are at this library, make a note of certain titles and authors which you have never heard of before. Then, when you are back home, ask a librarian, or check the Internet, to see if such titles/authors exist.
- If they do, it would be a proof that you have not been hallucinating! Or perhaps you would like to try a new career, see how it feels to become a teacher, or a singer, or a trapeze artist. Why not try it? You are the best judge on what you wish to accomplish!

*** *** ***

VI. Subsequent Visits to the Alternate Realities:

After the initial visit to the alternate reality, you will no longer need to use the Minzaar. As mentioned before, some students find it easier to look at the Minzaar for a while before attempting the visit, but it is not entirely necessary.

Gomatirach-Minzari "Gomu-Minzar"

- The best time to visit is your usual bed time. Before you go to sleep, just lie down on your bed. Generally, it is best to lie on your right side, to avoid pressure on the heart.
- Close your eyes.
- Think about the place you want to visit.
- Draw as clear a picture of it in your mind as you can.
- At this point, remember the way your hands were placed on the Minzaar, and imagine yourself behind your fingers.
- Tell yourself the first activity you wish to perform during your visit.
- For seven to ten seconds, do not think at all. Make your mind completely blank.
- Do not be startled – amazing things will begin to happen now. Images will float before your eyes, you will hear sounds, or noises. This is called "The buzzing of the mind."
- At this moment, the preliminary rapport is established between the necessary cell in your Conduit and your double in the alternate reality.
- The cell will zoom you there and your double will be your guide. In other words, the cell acts as your vessel, and the double as the pilot.
- As soon as you arrive, the double will stop all activities and instantly merge with you.
- Your visit has begun.

*** *** ***

VII. Benefits and Advantages:

Beside the pleasure and learning experiences that you gain through your trips to the alternate reality, there are several concrete advantages that will manifest themselves very soon in your normal reality.

- You will be less tense or nervous.
- You will gradually lose any phobia that might have tormented you for many years, perhaps all your life.
- Your physical health will improve.
- You will be able to work efficiently, since you will bring with you some very important creations, plans, or thoughts from your alternate reality.
- Such products or services will be performed in much greater speed since they have been "rehearsed" in the alternate reality.
- You can learn languages with surprising speed since you can actually learn them first in the alternate reality, and the memory is retained. That applies to other skills, such as computer skills, art, music, and many others.
- You will put every moment to good advantage.
- If you hate waiting in line, or sitting in the doctor's office, or listening to your boss droning on and on while of course you cannot put a stop to the conversation, just hop to the new reality for a few minutes, and do something fun or creative there. Of course, for these few moments you will be out of touch with your earth body, but you will be recalled back quickly as soon as needed. Obviously, using this quick "hop" you will never be bored again, ever.
- To complement this activity, it is advisable to always carry a notepad and a pen in case you wish to quickly record an experience.

*** *** ***

VIII. Returning to Your Regular Reality on Earth:

We must note that there is never any need for fear. Some people are concerned that the body that they have left on earth when visiting their alternate reality might be exposed to harm, perhaps even attacked.

Gomatirach-Minzari "Gomu-Minzar"

There is no reason for such fear. First of all, with the exception of the first time, when you originally build the Minzar, you will usually do it in the privacy of your own bedroom, and alone.

Second, no matter how long you will spend in your alternate reality, you will return to your body seconds after you left it in our reality here, since time flows very differently in the alternate reality, and the Conduit knows how to handle it.

The only thing you should be concerned about is not to come back into the body too quickly.

If you panic suddenly and zoom into your body, you may harm it by this speed.

You are perfectly safe, so come back easily and slowly.

The best procedure for a beginner is to spend the time and enjoy the stay in the alternate reality without worrying about coming back. The first few times would not take long, since you are so new at it, anyway.

After a while, your stays will be extended.

In both cases, after what seems to be minutes, hours, days, or months, since it really does not matter how long you are there, suddenly you will remember that you left your body behind. For a few seconds, you are not sure which part of you is real, and it may create the sense of fear discussed above.

Remember there is nothing to fear, your Conduit is in control, and it knows what it is doing. So when this moment arrives, allow yourself to relax, and in seconds you will be aware that you are back in the presence of your normal earth body.

Do not rush, and do not bunch yourself quickly into the body from either side. Instead, help your Conduit by hovering horizontally right above your body, and then settling peacefully into it.

Most likely that will be followed by a few minutes sleep, after which you will wake up refreshed and in complete memory of your activities in the alternate reality."

*** *** ***

Technique/Lesson 4

Gubada-Ari
The Triangle Of Life Technique

Term referring to the Anunnaki-Ulema "Triangle of Life", and how to apply the value of the "Triangle" shape to health, success, and peace of mind.

Most importantly, how to find the healthiest spots and luckiest areas on earth, including private places and countries, and take advantage of this.

Note: From Ulema Rabbi Mordachai's Kira'at (Reading). (Excerpts from the books "On the Road to Ultimate Knowledge", and "The Book of Rama-Dosh, both co-authored by Ilil Arbel and M. de Lafayette.)

108

Technique/Lesson 4
Gubada-Ari
The Triangle Of Life Technique

Ulema Rabbi Mordechai explained the concept, importance, and practical use. He said (Verbatim):
How this technique will enhance your life:
With the help of the triangle, you will able to find the perfect areas on earth where your health, success, and peace of mind will be at their optimum. You can work it on a large scale and find out the best countries to live in, or on a small scale, which would give you the best neighbourhoods in your own city or county.

I. Synopsis of the Theory:

- There are lines of energy spinning around the world. In this exercise, we will concentrate on the lines that are revealed by the use of the triangle.
- The energy flows in currents, both negative and positive, mostly underground, traversing the globe.
- Those who live above the positive lines, will have good health, success, and peace of mind. Those who live above the negative lines, will have bad health, lack of success, and will experience mind turmoil.
- The meaning of life is based on the fact that life is, in itself, a triangle.
- One corner of the triangle represents health.
- The second represents success.
- The third represents peace of mind.

Gubada-Ari

- You find meaning by placing the triangle you are about to draw on the world.
- The student might ask, where do I put the triangle? How do I choose the original location? The answer is, you put the triangle wherever you are.
- The student might ask, what if I change locations? The answer is, this technique is working within the dictates of the moment. Wherever you are, the triangle follows. Change it as many times in life as you need. It always works.

*** *** ***

II. Materials:

- This lesson can be accomplished with two different props. And they are easy to find.
- You can use a globe, or a flat map of the world.
- A globe (Earth Globe) gives a more precise directions, but it is expensive and sometimes hard to get.
- The student may instead use a flat map of the world.
- It is not as precise, but the distortion is so slight that it does not signify, and it is cheaper and readily available.
- If you are using a map, you will need lightweight paper which is somewhat transparent, a pen, a ruler, and a pair of scissors.
- If you are using a globe, you will need plastic wrap, the kind that is used to wrap sandwiches or leftovers in the kitchen, since it will adhere easily to a globe.
- You will also need a magic marker that can write on this material, a ruler, and a pair of scissors.

*** *** ***

III. The Technique:

- The drawings below show how the double triangle, or the six-pointed star, was created.
- To be most effective, an individual exercise should be used separately for Health, Success, and Peace of Mind.
- As you copy the template below, simply change the word on top for each exercise.

"Triangle A" was drawn as an equilateral triangle.

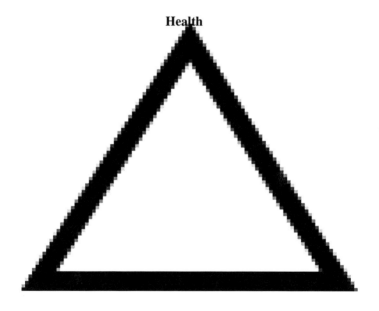

Figure 1: Triangle A

"Triangle B" was drawn by extending the lines on top of triangle A, and then closing these lines and thus creating a second triangle of the same size exactly.

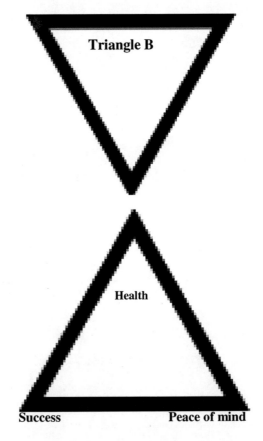

Figure 2: Triangle on the top is triangle B.

"Triangle A" was moved up and centered exactly on Triangle B. By doing this, we have created a six pointed star. We have numbered the four small triangles created on the sides of the star, as 1, 2, 3, and 4.

Figure 3: The six pointed star

Gubada-Ari

- Copy the template of the star on transparent paper if you are using a map, or on the plastic wrap if you are using a globe.
- Place the center of the star precisely on the location of the place you are living in now, at this very moment.
- All countries located inside these four small triangles are good for your health. Should you have a health issue, or a desire to live in the more healthy places, these are your choices

***   ***   ***

The Anunnaki-Ulema Triangle is a complex concept. Perhaps, to better understand its essence, revisiting Ulema Mordechai, and listening to him explaining to his student Germain Lumiere is a must.
Excerpt from his dialogue with Lumiere, reproduced from the books "On the Road to Ultimate Knowledge", and "The Book of Rama-Dosh, both co-authored by Ilil Arbel and M. de Lafayette.)

Ulema Mordechai and Germain Lumiere Dialogue

"We are going to apply the value of the triangle shape to real life and to the organization we call the Pères du Triangle. I am not sure if you are aware of it, but there are six Triangles on earth. Actually, they rule the earth."
Lumiere: "Are they political? Secret? Are they part of existing governments?" I asked.
"They are more important, far more so, than mere governments. Can you define for me what are the most important things in life?"
"Life itself?" I said.
"Yes, this is right within itself, but it does not answer the question." I was annoyed. Here we go again, I said to myself. I am arguing with an old Jewish Rabbi. They always go round and round, using semantics that get you nowhere. "How can I be right and wrong at the same time?" I asked.

114

Ulema Mordechai and Lumiere Dialogue

"Well, we will go about it in a different way," said Rabbi Mordechai. "What is the meaning of life on earth?"

"Family? Friends?" I said, knowing full well that he will argue again, and I was right.

"Family and friends make our life meaningful, of course," said Rabbi Mordechai, but they are not the meaning of life. The meaning of life is based on the fact that life is, in itself, a triangle. One corner of the triangle represents health.

The second represents success.

The third represents peace of mind. Visualize it like that." And he demonstrated by joining his two thumbs and his two forefingers, creating a triangle. "You find meaning by placing this triangle on the world." He leaned his hands on the large globe. "But the all important thing is to find the right spot to put the triangle on."

"I am not sure I follow," I said, dubiously.

"So let's demonstrate it with some props," said Rabbi Mordechai. He gave me paper, pencil, a ruler, and a pair of scissors. "Now," he said, "draw and cut a more or less equilateral triangle from this peace of paper." I did, trying my best to make an exact drawing, and cut it carefully.

"Now," he said, "put it anywhere on the globe."

I took the paper, and feeling like a fool tried to place the paper on the globe, knowing that it will fall off since I used no glue. Of course it fell, several times, until Rabbi Mordechai smiled rather cynically, an expression I have never seen on his face before. "Put it on again," he said, giving the globe a piercing look. I did, and the paper stuck to the globe. Another trick, I thought. I was tired of tricks.

"Spin the globe," he said. The triangle stuck and the globe was spinning.

"As this is happening," said Rabbi Mordechai, "realize that if the lines of the triangle were somehow continued, they would represent lines of energy around the world. Let's concentrate on the lines that occur when you extend the Health corner at the top of the triangle.

This energy flows in currents, both negative and positive, mostly underground, traversing the globe." This was beginning to make sense to me.

I span the globe again, the paper stuck, and I tried to imagine the continued lines that would follow the entire world. I was beginning to see the pattern.

"Those who live above the positive lines, will have good health. Those who live above the negative lines, will have bad health. But let's elaborate a little. Look at the drawing I am about to make."

He drew a triangle, wrote Health on the top of it, and said, "This is Triangle A."

Then, he extended the lines. "Close these lines and thus create a second triangle of the same size exactly, which we call Triangle B. Everything inside Triangle B will have good health. Now, make a copy, of an exact size, of Triangle A. Move it up and center it exactly on Triangle B. By doing this, you have created a six pointed Star of David."

By now I realized we were not doing any tricks, but studying a most fascinating and helpful technique. "How do we proceed?" I asked, poring over the drawing.

"We will number the four small triangles created on the sides of the Star of David

1, 2, 3, and 4. All countries located inside these four small triangles are good for health. Should you have a health issue, or a desire to live in the more healthy places, these are your choices."

"So I imagine that you can do the same for Success and Peace of Mind, to find the best of each quality?"

"Correct," said Rabbi Mordechai.

"Ah, but there still one problem here. Where do I put the triangle? How do I choose the original location? " I asked.

Rabbi Mordechai laughed. "For once, son, I encourage you to consider yourself the center of the world. You put the triangle wherever you are."

"However, Rabbi Mordechai, another question remains. At this moment I am in Budapest. I put the triangle on the map of Hungary and learn of my best locations. But next week, or next month, I am going back to France. Then, should I put it on the map of France?"

"Yes, of course," said Rabbi Mordechai.

"This technique is working within the dictates of the moment. Wherever you are, the triangle follows. And it always works."

Ulema Mordechai and Lumiere Dialogue

"I am a little surprised to see the Star of David involved in Ulema teachings," I said.

"Not at all," said Rabbi Mordechai. "You must realize that the Kabbalists share many of the Ulema techniques. There is much more to it, as this is only one of the seven great secrets of the Star of David," said Rabbi Mordechai. "The Kabbalists have been using it to great advantage for centuries."

"But the Triangle is used by the Pères du Triangle, so it is a universal symbol," I said.

"Good point. As you can imagine, the presence of the Star of David caused the usual Anti Semitic comments that the Jews are ruling the financial world. But this is sheer nonsense. The Pères du Triangle include people from all religions and nations, and they have very little affiliation to either.

The Star of David, even though it signifies in Judaism and is placed on the flag of the state of Israel, is entirely universal and many scholars claim its origin is Anunnaki." Indeed, so much of the Ulema knowledge comes from the Anunnaki, that it did not surprise me." (Source: The book "On the Road to Ultimate Knowledge", by Ilil Arbel and Maximillien de Lafayette)

*** *** ***

118

Technique/Lesson 5

Cadari-Rou'yaa

Name or term for a secret technique developed by the Anunnaki-Ulema, centuries ago, that enabled them to read the thoughts, intentions, and feelings of others.
It is composed of two words:
a-Cadari, which means a grid; a plasma-screen.
b-Rou'yaa, which means vision; perception.

120

Technique/Lesson 5
Cadari-Rou'yaa

Cadari-Rou'yaa is also a method to diagnose health, and prevent health problems from occurring in the present, and in the future, by reading and interpreting the rays and radiations, a human body diffuses on a regular basis.

In the West, it is called reading of the aura.

The following is an excerpt from an Ulema's Kira'at (Reading). It is herewith reproduced verbatim (Unedited), from a Kira'at, as it was given by an Anunnaki-Ulema in the Middle East.

Ulema Sadiq is talking to his students (Verbatim):

I. The Technique:

- **1**-You are going to learn wonderful things today. But you have to remember that you should stay calm, focused and relaxed all the time.
- **2**-You are going to succeed. But you should not give up too easy. Don't get frustrated and despair because it is not working right away. At the beginning, everything needs additional effort, a great deal of patience, and a strong belief in yourself.
- **3**-We are not asking you to have a blind faith. Leave faith to others. Use your mind. Follow the procedures. Practice, practice, practice. And everything is going to be just fine.
- **4**-I repeat again one more time. Don't get frustrated and anxious if it is not working right away. It is going to work, and your patience will pay off.

Cadari-Rou'yaa

- **5**-Now, go to a quite place. We suggest your office if you are sure nobody is going to interrupt your practice, or just your bedroom if you can be by yourself, alone, quite and distant from noises.
- **6**-You have to practice alone. Always alone.
- **7**-Good. Take a piece of paper. A plain sheet of white paper with no lines. Size: 7 centimeters by 6 centimeters.
- **8**-On the left side of the paper, draw a red circle. Size: 2 centimeters in diameter.
- **9**-Next to the red circle, and at a distance of 1 centimeter, draw a small black dot. Size: Half the size of a bean.
- **10**-Next to the black dot, and at 1 centimeter distance, draw a green circle. Size: 2 centimeters in diameter.
- **11**-All should be aligned equally and straight on the same line. (Same level)
- **12**-Now you have from left to right: A red circle, a black dot, and a green circle, all on the same line.
- **13**-Make sure the sheet of paper is placed 25 centimeters in front of you.
- **14**-Close your eyes for 4 seconds.
- **15**-Open your eyes, and breathe slowly and deeply.
- **16**-Close your eyes one more time for 2 seconds.
- **17**-Open our eyes, and breathe one more time slowly and deeply.
- **18**-Now, look straight at the black dot for just 2 seconds.
- **19**-Close your eyes for 2 seconds.
- **20**-Open your eyes now, and look one more time at the black dot for 40 seconds or so.
- **21**-Now, tell your left eye to look at the red circle, and your right eye to look at the green circle at the same time.
- **22**-I know, it is strange, and it seems confusing to you all. But don't worry.
- **23**-Try again.
- **24**-Keep on trying until you get it right.

Cadari-Rou'yaa

- **25**-Now, something is going to happen. Pay attention.
- **26**-You will start to see both circles getting closer.
- **27**-It is not an optical illusion.
- **28**-On the contrary, it is an optical adjustment, because now, your eyes and your mind are working together. Something you have not done before.
- **29**-Now, something very new and very unusual is going to happen.
- **30**-Keep looking at those circles.
- **31**-Do not loose concentration.
- **32**-Watch now what is going to happen.
- **33**-The blue circle on your left starts to look very different. It has something around it. Something you did not see before.
- **34**-The blue circle has some sort of a lighter color ring around it. It could be any color. It does not matter.
- **35**-Remember you are still looking at both circles at the same time.
- **36**-Don't leave one circle to go to another circle.
- **37**-Now the green circle on your right starts to look very different. It has something around it. Something you did not see before.
- **38**-The green circle has some sort of a lighter color ring around it. It could be any color. It does not matter.
- **39**-Remember you are still looking at both circles at the same time.
- **40**-Don't leave one circle to go to another circle.
- **41**-Keep looking at both circles for two minutes or so.
- **42**-Something is going to happen now. Pay attention.
- **43**-It would/could appear to you that the black dot is moving somehow.
- **44**-Don't let this distract you.
- **45**-Anyway, it will go away in a few seconds.
- **46**-Something very important is going to happen now. Pay attention.

Cadari-Rou'yaa

- **47**-The ring around the blue circle on your left is getting bigger and denser.
- **48**-The ring around the green circle on your right is getting bigger and denser.
- **49**-And you are still looking at both circles.
- **50**-You are doing absolutely great.
- **51**-Now, focus your attention on the blue circle on your left.
- **52**-Something very important is going to happen now. Pay attention.
- **53**-The longer you look at the blue circle, the stronger and brighter is the ring around it.
- **54**-Now the ring around the blue circle is getting denser.
- **55**-In less than 2 seconds, the ring becomes much much brighter and starts to radiate.
- **56**-Now move to the green circle on your right.
- **57**-Focus your attention on the green circle on your right.
- **58**-Something very important is going to happen now. Pay attention.
- **59**-The longer you look at the green circle, the stronger and brighter is the ring around it.
- **60**-Now the ring around the blue circle is getting denser.
- **61**-In less than 2 seconds, the ring becomes much much brighter and starts to radiate.
- **62**-You are seeing now something you have never seen before. And that is good.
- **63**-Breathe deeply and take a short brake. (One minutes)
- **64**-Repeat the whole exercise from the very top.
- **65**-This should do it for now.
- **66**-Tomorrow, you will practice again.
- **67**-You will do the same thing.
- **68**-Keep on practicing like this for 5 consecutive days.
- **69**-If it did not work, do not give up.

Cadari-Rou'yaa

- **70**-Be patient. It will work. It did work for many students. It is simply a matter or practice, perseverance, and patience.
- **72**-And hopefully, if it did work, the rings you saw around the circles were the vibrating auras of the circles.

Note: According to the Ulema, this exercise opens an extra visual/optic dimension for your eyes and your mind.
In fact, it did not open anything new, it has just activated your visual perception. You had it all the time, but you were not aware of it.

*** *** ***

126

Technique/Lesson 6
Chabariduri

Name of an Anunnaki-Ulema technique/exercise to develop the faculty of remote viewing.

The Ulema taught their students the art and science of remote viewing to improve their knowledge, enrich their awareness, and widen their perception of life, and not to spy on others, as it is the case in the West.

128

Technique/Lesson 6
Chabariduri

Herewith a synopsis of one of the Ulema remote viewing techniques as I recall it to the best of my abilities.
Below are excerpts from the Ulema's Kira'at.
Note: The Ulema hand over to each student two small stones of the same size.

The honorable Ulema said:

Stage One:

- **1**-Pick up any stone you want and write on it Aleph "A" (First letter in many Semitic and ancient Middle/Near Eastern languages)
- **2**-Squeeze on the stone, and try to feel something, anything, or try to think about something, anything you want.
- **3**-Put the Aleph stone on your desk.
- **4**-Pick up the second stone and write on it Beth "B".
- **5**-Squeeze strongly on the stone.
- 6-Try to feel something, anything, or try to think about something, anything you want.
- **7**-Put the Beth stone on your desk.
- **8**-Write down on the white paper what did you feel or what did you think when you touched stone Aleph.
- **9**-Draw a line, and write below the line what did you feel or what did you think when you touched stone Beth.

*** *** ***

Chabariduri

Stage Two:

- **10**-Now, use the other sheet of paper.
- **10**-Take stone Aleph, and put it in your right palm. Close your hand. Close your eyes.
- **11**-Breathe slowly and deeply. Squeeze on the stone, and ask yourself where did the stone come from. Ask yourself this question 4 times.
- **12**-Put down the stone on your desk. Open your eyes. Take the pen and start writing on the paper what you are thinking about. It does not matter what. Just write down what your mind is telling you.
- **13**-Now try to guess where did the stone come from.
- **14**-Try to associate the stone with places you know and places you don't know.
- **15**-Draw on the paper whatever you see in your mind.
- **16**-Think strongly. You may close your eyes if you want.
- **17**-You still have 2 minutes to finish the test.

*** *** ***

Stage Three:

Note: Now, the Ulema tells the students time is up.
One of the students is asked to collect the papers, and he deposits them on the desk of the Ulema. After having reviewed the students' answers, the Ulema directs those who passed the test to move to a designated area in the classroom, and he dismisses the others for now.
If all the students failed the test, the session comes to an end, and another test will resume the following day.
Now, the students are asked to do the same thing with stone Beth. Same instructions are given, and same procedures are followed. Those who pass the test stay in the classroom, and those who failed are dismissed.

130

Chabariduri

The Ulema continues (Talking to the students and adepts who have successfully passed the test):

- **1**-Now you are going to work with stone Aleph. Stone Beth is no longer needed.
- **2**-Now you are going to describe the place where the stone came from. You are going to write down everything you see or think of.
- **3**-Now you will write down on a new sheet of paper, anything you will be thinking about, anything and everything, no matter how silly or unrealistic it appears to you.
- **4**-Do not hesitate. Do not doubt yourself. Don't wait to have a second thought.
- **5**-Rush your visions, thoughts and feelings to the paper.
- **6**-Now hold the stone in your right hand, and squeeze on the stone firmly for one minute.
- **7**-Put the stone down, and start writing.
- **8**-Right down first what you thought first.
- **9**-If you feel, or if you think that you know something or anything about the place where the stone might have come from, write down right away the name and location of the place. Do not doubt yourself.
- **10**-Follow your instinct, follow your thoughts, follow your feelings, follow your vision, and stop there.
- **11**-Now you are there. And you start to see things; people, houses, shops, gardens, children, trees, water, bicycles, cars, animals...many many things, or maybe just few things. It doesn't matter how much you see. Write it down.
- **12**-Now, make a list of you are seeing.
- **13**-Describe what you are seeing.
- **14**-Be precise; give as much details as you can, and name things...be specific about colors, sizes, forms, shapes, dimensions, locations...anything around, below and above the items you see.

Chabariduri

- **15**-You don't need to follow any particular order in listing what you see. First, write down everything you see, later we will sort them out together.
- **16**-Now draw what you see. You don't have to make a masterpiece. Sketches are fine. Any kind of sketches. Even small icons, a few lines here and there, even a series of lines and geometrical forms...draw anything you see or you think you are seeing.
- **17**-Do not try to force yourself to give any explanation to what you are seeing or drawing. You will think later about that. Now concentrate on that place you have found and write down everything you see...draw more pictures...do not delete anything...add but don't delete.

Note: At the end of the session, the students' work is evaluated, and compared with the data and information about the place subject of the test, and safely guarded in numbered files.

This was a synopsis of the Ulema's instructions and guidance, and their students' orientation/training session.

This remote viewing exercise is repeated again and again on a daily basis for one full month.

At the beginning, you need an instructor (Ulema or just an instructor or a guide to tell you what to do).

But later on, you will do it on your own. After few practices, you know exactly what to do.

Technique/Lesson 7

Daemat-Afnah

How To Stay And Look 37 Permanently

Term for longevity, and halting the process of aging.
It is composed of two words:
a-Daemat, which means longevity.
b-Afnah, which means many things, including health, fecundity, and longevity.
According to the Anunnaki-Ulema, we are not programmed to age.

Technique/Lesson 7
Daemat-Afnah

Technique/exercise for how to stay and look 37 permanently

Herewith, an excerpt from one of the Ulema's Kira'at (Readings), reproduced verbatim, without editing:

Understanding human life-span and our body longevity.

The honorable Ulema said:

- **1**-Not all parts, membranes, tissues and organs of your body age the same way and at the same rate.
- **2**-Sometimes, your neck or the skin right under your eyes shows your age, while your very eyes remain vibrant and young. It is a matter of genes or cells. This is what science taught us.
- **3**-Although, it is true, we age because our genes get damaged, there are reasons for aging that are still unknown to science.
- **4**-Some of the non-physical aging factors cannot be detected in laboratories, because they are not created by purely terrestrial elements.
- **5**-They belong to another dimension, where your blue prints were conceived and stored.
- **6**-Humans are not programmed to age. I am neither referring to the early genetic creation of mankind (One million years ago or so), nor to the primordial seven prototypes created by the An. Na.Ki. (450,000 years ago or so).

Daemat-Afnah

- I am talking about the final specimen of humans that contained the original 13 mental faculties, some 65,000 years ago.
- 7-The Anunnaki who live outside time don't show any indication of aging, because time does not control their lifespan. Human life is controlled by time. Anunnaki's life is free of time, thus time cannot regulate their lives.
- 8-The Anunnaki have the ability to activate and reactivate their genes in their laboratories. Although, they are not immortal, and eventually their cells and genes deteriorate, the Anunnaki can activate the last fully functional and healthy cell, reproduce it in a large quantity, and activate each newly created cell separately, in conformity with the many copies and doubles of an Anunnaki stored in a reversed time-data-storage.
- 9-The Anunnaki can keep you young for ever, and easily postpone aging indefinitely. Two of the very first things they do are:
- A-Extending the longevity of your Double by rearranging your stored DNA and blueprints.
- B-By building a new genetic sequence aimed at resisting stress that causes damages to your genes in a terrestrial surrounding.
- 10-The Anunnaki can divide each sequence of your DNA, and add to this divided sequence, a new genetic code that extends your life span for thousands of years. Quantum physics and modern medicine sciences do not contradict this.

*** *** ***

Daemat-Afnah

Note: The following pertains to this topic, and I have reproduced herewith, a few pages taken from my book "Ulema Code and Language of the World Beyond".

Is it possible to stay young for ever? The Ulema said yes!
The Ulema's idea of staying young and feeling and looking 37 for the rest of your life:

From the Ulema's Kira'ats.
Excerpts from the readings of Master Li, Master Lumiere, and Master Ben Zvi

Translated verbatim in conformity with its authentic caché and linguistic expressions.

- **1-**You can reprogram yourself and adjust your genes. The Anunnaki, Ulema, and the sages of Melkart taught the enlightened ones and the righteous ones how to do it.
- **2-**Your body is a machine like so many other machines in the universe, here on earth and beyond.
- **3-**Some machines run on fuel, others on atomic energy...your body is very special, and a great mystery, because it runs on a substance known to very few people in the world. Is it your blood?
  Is it the oxygen you breathe in the air?
  Is it your soul? Is it the mind of God?
  Is it your essence, your Chi, your DNA?
  Or all of the above?
  Or perhaps something we cannot touch, we cannot see, we cannot measure, and consequently we cannot understand or be sure of?
- **4-**You were taught that the human body is created from a male's semen and a female's eggs. That is very true.
  But this semen and these eggs must have "something" extraordinary, something non-physical to allow a physical human body to perform physical/non-physical

137

Daemat-Afnah

acts such as writing poetry, epics, music, symphonies, and love letters, to measure light, to reader others' thoughts, to communicate telepathically, to fall in love, to think about new ideas, and possibly to escape laws of physics. This very special and extraordinary "something" is somewhere...not necessarily in the semen and the eggs...

- **5**-Although, we are all human beings...the truth is, we did not come from the same origin. Some were born here on earth, others were born somewhere else...in some other dimensions and far distant spheres. Yet, we have many things in common, because we were created by the same Khalek (Creator) and his assistants.

- **6**-We are not an assembly-line product. We are not like automobiles manufactured and assembled exactly the same way by the same plant.

- **7**-This is why each one of us is different. And this difference exists, because each one of us was created in a different plant, according to different specifications and very distinct genetic-programming process.

- **8**-Those who created us know these specifications and what went into our creation, thus, they can reprogram us, alter our properties, give us a new form, new faculties, and reduce or increase our life span.

- **9**-At the time we were created (Designed, produced, manufactured, etc.), three things happened to us, and are directly related to (a) intelligence, (b) luck/success in life, and (c) health/youth/longevity.

A-The Brain Motor:

A brain was designed and instantly tested.
The brain was created before the body took shape and form.
In this brain, all faculties were installed.
A copy or blueprints of the brain (Mind) was duplicated and stored in an etheric dimension "ED" (This is the best way we can describe this dimension for now.)

138

Daemat-Afnah

This ED is similar to a cosmic net that consists of trillions and millions of trillions of canals, stations, terminals and channels, all connected together, yet they function separately according to very specific frequencies and vibrations.

Once these faculties are installed and begin to function –no matter at what rate or level –, they become a permanent and final fixture of our thinking process, i.e. intelligence, logic, creativity, etc. However, these faculties will get better and better by constant learning and acquiring new knowledge.

This is only possible, if the Conduit (Installed by the An. Na. Ki or other non-terrestrials geneticists-creators in your brain's cells) has more room for improvement.

The capacity of the Conduit is usually detected at an early age, between 3 and 5.

Many of the greatest geniuses on earth manifested the Conduit's capacity and potentials during this short and early period of time.

B-Vibrations, Frequencies, and Luck in Life:

Creation of a place for the vibrations of our mind.

Nothing in the physical and non-physical dimensions exists, continues to exist, and functions without vibrations and frequencies.

When these rays (Vibrations and frequencies) get damaged or cease to radiate or emanate, the organism stops to function. In other words, the brain (Mind) as a motor dies out instantly. When our creators designed this motor during the first stage of manufacturing us, they carefully tested and measured the frequencies and vibes of the brain, and adjusted the level of its creativity. At this very moment, they created a space for this creativity, called the vibrational dimension.

Now, if these vibrations resonate in synchronization with the vibrations of the canals and channels of the cosmic net, the person who has this kind of vibrations will be a very luck person, but not necessarily a righteous one.

Daemat-Afnah

In other words, either you were born lucky, or unlucky, and you are going to stay lucky or unlucky for the rest of your life, and there is nothing you can do to change your luck.

However, Master Li said: "It is not totally so...although you have no control over your destiny and luck, your Conduit will be able to ameliorate your chances if it is activated by your Double. The sad part of this story is that many of us either do not believe in a Double, nor accept the idea that a Conduit does in fact exist in our brains' cells."

*** *** ***

C-The Conduit=Health/Youth/Longevity:

Those who have read my books are now familiar with the Conduit. For those who didn't, here is a brief description of the nature of the Conduit.
Basically, the Conduit is a depot of everything that is YOU; intelligence, emotions, feelings, attributes, qualities, talents, health, dreams, physiognomy, abilities to learn many languages, creativity, endurance, and yes, your future as well.

At the time you were born, a Conduit was installed in the cells of your brain. If the Conduit has been activated, then everything you touch will turn into gold, all your deeds will become honorable, and you will be destined to greatness. If the Conduit remains inactive, you will live a normal life, nothing spectacular about it, and you continue to live a very ordinary life like all the others.

A miniscule, an infinitely small part of the Conduit deals with health, youth, and longevity. And this very small part has been already programmed by those who created you. You can't deprogram it. You can't find it. And you can't reach it. It is way beyond your reach and comprehension. So let's leave it like that for now.

In the Conduit, your life-span has been formulated and its length and/or continuity has been decided upon genetically.

140

Some people will die young, other will live 100 years. Some people will grow up to be very tall and physically strong despite lack of nutrition and a good diet, while many others will stay short, fat, or weak despite their healthy life style, good diet, and impeccable hygiene.

Physicians and scientists are so quick to say: It is in the genes! And they stop there! But one thing they don't know for sure is what or who created those genes, and according to what guidelines, specs., and creation process?

They don't know. Well, the Ulema do know, because they learned it from their teachers the An. Na.Ki.

You can't control longevity, youth and your life-span by deprogramming their genetic codes, because first, you don't know where to find these sequences, second, you have no control over the Conduit, and third, you don't know how much to add or to subtract from and to the genetic codes.

If you do, if you know for a fact, how to prolong the vibrations of these sequences and how much "stuff" to add to the Conduit, then, and only then, you will be able to control your life-span. Ulema Marash said: "It is like when you fill your automobile gas tank. The more fuel you put in your tank, the more mileages your car will run.

The difference is that, at the gas station, you are in control, because you can decide how much gas you want to buy, but when it comes to living young for ever, first, you don't know where the youth station (In comparison to the gas station) is, and second, you are not in control of your Conduit (In comparison to your car)."

"The good news", said Ulema Albakr" is that a Conduit can be activated and/or reactivated if training and orientation programs are completed...Enlightenment and blessings are not the monopoly of few..."

All these statements are fascinating, but is there a pragmatic and an effective way to either activate the Conduit or to stay and look younger for ever? "What do I have to do to stay young? And yes, I am over 37, but I want to look 37, can you teach me how to do this?" you might ask.

Daemat-Afnah

Well, here are some of the guidelines and techniques according to the secret doctrine of the Ulema.

*** *** ***

Some of the Ulema's guidelines and techniques

Introduction:

- You do not need to buy anything.
- No equipment is needed.
- No physical training is required.
- No diet is imposed.
- No pills to take.
- All what you need is your mind; believing in yourself; convincing yourself that you are determined to succeed; a great deal of optimism and patience. Nothing else.

The honorable Ulema said (Translated verbatim):

- **1**-Your environment conditions your state of mind, and your way of life. This is very true.
- **2**-Equally true is the fact that your mind (No matter how educated or uneducated you are) can also condition your environment and way of life.
- **3**-It is up to you to decide: Would you like to be permanently at the mercy of your environment and what life and others have imposed upon your, or would you rather use the power of your mind to change your life for better? It is up to you!
- **4**-Your mind can do miracles for you if you let it. Just believe in it.
- **5**-Your mind has the power to make you look healthy and much much younger.

142

- **6-**Your mind is much powerful and durable than your genes and your pumped muscles. Because your mind can influence your genes and your muscles.
- **7-**In doing so, your mind can "freeze time" in your body and postpone aging. O yes, you will grow older, but you will look much younger, despite your old age.
  In fact, your body will never show sign, or any indication of aging if you let your mind create a new mental setting for your body, and I am going to show you how...
- **8-**First, you choose an age of your choice; this age will stay the same indefinitely, this is the age that is going to freeze time, and at which you stop to get older. Wonderful.
- **9-**Second, you tell yourself I want to stay 25 or 45 or 37 year old for the rest of my life, it is up to you (This depends on the age you have chosen.)
- **10-**We recommend that you choose the age of 37 if you are older than that. If you are younger, stay where you are and count your blessings.
- **11-**Do not think for a second, just because you have told yourself you want to stay 37 for ever, that you are going to stay 37 for ever. No! It requires much more than that.
- **12-**For 37 consecutive days, you will tell yourself as soon as you wake up in the morning: "I am going to stay 37 for ever." And immediately, you start to think about all the happy days and wonderful things you enjoyed when you were 37. You have to do that, otherwise it will <u>never</u> work.
- **13-**You have to convince your mind that really you want to stay 37. Once your mind is convinced, it starts to work on your genes. Do not ask why and how. It is too complicated. After all, do you want to eat grapes or chase the bear in your vineyard? Don't ask too many questions.
- **14-**Now, we have to use some imagination here. O yes, imagination creates wonders. So, you start to tell yourself, you are going to relive the time when you were 37.

Daemat-Afnah

- **15-**First thing to do is to refresh your memories and remember (as much as you can) all the wonderful places you have visited when you were 37, the kind of sport you practiced, the fashion you followed, the movies you saw, the music you listened to, the car you drove, the entertainment you enjoyed, all the gifts and presents you received, and do not forget the young and beautiful girl or man you dated...all these things must pop up together and simultaneously in your head.
- **16-**You will fantasize about all these things, and you will revisit all these things, you relive and feel all these things the way you felt them when you were 37. You have to relive these times in your mind every single day for 37 consecutive days. Do not miss one single day.
- **17-**Before you go to sleep, and while you are still awake in your bed, choose one of those places you have recently visited in your mind. Any place you want. Very good.
- **18-**Go there now. See what is going on there.
- **19-**See if your buddies are there.
- **20-**Try to find one. You got to find somebody, a pal, a friend, somebody you had good time with. Good.
- **21-**Start talking to your friend. You got to believe in this. No, you are not crazy, you are doing just fine, and your mind is working perfectly.)
- **22-**Engage into a real chat with your friend. Tell jokes. Laugh. Feel the energy of being young again.
- **23-**Now do something else. Tell yourself you want to go on a date. Call your date. Pick up a place you used to love so much.
- **24-**Pick up your date, head straightforward to that place, be brave, kick the door, and step in.
- **25-**Once you are in, you are going to meet lots of good friends, and you are going to have a ball; eat, drink, sing, dance if you can, enjoy yourself.
- **26-**Probably you are sleeping now, and that is good for now. Your mind needs a rest. Go to sleep.

- **27-**Every single day for 37 consecutive days, keep on doing this. Of course, every time you revisit your life, do something different, but similar to what you used to do when you were 37.
- **28-**Do not do anything different or differently.
- **29-**You are still living your normal life; the one you are currently living. And I bet, now and then you are having some hard times, and of course some good times too. Now, you have to remember you have another wonderful life beyond this one.
- **30-**The one you visit in the morning and before you go to sleep. So why don't you go there right now and dump all these troubles you are having, and come back in the morning.
- **31-**Stay there overnight. It is good for you. Keep telling this to yourself. And every time you feel bad about something, or somebody is disturbing you, and you become anxious, exhausted and unhappy, you have to remember that you have a magical formula nobody knows about...it is your secret...you have the wonderful life you visit from time to time. It is there. It exists. It continues to exist, but you forgot about it, because you are living at a different pace and speed, and you worry so much.
- **32-**Now you have been visiting your youth, let's say for two weeks. And that is fine. At the end of the third week, you are going to feel so good, you are not going to believe it. You are going to feel so good about yourself, I guarantee it.
- **33-**Continue to visit your new world. At the end of the 37 day period, your life will change to better. You will see the difference. But that is not enough.
- **34-**Nothing physically in you has changed yet. Don't worry. It will happen sooner than you think. But now, you are shifting gear, you are steamed up, you are happy about how you feel about yourself, and so, you decided to visit more often the wonderful place, life and time when

Daemat-Afnah

- you were 37. So go ahead, go there as often as you can, and as much as you want. It belongs to you. It is yours!
- **35-**If you keep doing this for 6 months – non stop –, you are going to see a major and mind bending physical transformation in you. Especially on your face. I will explain...
- **36-**Your hair color will not change. If you had grey hair before, well, the grey hair is still there. If you were bald, sorry, you are still bald. But your face now is much much much younger, and you start to look almost 37. You will believe it when you will see it, and you are going to see it.
- **37-**Gradually, you start to regain your youth, but you are not stopping the time clock. But what do you care?
- **38-**You are not showing sign of aging. You will not have wrinkles on your face for many years to come. Everybody around you will see the difference. And those who will meet you for the first time will never guess how old you are! You will never look your age.
- **39-**It is at this very stage of your life, when you will realize for the first time, that age is not a state of mind, but what mind can do to stay that way."

*** *** ***

Technique/Lesson 8

Da-Irat

Name for Anunnaki's "Circle Technique"
Da-Irat is known to the enlightened ones and Ulema' adepts as the "Circle Technique" (Da-Ira-Maaref), which means the circle of knowledge.
This technique eliminates stress, through one's self-energy. In other words, it is an Ulema technique used to energize one's mind and body, and to eliminate worries that are preventing an individual from functioning properly everywhere, including the office, home, social gatherings, etc.

148

Technique/Lesson 8
Da-Irat

In the West, zillions of techniques to reduce stress and counter bad vibes were proposed. And many of those techniques work very well. The following will explain the Ulema's techniques that were in practice for thousands of years in the Near and Middle East. No physical exercise is required.
It is purely mental, although some of the steps to follow might look esoteric or spiritual in nature.

These techniques were developed by the early Ulema and members of the "Fish Circle", a brotherhood of the ancient island of Arwad, where allegedly, remnants of the An.na.Ki (Anunnaki) lived, and developed the Mah-Rit in sophisticated genetic labs.
The Da-Irat Technique (The Circle Technique) as used by the Fish Circle Brotherhood.
Terminology:
1-In Ulemite, it is called Da-Irat (Circle; sphere).
2-In Ana'kh, it is called Arac-ta.
3-In Phoenician, it is called Teth-Ra. Teth is circle or good thing. Ra is creative energy or first source of life.

***   ***   ***

Application and Use:

Excerpts from the Anunnaki-Ulema Kira'ats.
Note: Translated verbatim (As Is) from the original text and readings in Ulemite and Phoenician:

- **1**-You have to create a space, or find a new space where your mind can manifest itself.

Da-Irat

- **2**-You live through your mind, and not through your soul.
- **3**-Therefore, no spiritual exercise is required.
- **4**-A mental exercise is a prerequisite.
- **5**-You can create a space for your mind by putting aside for a short moment all your worries, thoughts and other activities.
- **6**-You enter your private room, and you sit there for five seconds, doing nothing, and trying to think about nothing.
- **7**-Find a comfortable spot.
- **8**-Untie your belt and take off your shoes.
- **9**-Bring your arms close to your hip. This position is called Kaph.
- **10**-If you managed to stop thinking about anything and everything, this would be great. If not, do this:
- **11**-Speak to your mind vocally. Do not be embarrassed. Nobody is going to think you are crazy, because you are alone in your room.
- **12**-Tell your mind that you want to see right before your eyes a large white door on your right, and a small blue window on your left. This exercise is called Qoph. It is a Phoenician word, and it means the eye of the needle. In Ulemite, it is called Qafra. In Ana'kh, it is called Kaf-ra-du.
- **13**-Tell your mind you are knocking at the door, and you are getting ready to walk in.
- **14**-Knock at the door. Yes, you can raise your hand and knock on the door. Do not hesitate. You will go through. It is guaranteed.
- **15**-Before you enter, look to see if the window is closed.
- **16**-If the window is closed, that's fine, open the door and get inside.
- **17**-If the window is open, close it. Make sure it is close.
- **18**-Now, proceed and get in...
- **19**-As soon as you step in, shut the door behind you.

- **20**-Your mind is free now.
- **21**-Close your eyes. Do not open your eyes, until I will tell you when.
- **22**-Your mind is no longer distracted by other things.
- **23**-You are now in a state of serenity.
- **24**-Your mind is getting settled.
- **25**-Your mind is finally finding its place. This stage is called Taw in Phoenician, and it means mark. You are marking now your state of mind.
- **26**-This is the place where you are going to dump your worries.
- **27**-You start to feel very quite, calm and relaxed. And that is good.
- **28**-Keep your eyes closed.
- **29**-Now, your mind is ready to listen to your command and wishes.
- **30**-Tell yourself you are entering inside your body.
- 31-Tell yourself you want to enter inside your head. This stage is called Resh in Phoenician, and it means head. In Arabic, it is called Ras. In Ulemite is called Rasha. In Ana'kh, it is called Rashat.
- **32**-Bring yourself very close to your forehead.
- **33**-Direct yourself toward your eyebrows.
- **34**-You are seeing now a calm stream of water.
- This stage is called Mem in Phoenician, and it means water. In Ulemite, it is called Ma'. In Arabic, it is called Ma' or Maiy.
- **35**-The water is running very smoothly.
- **36**-Flow with the stream.
- **37**-Become one with the stream.
- **38**-The stream is showing you now beautiful sceneries.
- **39**-The stream is branching out very gently and is diving itself into small canals. And that is good.
- **40**-Can you count how many canals are you seeing?
- **41**-Follow the canals and count how many are they.
- **42**-Can you try to join them together?

Da-Irat

- **43**-Try again.
- **44**-Let your mind help you.
- **45**-Ask your mind to grab all these canals.
- **46**-You see, you are doing it. This stage is called Heth in Phoenician, and it means fence.
- **47**-You are feeling so good.
- **48**-Now, breathe slowly and gently.
- **49**-Continue to breath.
- **50**-Now tell yourself you want to continue going inside yourself.
- **51**-Can you manage to bring the river inside your body?
- **52**-Try.
- **53**-The river is coming closer to your chest.
- **54**-You start to feel it.
- **55**-Yes, the canal is entering your chest. And you are feeling so good, fresh, energized.
- **56**-Tell the canal to clean everything in your body.
- **57**-Everything...everything...
- **58**-You are feeling now the fresh and cool water everywhere in your body. This is a true feeling.
- **59**-The beautiful fresh water is cleaning all the mess and dirt inside your body.
- **60**-Command the water to flush everything out.
- **61**-Tell your mind to close your body.
- **62**-Nothing now can enter your body. It is sealed. It is clean and sparkling, and you feel it.
- **63**-Now, you want to visit your knees.
- **64**-Go there. Turn around your knees.
- **65**-Turn one more time.
- **66**-You are going to see now white spirals of light surrounding your knees.
- **67**-Stay there.
- **68**-Let the light turn and turn and turn around your knees.
- **69**-Now the light is going down...down toward your feet, and that is good.

152

- **70**-Your feet feel good.
- **71**-Your feet are floating now.
- **72**-Let them float.
- **73**-You start to feel as if you are sliding gently...
- **74**-You are, but you are floating. And that is so good.
- **75**-Tell yourself your heart is strong and healthy.
- **76**-Tell your lungs they are clean and healthy.
- **77**-Tell your body how wonderful and strong it is.
- **78**-Tell yourself how wonderful and strong you are.
- **79**-Thank your mind for this wonderful journey.
- **80**-Tell your body that your mind is standing by your body and is going to take care of it.
- **81**-Breathe slowly and deeply three times.
- **82**-Tell yourself you have done a good job and you are going to open your eyes now.
- **83**-Open your eyes.
- **84**-Stretch your arms gently.
- **85**-Stay put for 5 seconds.
- **86**-Stand up.
- **87**-Take a nice hot shower.

Ulema Win Li said:

- Repeat this exercise twice a week.
- The second time you do this, you are going to feel much better, and the exercise will look more pleasant.
- After the second exercise, you are going to notice a great improvement in your mental and physical health.
- Take note of your progress, and compare notes.

*** *** ***

154

Technique/Lesson 9
Dudurisar

Name for the act or ability to rethink and examine past events in your life, change them, and in doing so, you create for yourself a new life and new opportunities.

To a certain degree, and in a sense, it is like revisiting your past, and changing unpleasant events, decisions, choices, and related matters that put you where you are today.

156

Technique/Lesson 9
Dudurisar

Excerpts from Ulema Anusherwan Karma Ramali Kira'at, number 165, Introduction to Dudurisar, Fasel Wahed (Part one) March 1961, Alexandria, Egypt. Verbatim. Unedited.

The Concept:

The honorable Ulema spoke:

- **1**-You are not totally satisfied or happy in your current situation, in what you are doing, and where you are today. You wish you had a different life, a better job, more opportunities, less troubles and worries.
  But there is nothing you can do about it, because the past is the past, and nobody can change the past. It is done.
- **2**-True, it is very true, you cannot change your past, because it was Maktoub (Written) in the pages of your fate and destiny book, the day you were born.
- **3**-Besides, changing or altering the past creates global chaos, confusion, and dysfunctional order among people, communities and nations.
- **4**-But you don't have to change your whole past (All events) to become happier, more successful, and put an end to your misery and tough times.

Dudurisar

- **5**-All what you need to do is to change the part or segments (Days, months, years, places, decisions) that have created hardship, misfortunes and mishaps in your current life; and this is permissible, possible, ethical and healthy.
- **6**-What part of your life you wish to change or alter, how to do it, and the reason(s) for doing it are the paramount questions you have to ask yourself very honestly.
- **7**-Once you have decided to alter a portion or a segment of your past, and replace this specific segment with new wishes and decisions, you cannot change, modify or alter the changes you have made.
- **8**-You have to live with it, and you will not have another chance.
- **9**-Something else you should think about (and you should never forget it): Your family, your children, your current obligations, your commitment to others, and all the promises you made to people. Because, once you have changed a major part of your life (Past or present), all these things that you are dealing with right now will change too, and you might not like it, or perhaps you might? Everything depends on your intentions, needs and desires.
- **10**-Avoid at all costs and at all time selfishness, greed, escaping from responsibilities, and vicious intentions. No, you can't go back in time and kill all those people who did you wrong, or hurt the woman who turned you down.
- **11**-You go back in time/space for one reason: Changing unpleasant events and decisions that unfairly have caused you grief, failures, pain, and unhappiness.
- **12**-So the keyword here is "Unfairly". But how would you know what is fair and what is unfair, as far as your past, your job, your luck, your fortune, your bank account, you relationships, promotion in your career or profession, health conditions, peace of mind, and success are concerned?

- **13**-You will, once you have crossed the frontiers of the present-past sphere.
- **11**-You will not be able to lie to yourself. Once you are behind that thin curtain, you become a different person; un-materialistic, honest, sincere, simple, and wise.
- **14**-The world you will enter is as real as the one you live in right now.
- **15**-However, it is much much bigger, prettier, serene, meaningful, and confusing at the same time, because it has different purposes, unlimited borders and levels, it is ageless, multidimensional, and contains places, dates, times, people, unfamiliar creatures, humans and non humans (Women, men, children, even animals and strange non-physical creatures) you have not met yet in your life, because they either belong to the future, and/or to different, multiple, vibrational, parallel worlds.

*** *** ***

II. The Technique: It works like this

Note: This might frustrate you, because it requires a great deal of patience. Without patience, a strong will, and perseverance, you will not achieve a thing. This technique works.
It is up to you to make it work for you.

- **1**-First of all, you have to understand that you cannot revisit and change your past at will, or as you please. There are rules you must follow. And these rules are closely connected to time, the place where you live, your intentions, and the specific events you wish to change.
- **2**-For instance, you cannot return in time/space to take revenge, to kill a person you dislike, or prevent that person from evolving or competing with you.

Dudurisar

- **3**-There are limits to what you can do. You cannot return in non-linear time/space and create wars or bring destruction to people and communities. Changing a part or a segment from your past is limited to your sphere.
- **4**-Sphere means your very personal life, your personal actions, your personal events; things that are closely and exclusively related to you.
- **5**-You have no powers over others.
- **6**-Also you have to understand that you cannot return to the past any day you want. There is a calendar or more precisely a time table you should fit it. This means, there are days and hours that are open to you; these days and these hours allow you to zoom back into your past.
- **7**-Consequently, you must find out what are these days and these hours. You have to consider yourself as if you were an airplane.
- **8**-An airplane cannot take off or land without a flight schedule, and an authorization. Consequently, you have to schedule your trip to the past according to a trip schedule.
- **9**-The trip schedule is decided upon by many factors. The two most important factors are: a-The activation of your conduit; b-The most suitable hour for your trip; this happens when your Double, or at least your astral copy is in a perfect synchronization with the Ba'ab's opening. Possibly, you are getting confused with all these words and conditions. I will try to simplify the matter for you.
- **10**-To find out what is the most suitable hour to schedule your trip to the past is to do this: All the letters of the alphabet have a numerical value in the Ulemite literature, and were explained in the Book of Rama-Dosh Refer to Book 2). These numerical values are as follows:
- A numerical value: 1.
- B numerical value: 3.
- C numerical value: 5.
- D numerical value: 7.

160

Dudurisar

- E numerical value: 11.
- F numerical value: 15.
- G numerical value: 16.
- H numerical value: 21.
- I numerical value: 32.
- J numerical value: 39.
- K numerical value: 41.
- L numerical value: 42.
- M numerical value: 44.
- N numerical value: 49.
- O numerical value: 56.
- P numerical value: 58.
- Q numerical value: 62.
- R numerical value: 75.
- S numerical value: 81.
- T numerical value: 83.
- U numerical value: 89.
- V numerical value: 95.
- W numerical value: 98.
- X numerical value: 102.
- Y numerical value: 111.
- Z numerical value: 126.
- **11**-Let's assume your name is Kamil. Now, let's find out the numerical value of Kamil.
- **K=41**. Add 4 + 1=5. The number 5 is the numerical value of K.
- **A=1**. A is a single digit. The number 1 is the numerical value of A.
- **M=44**. Add 4 + 4=8. The number 8 is the numerical value of M.
- **I=32**. Add 3 + 2=5. The number 5 is the numerical value of I.
- **L=42**. Add 4 + 2=6. The number 6 is the numerical value of L.

Dudurisar

- **12**-Now, let's find out the complete numerical value of the whole name of Kamil. Add the numerical values of all the letters of the word Kamil.
- **13**-We have here: 5+1+8+5+6=27.
- **14**-The numerical value of Kamil is 27. Now add 2+7=9. The number 9 represents the 9th hour on Kamil's trip schedule. Always use night hours. This means that you can't zoom into your past at a different hour. Just tell yourself you got to be at the gate at 9 o'clock, exactly as you do when you take a regular flight at any airport. You have to be on time.
- **14**-Now, we have to find out the day of the trip (Zooming into the past.) Only on this day you will be able to do so.
- **15**-Take the "Triangle" you have used in practicing your technique/lesson 4 "Gubada-Ari".
- **16**-Place the Triangle on the globe. If you have done this previously and found out your best spots on the globe, then, take the number corresponding to that particular spot. Remember there are 4 small triangles, and each triangle has a number on it (From 1 to 4 on the Six Pointed Star.)
- **17**-Let's assume that the corresponding small triangle's number is 3. What does 3 represent? Or any of the 4 numbers of the four small triangles in any case?
- **18**-On Earth, the week consists or 7 days. In the Anunnaki-Ulema Falak, there are no weeks, no days and no time, because time is equated differently beyond the third dimension. Instead, the non-terrestrial beings have four spatial sequences, each representing four different spheres beyond the fourth dimension. Don't worry about these spheres. For now learn this: The number 3 you found on the globe means the third day of the Anunnaki-Ulema calendar.
- **19**-The Anunnaki-Ulema calendar consists of the following: 4 days (So to speak). And the four days are (In a figurative speech) 1-Tuesday; 2-Wednesday; 3-Friday; 4-Saturday. Forget all the other days.

- **20**-This means that your zooming day is Friday. And the departure is at 9 (See bullet#14).
- **21**-Now, we know the day and the hour. What's next?
- **22**-Now, we have to find the gate (Ba'ab).
- **23**-The gate is usually very close to you. This gate is not the "Spatial Ba'ab", but your mental launching pad.
- **24**-The most practical launching pad is any place where nobody can interfere with this technique.
- **25**-Use your private room, and make sure that nobody is around.
- **26**-Place the Triangle on your desk, or on any solid and stable surface.
- **27**-Sit in a comfortable chair behind your desk, close enough to place both hands parallel to the triangle.
- **28**-Take a deep and long breath, approximately four or five seconds. Repeat this three times.
- **29**-In your mind, project two lines exiting from the top corner of the triangle. In other words, let the lines of the both sides (left and right) of the triangle continue outside the triangle leaving from the top corner.
- **30**-In your mind, create a new triangle starting from the top of the triangle you already have on the desk, and just formed by the extension of the two lines you have mentally created.
- **31**-Now you are looking at this new triangle sitting on the top of the other triangle. We are going to call it "Mira".
- **32**-At each corner of the Mira, you are going now to put something.
- **33**-For example, at the base, which is upside down (left side), choose the year you want to visit.
- **34**-At the base, which is upside down (right side), pick up the event you want to revisit. By event, I mean something you have done, such as a decision, a job you had, a responsibility you have assumed, a trip you made,

an encounter you had. In other words, the thing you want to change or alter from your past.

- **35**-At the lower corner of Mira which is joining your triangle on the desk, put the "new thing" or "new wish" you want to use to change or alter something you have done. Remember: You have already chosen what you want to change; it is already placed at the right side (upside down) of the triangle (See bullet#34).

- **36**-Now, everything is in place. You have on the left side, the year you want to visit; on the right side, you have the event or the thing you want to change, and on the reversed corner of the triangle you have the new thing you want to bring to your past so it could change or alter the things you want to remove from your past.

- **37**-Your final mental projection is this: Draw in the triangle a circle, and make it spin or rotate in your mind.

- **38**-Let the circle spin as fast as possible.

- **39**-Keep telling your mind to order the circle to spin. And concentrate on the rotation of the circle as strong as possible. Stay in this mode as long as it takes until you see the circle increasing in size.

- **40**-When you begin to feel that the circle is getting big enough to contain all the corners of the triangle, at this very moment, and in your mind, push out of the circle all the contents of the right side corner, and immediately refill it with your wishes.

- **41**-Bring the refill to the left side corner.

- **42**-Anchor it in the chosen year.

- **43**-In your mind, close the right side corner.

- **44**-In your mind, close the bottom corner of the triangle.

- **45**-In your mind, stay with the year you are visiting now.

- **46**-You are now seeing lots of things; scenes from your past, people you knew, it depends where you are, in other words, your past as it happened at that place and during that year has been reconstructed. Not hundred per cent physically, but holographically, and in this holographic projection, the essence, fabric and DNA of everything that happened are brought back to life in a different dimension, as real as the one you came from.

- **47**-Remember, nothing is completely destroyed in the world. Nothing comes to a total and permanent end. Everything is transformed, retransformed, and quite often recycled. You can recreate the original fabric of everything that happened in your past by recreating the DNA sequence of past events, in revisiting the parallel dimension that has never lost the print and copy of original events. It is this very parallel dimension that you are revisiting now mentally. Ulema enter that dimension physically and mentally. But because you are still a student, you will only revisit that dimension mentally and holographically.

- **48**-You are now revisiting and re-living past times in another dimension. Even though, you are experiencing this extraordinary phenomenon and interacting with re-structured events, you will not be able to bring to your physical world the changes you have made in the parallel dimension, because you cannot transport them to a different dimension. They exist only in that holographic reality, which never ceased to exist.

- **49**-However, you will be able to bring back with you the effects and positive results that such changes have created by altering the past. Those results created in a different dimension will materialize physically in your real life, and you will be able to sense and recognize their effects in a very realistic manner, in all things closely related to their nature.

- **50**-In fact, what you have done is changing or totally eliminating the negative and destructive effects of things and decisions you have made in your past. And this is what really counts. Because you have substituted bad results with good results.

- **51**-Those results will continue in your current life when you return to your physical world, and will prevent future bad incidents and bad things from occurring again in your current life. Worth mentioning here that the kind of bad experiences you had in your past will never happen again to you. You have blocked them for good.

*** *** ***

How real is the holographic/parallel dimension you are visiting?

It is fantasy?
Is it hallucination?
Is it day-dreaming?
It is wishful thinking?
None of the above. It is as real as your physical world. Everything you see and feel in this materialistic/physical world exists also (Identically) in other worlds.
But their properties are different. Nevertheless, they look exactly identical. Even the smallest details are preserved. So what you will be seeing during your trip is real. What happened in the past still exists in other dimension, and follows rules that our mind cannot understand.
That incomprehensible and wonderful dimension does not only contain events, peoples, and things from your past, but also whatever is currently occurring on Earth.
In other words, you as a human being living on this planet, and working as a teacher or as a physician, you are simultaneously living and working as a teacher or as a physician in a parallel dimension. You may not have the same name or nationality, but your essence, persona and psycho-somatic characteristics are the same.
In fact, you live simultaneously in many and different worlds. Perhaps, and as we speak, there is another person who looks exactly like you in a different dimension is trying to visit you here on Earth, or perhaps, as we speak he/she is so curious to know if you look like him/her, what are you doing, are you aware of him/her in other dimension? Highly advanced copies of you are fully aware of your characteristics and existence on this planet.

If he/she is older than you in linear time, then he/she is from your past. If he/she is younger than you, than he/she is from your future. But in all cases and in all scenarios, you are one and the same person living at the same time in different places, each place functioning according to different laws of physics, or lack of laws of physics.

So, when you revisit your past in a different dimension, prepare yourself to meet another copy of you, or simply YOU in a different non-linear space/time existence.

Many adepts who have visited that dimension did not want to return back. In fact, some Talmiz-Ulema remained there. But as you know by now, their copies remained on Earth.

Final words on your visit to the parallel world you have visited using the Dudurisar technique. While you are there, you will not have terrestrial sensorial properties, because your physical body is still in your room, where you began, however, a sort of a spatial memory you will pick up on your way to the parallel dimension, and will substitute for physical feelings and impressions. This spatial memory you had in you all your life, but you never knew you had it, because you have not entered another non-linear dimension before now. It will come handy, and will help you to remember or identify things.

While you are there, you will have all the opportunities of :

a-Meeting many of your past friends (Dead or alive, so to speak in terrestrial terms), perhaps loved pets you lost;

b-Making new friends, and this could sadden you knowing that you will be returning home;

c-Watching the re-happening of future events, as if you were watching a film (you saw before) backward;

d-Learning from new experiences and results you can use when you return home.

The time will come, when you become capable of realizing and understanding the many lives and existences you have now, had, or will acquire in the future.

*** *** ***

Some of the benefits:

- **1**-Your mind (On its own) knows when it is time to return home.
- **2**-Some people have reported the sadness they felt when they realized that they had to return home. Many did not want to return home, because they have discovered a better place, made new friends, and lived a life –even though extremely short – free of worries and troubles. This could happen to you. But your brain is stronger than your wishes, and you will return safe.
- **3**-On you way back, your mind will reassure you that everything is going to be just fine, and that you have succeeded in removing some stains, copies of disturbing events from your past, and above all the effects of past actions and events that have handicapped you in this life.
- **4**-Your mind will retain all the knowledge you have acquired, and will guide you more efficiently in all your future decisions.
- **5**-Numerous people have reported that their journey was beneficial, because for some incomprehensible reasons, many of the problems and difficulties they have faced before evaporated in thin air.

Closing the Technique:

- **1**-For this particular technique, you mind will close the technique by itself.
- **2**-You will wake up, and you will realize that you were somewhere else, far, far away from your room.
- **3**-You open your eyes, and all of a sudden, a delightful and reassuring sensation will invade your being. You feel energized, more confident, and in a total peace with yourself.

*** *** ***

Technique/Lesson10

Arawadi

A term for the supernatural power or faculty that allows initiated ones to halt or send away difficulties, problems and mishaps into another time and another place, thus freeing themselves from worries, anxiety and fear.

A very complex concept that touches metaphysics, esoterism and quantum physics. Ulema Stephanos Lambrakis said that it is very possible to get rid of current problems by "transposing" them into a different time frame.

He added that "all of us live in two separate dimensions so close to us.

One we know and we call it our physical reality, the other is the adjacent dimension that surrounds our physical world.

Enlightened ones visit that dimension quite frequently.

It is a matter of a deep concentration, and perseverance.

In fact, it is possible to enter that parallel dimension and leave there all your troubles, and return to your physical world free of worries and problems."

In fact, it is possible to enter that parallel dimension and leave there all your troubles, and return to your physical world free of worries and problems."

170

Technique/Lesson10
Arawadi

The Arawadi Technique:

Ulema Micah Naphtali Irza said: "To explain this concept is not an easy task. However, those who have earned the 8th degree are fully aware how Arawadi works. It requires a lot of imagination, discipline, and mental activity. In essence, it works like this…":

- **1**-You are facing problems and experiencing tough time, all sorts of problems, financial, emotional, and physical.
- **2**-You are overwhelmed by all this, and it seems there is no way out.
- **3**-But there is.
- **4**-First, you bring together all these problems and you dumped them in one bag.
- **5**-Be patient. Use a bit of imagination. Just tell yourself that you have a bag. And you want to dump in this bag all the troubles, back luck and horrible things happening to you.
- **6**-You have to convince your mind that indeed you are holding a bag in your hand.
- **7**-If you don't, it would not work.
- **8**-Now, hold strong on this bag.
- **9**-Place the bag on the floor.
- **10**-Go back to your mind, and tell your mind you want to get rid of this damned bag.
- **11**-Stay calm. Don't rush things.
- **12**-Lay down, flat on your back.

Arawadi

- **13**-Close your eyes and take a deep breath.
- **14**-Do not open your eyes yet. Keep breathing slowly and deeply. Spread you arms and your legs.
- **15**-Give a name to your right foot. Any name you wish.
- **16**-Give a name to your left foot. Same story; any name you want.
- **17**-Call you right foot by its name and tell your right foot to command your left foot to go to sleep.
- **18**-Call your left foot and tell your left foot that it is going to sleep now.
- **19**-Call your right foot now and tell your right foot to go to sleep immediately.
- **20**-Now, you will begin to feel something strange. Stay calm.
- **21**-Repeat exactly the same procedures (Step-by-step) if nothing happens within two minutes.
- **22**-Now, you give a name to your body and you call your body by its name, and you command your body to go to sleep.
- **23**-Repeat this 4 times.
- **24**-Now, you tell yourself: I am floating.
- **25**-You repeat this 5 times.
- **26**-You wait. Don't move. Any way, you are not going to move at all, because you are already sleeping, or you are in a state of trance.
- **27**-You start to feel as if some heavy weight is entering your head. That is good. Stay calm.
- **28**-All of a sudden, you feel that you are floating.
- **29**-Tell yourself you want to go somewhere else.
- **30**-Tell yourself you want to go somewhere far, very far.
- **31**-Tell yourself to take you to the sea.
- **32**-You are there now. And you begin to see the sea.
- **33**-Lower yourself, you are still floating too high.
- **34**-Come closer to the surface of the sea.
- **35**-Open the bag.

Arawadi

- **36**-Don't worry. You did not forget the bag, because your mind knew you will need it. So your mind brought the bag with you.
- **37**-Open the bag. Spit on the bag.
- **38**-Dump everything in the sea.
- **39**-Go up in the air now.
- **40**-Tell yourself you have dumped all your troubles in the sea.
- **41**-Ask your mind to repeat to your body that you have dumped all your troubles in the sea.
- **42**-Tell your body to take you back home.
- **43**-Come back home now.
- **44**-Enter your room and tell your body to wake up.
- **45**-Your eyes are open now.
- **46**-Immeditely look at the bag.
- **47**-What you are about to see will amaze you.
- **48**-Do not doubt what you have just seen.
- **49**-Get rid of the bag.
- **50**-Take a shower.
- **51**-Think briefly about the sea you visited in your journey.
- **52**-Wait until tomorrow.
- **53**-Good news are coming your way...

*** *** ***

Technique/Lesson11

Baaniradu

Baaniradu is the Anunnaki-Ulema term for the healing touch technique. It was first used by the priests of Melkart in Ancient Phoenicia, Ugarit and Arwad.

It is extremely important to bear in mind, that this technique does not in any shape or form replace any scientific and medical treatment (s). Baaniradu has not been fully explored and used in the West.

176

Technique/Lesson11
Baaniradu

Excerpts from the Anunnaki-Ulema Kira'at

I. Prerequisites and Preparation

The Honorable Ulema said (Verbatim and unedited):

- **1**-Before you learn how to heal, you should know first if you can heal, and if you have the power to heal without learning.
- **2**-Training and learning will show you the way, but not necessarily the blessing of healing others.
- **3**-Training will teach you the techniques of healing by touch and/or healing without touching. But success depends on the quality and quantity of the healing power you have in your "Conduit".
- **4**-Also you have to remember that if you are intoxicated, or under the influence of drugs, medicine, pills, addictive substances, narcotics, caffeine, tobacco and similar substances, you will not be able to heal others.
- **5**-If your body is not clean, you will not be able to heal others. Your hands most be sparkling clean all the time.
- **6**-If you have been sick yourself for the past 40 days, you will not be able to heal others.
- **7**-If you have committed an act of violence, perjury, false testimony, adultery, theft and/or any hideous act (For the past 2 years), you will not be able to heal others. However, if you have been purified by the Ulema, and if you have fully compensated others (Humans and animals) for all the damages, losses, hurting, pain and suffering

you have caused them, your chances of healing will increase considerably.

- **8**-Do not come close to a sick person, and do not attempt to heal a sick person, if you have sinned in action and in thought. Only, when you are pure in heart and mind you can do so.

Because you will be generating a strong energy current with your hands, you have to keep in mind three important things:

A-Do not rotate both hands in opposite directions over one area of the sick body.

B-Do not use physical strength in moving your hands;

C-Do not constantly concentrate on one particular area of the sick body. Work around it as the healing touch progresses.

The Ulema continues:

- **1**-Our bodies were created to heal themselves.
- **2**-Our bodies were programmed from the time we were born.
- **3**-We cannot change what was written in our "Essence" (Similar to DNA).
- **4**-But we can improve on it.
- **5**-Our bodies consist of many things, including mental memory, physical memory, spatial memory, and etheric memory.
- **6**-Each memory has its own health condition, limitation and sphere.
- **7**-We can be sick in one sphere, and perfectly healthy in another.
- **8**-The mental affects the physical, and vice versa.
- **9**-We can overcome mental and physical difficulties and disturbances by balancing our physical state (Physical milieu) with our mental sphere (Astral and/or non-physical dimension, also called Zinnar (Etheric Belt surrounding our body).

- **10-**This helps a lot. Because when we feel pain in certain part of our body, this part can be transposed into the Zinnar sphere for self-healing.
- **11-**Once it is healed, this part will return to its physical origin. This is an exercise/technique only the Ulema can accomplish. But students like you can heal the painful part of your body without transposing it into a non-physical sphere. You can heal that part with "Talamouth" (A gentle synchronized energetic touch), and "Tarkiz" (Even without touching the suffering part, and simply by directing beam of energy from the brain's cell "Conduit").
- **12-**You have to consider your body as a battery, or like an electrical current. Both have negative and positive terminals. Your body too, has a positive area, and a negative area.
- **13-**Some individuals have negative terminal in the left side of their bodies, and a positive terminal in the right side of their bodies. Others, just the opposite.
- **14-**Thus, it is very important to discern between the two terminals, and know where exactly the negative and the positive terminals or stations are located within the body.
- **15-**If you don't know how to localize these two terminals, and you try to heal a sick person, you could disorient the energy in his body and cause severe injuries.
- **16-**A well-trained student knows how to find these two terminals by dowsing, using his both hands as rods.
- **17-**Before you start dowsing, you have to know upfront, which one of your hands is positive, and which one of your hands is negative.
- **18-**If you don't know, and you begin with your healing touch process, you could disorient the energy flux in the body of the sick person, and cause severe damages to his health.

Baaniradu

- **19-**If your right hand has a positive charge, then this hand should "hover" over the positive terminal of the sick person.
- **20-**If your right hand has a negative charge, then this hand should "hover" over the negative terminal of the sick person.
- **21-**The same thing applies to the other hand.
- **22-**You should not wear jewelry or metal during the healing touch therapy.
- **23-**You should not perform the healing touch therapy nearby an electrical outlet.
- **24-**You should not perform the healing touch therapy nearby pets, because pets sense diseases, illness and negative energy. They are vulnerable to these conditions and could absorb their frequencies and vibes, thus disrupting the healing process.
- **25-**Do not come too close to the body of the sick person. Keep at least 20 centimeters of distance between yourself and the sick person.

- **26-**You should stop your healing touch immediately if you notice that the sick person is having trouble breathing.

The healing touch training requires patience, perseverance, practice, and time. Usually, to complete the training program, a student spends at least 3 months studying and practicing. In some instances, the period could stretch to 6 months.
Everything depends on the personal effort and commitment of the Talmiz (Student). There are several steps to follow. And here they are:
The honorable Ulema said: Your hands are an extension of your mind. Use them wisely and for the good of mankind. Talk to your hands. Explore them. Get to know them.
Find out what they can do, and try to discover how many beautiful things they can create. Watch what usually a good concert pianist does before he starts to play.

He examines his hands, he communicates with his hands, he flexes his hands. Do the same thing.
Get to know your hands.

This exercise/technique will show you how.

II. The Technique:

Stage One:
- **1**-You need to practice 3 times a week.
- **2**-Each practice session will take approximately one hour.
- **3**-You practice alone.
- **4**-No people, and no pets should be around you.
- **5**-Select the most suitable three days of the week and stick to this schedule: Meaning you practice only on these three days.
- **6**-Same hours are highly recommended.
- **7**-You have to build in your system a new "practice-memory".
- **8**-First of all, you take a shower. You must be clean and your hands must be spotless.
- **9**-Enter your room, and sit comfortably in a wooden chair.
- **10**-Do not use metallic or plastic chair.
- **11**-Stay put for 5 seconds.
- **12**-Breathe deeply and gently.
- **13**-Extend both arms straight ahead.
- **14**-Join both hands, palm against palm.
- **15**-Keep them like this for one minute or so.
- **16**-Separate both hands approximately two centimeters apart, not more.
- **17**-Focus sharply on these two centimeters for one minute.

Baaniradu

- **18-**Drop your hands down.
- **19-**Repeat this exercise (Joining and separating hands) three times.
- **20-**Drop your hands down.
- **21-**Stand up and breathe slowly and deeply three times.
- **22-**Sit down in your chair.
- **23-**Raise both hands, (palms facing the ground), and stretch them as far as you can (Not higher than your shoulders).
- **24-**Bring both hands close to your chest in an horizontal motion (Palms always facing the ground).
- **25-**Start to rotate both hands in a circular motion, and keeping a 15 centimeters distance between the rotation movements.
- **26-**Keep doing this for two minutes.
- **27-**Now, bring your hands together. Palm against palm.
- **28-**Keep both hands in this position close to your solar plexus for two minutes.
- **29-**Close your eyes for approximately two minutes.
- **30-**Now, tell your mind to enter a golden ray of light inside your solar plexus.
- **31-**Let the light enter your solar plexus.
- **32-**Keep your hands close to your solar plexus.
- **33-**Now, tell your mind you want your solar plexus to send the golden light to your hands.
- **34-**Tell your solar plexus to send the light right away.
- **35-**Tell your hands to receive the light and hold on it for one minute.
- **36-**Press strongly one hand against the other. Both palms are very firm.
- **37-**Stay like this for 2 minutes or so.
- **38-**At the end of the two minutes or so, you will start to feel some sort of heat in your palms. And that is good.
- **39-**Do not loose this heat. Hold on this heat.
- **40-**Do not let this heat leave your hands.
- **41-**Take a long and deep breath.

- **42**-Separate your hands.
- **43**-At this moment, you might feel a minor fatigue in both shoulders or a sort of a small muscle cramp in your neck. Don't worry. You will be fine in a few seconds.
- **44**-This is the end of the first session.
- **45**-Take a shower.

Note: Repeat this exercise three times a week for a period of one month.

***   ***   ***

Preparation for stage two:

During this stage you should not smoke, consume alcohol, or eat meat. And never ever touch addictive substances and narcotics!! This training stage shall take place outside your room. You are going to find a calm spot close to nature, far from cement, steel, noisy surroundings, and people.

We recommend a wooden area, a park, perhaps your backyard if it is not exposed to your neighbors, a river bank, or the beach when nobody is around. The most suitable time is always early in the morning around 5 o'clock. The day should be sunny but not hot. Dress in white. Very light.

Do not wear metal or jewelry. And do not eat before the practice. Drink plenty of water before you start your exercise.

You don't have to bring anything with you. Mother nature and a serene ambiance is all what you need.

Stage Two:
The honorable Ulema said:

- **1**-You are now starting stage two.
- **2**-You have spent one month practicing in stage one. And you have made an important progress: You have discovered that you hands can hold heat.

- **3**-We prefer to call that heat Energy.
- **4**-Now, we are going to make this energy a positive energy.
- **5**-If this energy is not developed into a positive energy, it will remain worthless, and will disappear before you know it.
- **6**-So, we are going to hold on it, and make it work as a healing energy; a sort of positive vibes; a therapeutic touch.
- **7**-You are going to succeed, as long as you have patience, you keep on practicing, and you are determined to use this wonderful power for the good of mankind.
- **8**-Different practices apply to different places.
- **9**-For instances, if you have chosen a river bank, you will be using river stones to practice with. If you have chosen a wooden area, you will be using leaves, or a piece of bark. If you have chosen the beach, you will be using sands or seashells.
- **10**-You will always practice with pure elements of Mother Nature.
- **11**-You will not touch synthetic products, plastic, metal or technological gadgets.
- **12**-Let's assume you have chosen a river bank. And that is good.
- **13**-Now you sit comfortably anywhere around the river bank.
- **14**-But make sure that the area is clean, calm, and you are alone.
- **15**-Take your shoes off.
- **16**-Sit for a few seconds, and try to "empty your mind".
- **17**-We have already taught you how to "empty your mind".
- **18**-We are going to use this technique in stage two.
- **19**-Take a deep and a long breath.
- **20**-Find two clean stones. Not too big, and not too small; the size of a small apple.

- **21**-Place one stone in each palm and close both hands.
- **22**-With firmly closed hands squeeze the stones as strong as you can for one minute or so.
- **23**-Open both hands.
- **24**-Keep them open for ten seconds.
- **25**-Close both hands now, and squeeze one more time on the stones for another minute or so.
- **26**-While squeezing tell your mind to bring the golden light to the stones.
- **27**-Ask your mind again one more time.
- **28**-Imagine the golden light entering your hands.
- **29**-Direct the golden light toward the stones.
- **30**-Keep focusing on this for two minutes.
- **31**-Now something is going to happen. Pay attention.
- **32**-The stones are getting hot.
- **33**-Keep squeezing.
- **34**-You start to feel some sort of heat in your hands, and that is good.
- **35**-Now you tell yourself you are going to send the heat away.
- **36**-You tell yourself you are going to absorb the heat.
- **37**-Your order the heat to enter your body.
- **38**-You start to feel the heat entering your body, and that is good.
- **39**-Now you tell yourself your hands are no longer feeling any heat.
- **40**-There is no more heat in your hands.
- **41**-You open both hands.
- **42**-Now something very important is going to happen. Pay attention.
- **43**-Look at the stones.
- **44**-You are going to see something around the stones.
- **45**-What you are seeing now is the vapor of the heat that was left inside the stones.
- **46**-In a few seconds, the vapor will dissipate.
- **47**-You have made a tremendous progress.

Baaniradu

- **48**-You were able to direct and to move the heat from one place to another.
- **49**-That is correct, because you have perfectly succeeded in bringing the heat to the stones.
- **50**-Also you have succeeded in storing the heat in the stones; and finally in directing the heat toward your body. That is remarkable.
- **51**-We are almost at the end of the exercise.
- **52**-You have to keep the two stones you worked with.
- **53**-Do not loose them.
- **54**-Put the stones in your pockets.
- **55**-Breathe slowly and deeply.
- **56**-Stay put for ten seconds.
- **57**-Stand up and you are on your way...

Note:

A-Repeat this exercise three times a week for a period of one month.

B-In a wooden area, you can use leaves or a piece of bark, or stones, whatever is accessible.

C-In the future, and once your Conduit is fully operational, you will be able to use this technique/exercise with various materials, including metal and substance originally made from liquids.

*** *** ***

Stage Three:

Introduction:
This final stage is extremely important because it concentrates on:
a-Cleansing your hands;
b-Nourishing your hands;
c-Protecting your hands;

Baaniradu

d-Experimenting with your hands.

The Technique:

The honorable Ulema said:

- **1**-For a period of one month, you should not touch any substance or product made out of animal fat.
- **2**-Do not touch any toxic element.
- **3**-Do not use tobacco or consume alcohol.
- **4**-Use of addictive substances or narcotics is absolutely forbidden.
- **5**-Every day for a period of 10 minutes, hold the two stones (you found on the river bank) in your palms (One in each hand), and gently flip the stones in any direction you want.
- **6**-Close your hands, and visualize yourself sitting on the river bank.
- **7**-Try to capture the sceneries of the river in your mind.
- **8**-Repeat this exercise once a day for thirty days.
- **9**-For five minutes or so everyday, bring both hands close to a healthy plant, and keep both hands at 10 centimeters distance from the plant.
- **10**-Avoid touching the plant. Just surround it with your palms.
- **11**-Focus on the greenest part of the plant or on the very top of the plant.
- **12**-Select a specific part of the plant and concentrate on this part. Preferably around the bottom or the roots.
- **13**-Repeat this exercise daily for thirty days.
- **14**-While concentrating on the chosen area of the plant, remind your mind of the properties and energies of the green colors which are:
- **A**-Modifying energy.
- **B**-Natural healing ability.

- **C**-Restful state.
- **15**-Tell yourself you are absorbing the energy, the natural healing ability and the serenity of the plant.
- **16**-So far you have practiced with stones and plant. Now, you are going to practice with water.
- **17**-Fill a flat container with boiled water.
- **18**-Wait until it cools off.
- **19**-Immerse both hands in the water.
- **20**-While immersing your hands in the water tell yourself that your hands are absorbing the blue light.
- **21**-Remind yourself of the properties and characteristics of the blue light which are:
- **A**- Balanced existence.
- **B**-Sustaining life.
- **C**-Easing the nerve system.
- **D**-Transmitting forces and energy.
- **E**-Balance of the mind.
- **F**-Receiving and/or transmitting information in a telepathic communication.
- **22**-Tell yourself once again that the blue light is entering your hands and solar plexus.
- **23**-Repeat this exercise twice daily for thirty days.
- **24**-We are almost done.
- **25**-Your final practice is with fire now. Nothing to be afraid of.
- **26**-You will be practicing with a gentle candle.
- **27**-Light up a white candle. Never use a black candle.
- **28**-Bring both hands close to the candle, and keep your palms at five centimeters distance from the candle.
- **29**-Focus on the flame for 2 minutes or so.
- **30**-Soon, you will start to see a purple color emerging from the blue flame. And that is good.
- **31**-Tell yourself the purple color is entering your palms and solar plexus.

Baaniradu

- **32**-Indeed the purple color and the gentle warmth of the candle are entering your solar plexus and nourishing your palms.
- **33**-Remind yourself of the major property and effect of the purple color which are:
- **A**-Spiritual thoughts.
- **B**-Gentility, tenderness.
- **34**-Repeat this exercise twice daily for thirty days.
- **35**-Stage three comes to an end now.
- **36**-You are done. You have completed the orientation and training program.
- **37**-It is very possible that you have acquired a healing touch.
- **38**-You have to believe in the positive powers of your hands.
- **39**-You will find out very soon.
- **40**-Use your hands wisely and for the good of mankind.

*** *** ***

Technique/Lesson 12
Bari-du

Baridu is the Anunnaki-Ulema term for the act of zooming into an astral body or a Double.

We have used the expression "Astral body", because of the Western readers' familiarity with what it basically represents. This representation is not the depiction usually used by the Ulema, but it is close enough, to use it in this work.

Technique/Lesson 12
Bari-du

Bari-du: The Concept

Anunnaki-Ulema explained Bari-du as follows:
Verbatim; Excerpts from a Kira'at:

- The initiated and enlightened ones can zoom into their other bodies, and acquire Anunnaki supernatural faculties.
- I have used the words supernatural faculties instead of supernatural powers, because the enlightened and initiated ones are peaceful, and do not use physical power, brutal force or any aggressive means to reach their objectives.
- The use of violence against humans and animals, even aggressive thoughts and harmful intentions annihilate all chances to acquire Anunnaki's extraordinary faculties.
- Your Double can easily read your thoughts.
- If your thoughts are malicious, your Double will prevent you from zooming yourself into its ethereal molecules.
- Therefore, you have to control your temper, remain calm, and show serenity in your thoughts, intentions and actions.
- You Double is very delicate, even though it can accomplish the toughest missions and penetrate the thickest barriers.
- Any indication of violence or ill intention triggers a pulse that blocks your passage to the ethereal sphere of your Double.

Baridu

- Once you enter your Double, you will be able to use it in so many beautiful and effective ways as:
  1- A protective shield against danger,
  2- An effective apparatus to protect yourself in hostile and dangerous situations,
  3- A tool to develop your abilities to learn many languages, and enhance your artistic creativity,
  4- A stimulus to increase the capacity of your memory,
  5- Instrument to heal wounds and internal injuries. No, you will not become a surgeon, but you will be able to stop internal bleeding, and eliminate pain,
  6- A vehicle to visit distant places and even enter restricted areas for good causes. The possibilities are endless.
- Once you are in a perfect harmony with your Double, and your physical organism is elevated to a higher vibrational level through your union with your Double, you will be able to walk through solid substances such as walls, sheets of glasses and metal.
- You become effective in controlling metal and de-fragmenting molecules of any substance. This will allow you to transmute, change and alter the properties of any object known to mankind.
- But if you use these supernatural faculties to hurt others, or for personal and selfish gain, you will loose them for good, and you will be accountable for such malicious use in the other dimension. And this could delay your entrance through the Ba'ab.

*** *** ***

Excerpts from their Kira'ats "Reading"

Ulema Al-Mutawalli said, verbatim:

- Before you were born, and before your body took shape, you (as a human being) have existed somewhere as an idea.
- What is this idea? We will give you an example. Before a product is mass produced, inventors and artists design and create a model or a prototype of each product. And everything begins with the drawing board.
- On this board, shape, form, dimensions, colors and specifications of the product are defined and illustrated. It started with an idea. The idea became a project and the project found its existence on the drawing board. In fact, everything in life started with an idea, continued with a sketch before it reached its final form, and eventually the market.
- Your physical body is a perfect product. And this product came from an idea like everything that has been created. Nothing comes from nothing.
- Who came up with this idea? This depends on your religious beliefs. If you believe in the Judeo-Christian tradition, then, your God is the originator of this idea. He created the first draft of your physical body on his drawing board.
- Most certainly, God had to think about how your body should look like. On the Judeo-Christian drawing board of the creation of mankind, God decided how the physical body should come to life.
- You are much more important than a commercial product or a commodity like a car, or a soda bottle. The designers, artists and engineers at the automobile factory and plant spent many hours designing the model of the car, and the manufacturers of the soda bottle spent some good time going through various designs of the

Baridu

- shapes and looks of bottles before they chose the most suitable design for their product.
- Now, if you think that you are more important than a car or a bottle, then, it is logical to assume that somebody has spent some time designing you, otherwise, you will surface as a non-studied and not well-researched product.
- If you look at your body very carefully, you will find out that your body is an extremely complicated machine and your brain consists of a very intricate wiring system that requires an engineer or at least a first class designer.
- In summary, you did not come right away without a plan, without a well-thought design, and without an idea that created the design and execution of your physical body.
- At the very beginning and early stage of the creation of your physical body, the "Divine" or "Superior" architect-engineer conceived your physical looks as a picture in the astral world.
- And the astral world for now call it: The world of ideas; a non-physical world. In a non-physical world, everything is non-physical, it is astral, it is ethereal.
- When the ethereal image or idea becomes reality and adopts physical properties like eyes, legs, feet and bones, this idea or your "prototype" becomes a physical body and enters the physical world via the womb of your mother.
- Yet, it remains deeply and directly connected to the draft of the first copy of your physical body.
- Since the first draft of your non-physical body and your recently acquired physical body (Or about to be developed in the womb of your mother) are still connected to each other, both bodies (The Idea or Draft and your physical body) co-exist.
- The physical body is inside your mother, and the non-physical body called double or first body exists outside the physical world.

- The other copy, or more precisely the first copy of YOU is called your Double.
- As soon as you begin to develop as a small physical body (a small fetus) inside the womb of your mother, the idea or draft that created you before you entered the womb of your mother begins to feed your brain's cells and program your intellect.
- In other words, your brain begins to receive all the information and characteristics that will create and define your personality, temper, character, persona and nature.
- During the very first 40 days, everything your "Creator" wanted you to be or become start to "go inside your brain" and in the physiology of your body.
- During this very critical intellectual and physical formation, the other aspect of you, your Double, enters a dimension very close to your mother, and once your mother delivers you, your double, the non-physical body will leave the "surroundings" of your mother and follow you.
- From this moment on, your Double will stay with you until you die.
- The double interacts with us in a most fascinating way, noticeable only to the "small child we are", and not to the others. Many children have seen their double. And many of them spoke to their double, and played with their double.
- In many instances, babies and children called their double "my friend", or "a friend who came to visit me." Unfortunately, many parents discouraged their small children from talking about their "imaginary friends", or fantasizing about the visits of their unseen friends." This is very common.
- Ulema children are encouraged to talk about their "imaginary friends".

Baridu

- These are very precious moments in our lives, because during this stage, the infant and later on, the small child, has a direct access to his/her double.
- If the child is deprived from this contact, the Double could dissipate for ever.
- Of course, in the future, the Double might appear again on certain occasions.
- But, because we have lost touch with our Double, and we no longer remember the beautiful and friendly visits of our forgotten imaginary friends, our mind and common sense will automatically dismiss the sudden apparition of our Double as a reality. In these instances, people quite often say: "I am seeing things", or "Am I hallucinating?" Therapists rush so quickly to explain the phenomenon as a trick by the mind.
- It is not a trick at all. It just happened that your Double is paying you a visit. Instead of questioning your sanity, you must rejoice and welcome your "friend". In fact, your Double is the most truthful, caring and best friend you ever had, simply because it is YOU!
- Your Double appeared to you for many reasons.
- Your "double" always watches over you. It cares about you. Its presence is a sign of friendship, sometimes necessary and indispensable for solving your problems and finding a way to get out of trouble. You should welcome your Double and listen to.
- The initiated ones can contact their Double; it is a matter of learning, practice and patience. However, you have to remember, that the living cannot contact the dead. By reaching the sphere of your Double or Astral Body, you are reaching yourself, not a dead substance, a departed entity or a spirit.
- Untrained persons cannot contact their Double, but can be trained and taught by the Ulema. And the training has nothing to do with magic, spiritism or religious trances and state of ecstasy. It is purely mental, intellectual, and scientific.

- Here, we will be talking about two situations:
- First situation: Your Double materializes before you on its own,
- Second situation: You initiate the contact with your Double.
- Sometimes, the Astral Body materializes before you eyes, even though you did not try to contact it. This apparition has many meanings, and could be interpreted differently according to the circumstances.
- Sometimes, your Double appears to you to warn you against an imminent danger. Sometimes, to guide you in a moment of despair and difficulties.
- Some other times, when you "see yourself" as a fragile ectoplasmic thin substance like a fog for instance, your Double apparition is telling you, that a very important event is going to happen and it could change the course of your life.
- In rare instances, this apparition could mean that your days are numbered. Short after Lord Byron saw his Double he passed way.
- In the second situation: Now, you are trying to contact your Double. You initiate the contact. If you are not one of the enlightened persons, you would not know what to do, and where to start. Like everything in the universe, including speeches and lectures...everything begins with an introduction and ends with an epilogue. This is the right path. In contacting your Double, you must have an introduction that comes in the form of an entry or entrance into the "Al-Madkhal".
- Al Madkhal means verbatim: Entrance and/or where you step in. Ba'ab is a spatial place that exists around the physical dimension of our world. In the Anunnaki-Ulema vocabulary, Ba'ab means verbatim: Door. And from and through this door you enter the other dimension where your Astral Body (Your Double) exists.

Baridu

In the West, ufologists, and even space scientists nickname Ba'ab "Stargate." It is not totally correct, because to them, stargate is a gate through which spaceships can travel through the infinity of space and conquer space-time, thus reducing the enormous distances between stars and planets, and reaching destinations in the universe at a speed greater than the speed of sound and light.

For the Ulema, the Ba'ab can be used as a spatial stargate, and a mental means to reach the non-physical world as well; no spaceships are needed to communicate with your Double.

*** *** ***

Technique/Lesson 13
Bisho-barkadari "Bukadari"

Bisho-barkadari "Bukadari" is the Anunnaki-Ultma term for the technique used in blocking bad vibes that negatively affect human beings.

It is composed from two words:

a-Bisho, which means bad; negative.

b-Barkadari, which means flames; rays, vibes; beams.

Technique/Lesson 13
Bisho-barkadari
"Bukadari"

On this subject, the Anunnaki-Ulema said:

Excerpts from their Kira'at, verbatim

Negativity is atrociously destructive. It affects your mind, your body, your relationships with others, and your very environment. Negativity comes from three sources:
1-Others; their thoughts, intentions, and actions,
2-Yourself; your thoughts, intentions, and deeds,
3-Your environment; where and how you live.

Ulema Sadik said (Verbatim):
- Thoughts can take a physical form.
- Thoughts can materialize in physical and non-physical dimensions.
- Enlightened ones can project and materialize healthy and positive thoughts.
- Deviated and succumbed seers can project, emanate and materialize negative and destructive thoughts.
- Bad and destructive thoughts directed toward you or against you can harm your mental and physical abilities, as well as your health, your progress, and your environment, including your home, your office, your car, and any place where you live and work.
- Malicious seers can either target your "Double" (Astral Body) and/or your physical body.

Bisho-barkadari

- They can also send harmful vibrations to your mind, to your body, and to the objects you touch, including tools, materials, equipments and instruments you use, such as a computer, a camera, a car, an elevator, a desk, even a can-opener. We will talk about all this in due time.
- These bad vibes can be intentional or unintentional.
- They are intentional when they are sent by others to harm you.
- They are unintentional when you discover or when you sense them on your own. In this situation, you can take an immediate action to stop their negative effects on you.
- For instance, you walk into a room or you mingle with people in a social gathering, and all of a sudden, you feel uncomfortable or disturbed in the presence of one or more individuals.
- You get the feeling that you are not at ease being around them, or something is bothering you about a particular person or a group of people. Usually, you get this feeling toward a particular person who has just passed by you, or looking at you, or just standing by.
- Sometimes you know what is bothering you about this guy, and sometimes you don't. Don't think much. Don't philosophize about it. You can stop this disturbing feeling on the spot. And I am going to show you how.
- But first, you must understand what has created this unpleasant and irritating feeling, and caused a negative current to circulate around you.
- Since this unpleasant feeling you have sensed was not intentionally created by others to hurt you, no serious harm will come to you.
- But if you do not stop it right away, it could cause further discomfort and additional nuisances.
- The person who has created this negative current around you is usually unaware of it. It is beyond his/her control.
- In most cases, the unpleasant vibes you felt toward that person, and the negativity you sensed are created by one or all of the following factors:

A-The person is physically sick. And the sickness is diffusing unhealthy vibrations.

B-The person's diet; the quantity of unhealthy food and addictive substances he/she absorbed.

C-The temper and character of the person; if he/she is a bitter and unhappy individual, the disharmonious and unbalanced frequencies of his/her unhappiness and bitterness will hit your Double, the perimeter of your aura, and all your sensorial faculties.

Those frequencies are charged with negative energy usually diffused through grayish rays undetected to the naked eyes, but could be seen, detected and analyzed in laboratories.

This is factual. In many instances, these negative vibrations can prevent your machines and equipments from working properly. All of a sudden, your computer crashes, your car does not start, your cellular phone is dead, your TV is shut off, and many of your electrical gadgets stop working. All these weird things happen while that person is around you.

Do not get frustrated. Do not lose your temper. Soon, everything will be just fine. In the following chapter, you will learn how to block negative vibes.

Two situations to deal with:

How many times did you tell yourself or others?

☐ I can't work when my roommate is in the apartment.

☐ I can't write when she is around!

☐ He drained me out completely!

☐ I feel nervous when he is around and everything stops working.

☐ I had to wait until he leaves before I could start working again.

☐ He gives me the creeps.

Basically, you have two situations to deal with:

1-Situation #1: What you should and could do if you can control your environment or place;

2-Situation #2: What you should and could do if you can't control your environment or place.

Bisho-barkadari

It is paramount to understand how the energy field surrounding you, and emanating from others plays a paramount role in conditioning and affecting your mind and your health.

You can't measure it or see it with your naked eyes, but most certainly you have felt it many times. Everything around you can affect you.

It can even affect your luck, fortune and business. Master B. Ushah was so right when he said that the energy field can be thought of as a grid of fine lines which run crisscross throughout the whole universe and through every living being, thereby connecting every part of creation to each other.

Wherever you go, you become part of the environment, even part of a street sign, and people crossing the street.

The Ulema call this energy field "Ih-tikah'k", meaning contact with others on different plane. Western teachers refer to it as Aura, based upon Eastern traditions.

This energy field (Ih-tikaah'k or Aura) is the electromagnetic field surrounding an object, including yourself, your friends and foes. Even your pets.

It surrounds all living things such as people, plants and animals as well as non-living things such as rocks. These fields change with time, sometimes without warning, due to various positive and more often negative influences.

This field surrounds and runs through the body, holding within it information which reflects the current physical mental and emotional condition of the individual.

It also contains the original "blueprint" of health.

The human energy field is part of the life force energy field and is like a template or network of energy points with which the physical molecules of the body are aligned. (Source: B. Ushah.)

The Ulema said that the field, within and outside of our bodies stores information including our thoughts, past and present. This energetic system comprises of several layers such as:

1-You physical body
2-Others' physical bodies,
3-You Double,
4-Others' Double,

5-Your electro-magnetic vibes,
6-Others' electro-magnetic vibes,
7-Your astral blueprints,
8-Others' astral blueprints,
9-Your Chakras,
10-Others' Chakras,
11-Your meridians,
12-Others' meridians,
13-Your past, present and future,
14-Others' past, present and future,
15-Your Conduit (Active or dormant),
16-Others' Conduit (Active or dormant).

Our personal energy field is in constant contact with the outside world because it is part of it:
- It absorbs slow frequencies from electrical equipment,
- It collects other people's negative energies,
- It stores the memory of upsetting interactions with others,
- It carries the memory of our past illness, distress and life experience. ((Source: B. Ushah.)

*** *** ***

Case study:
Employees In the United States:
Contemporary Ulema have found that negative vibrations and transmission of negative energy rays vary in intensity and degree of harm in virtue of many factors.
1-In the United States, negative and bitter people are more likely to emit negative energy that can deeply affect you mentally and physically on Monday and on Tuesday than on any other days of the week.
2-Employees who are dissatisfied with their jobs and who dislike their boss diffuse intense bad vibes during the early and late hours of the day of their shifts.

Bisho-barkadari

3-These vibes become more intense upon returning home, and especially during the first 40 minutes.

4-The negative vibes dissipate short after, however their subconscience retains their dissatisfaction and anger for the rest of the day.

5-Thus, the Ulema suggest that you give those people enough room to relax and enough time to forget about the job they hate before you discuss with them any delicate or sensitive matter, because they will explode.

6-It is highly recommended to have pets around depressed and tired people. Pets provide therapeutic and curing vibes. However, if these people are going through intense rage or anger state, pets should not be left around them.

7-The negative vibes of bitter and angry people can cause damages not only to humans and pets, but also to domestic appliances.

*** *** ***

Excerpts from the Ulema's Kira'at (Verbatim):

How to stop attracting negative people to your life. How to block negative vibes:

Master Win Li said: "There is a major difference between the Western approach and the Ulema's technique to blocking negative vibes that can harm your well-being. However, Western therapists and Ulema agree on two things:

1-Negative vibes are either produced by ourselves or by others.

2-Without knowing many attract negative and destructive people to their lives.

In both situations, the consequences can be disastrous.

Are there techniques to block harmful negative vibes, and to stop attracting bitter and negative people to our life and to what we do for a living?

The answer is yes!"

*** *** ***

The Ulema technique: How to block negative vibes

- 1-For the untrained, it is difficult to pinpoint the source of bad vibes. Therefore, we will be providing you with general guidelines useful in many cases.
- 2-It is very easy to protect yourself from bad vibes by creating a mental shield around your body.
- 3-Everything starts with your mind.
- 4-You start the first steps in the privacy of your room.
- 5-You sit comfortably in a chair in your room.
- 6-Take off your shoes.
- 7-Remove your jewelry, your belt, your tie, your watch, and any metallic substance you are wearing.
- 8-Change into white clothes. Never wear dark colors clothes during this exercise.
- 9-Close your eyes and take a deep breath.
- 10-Breathe deeply three times.
- 11-Keep your eyes closed.
- 12-Visualize your body standing before your eyes. It is very simple. Just tell yourself I want to imagine my body right here standing before me. It is not going to happen physically, but just say that to yourself.
- 13-Repeat it one more time. Repeat the very same thing you just said.
- 14-Everything is going to be fine.
- 15-Breathe deeply and slowly one more time.
- 16-Stretch your arms (Straight) and move them or rotate in any direction you want as if you were swimming.
- 17-Keep on breathing very slowly and gently.
- 18-Imagine yourself swimming in a beautiful crystal clear lake.
- 19-Continue to swim until you reach the bank or the edge of the lake.
- 20-You are there now. Look for a comfortable spot and sit there.
- 21-You start to feel a fresh breeze and that is good.

Bisho-barkadari

- 22-Keep your eyes closed.
- 23-Look at the other edge of the lake. You will find it. The edge from where you started to swim.
- 24-Good. You found the edge.
- 25-Clap your hands now.
- 26-You hear the clapping of your hands.
- 27-Tell yourself you are leaving the sound of clapping at the edge of the lake.
- 28-Leave the clapping at the far end (The edge) of the lake, and return to your spot where you were sitting.
- 29-No, you will not swim again to return to your spot.
- 30-Your brain is so fast now, and understands what you need...it will take you right away to your spot.
- 31-That is wonderful. You are there now, sitting calmly.
- 32-You are still enjoying the fresh breeze.
- 33-Breathe and smell the fresh breeze.
- 33-Tell the breeze to move faster and faster.
- 34-Repeat your command one more time.
- 35-The breeze is moving fast now.
- 36-Let it move and move and move.
- 37-Tell the breeze to get thicker and ticker.
- 38-The breeze is getting ticker...very very thick.
- 39-Thank the breeze.
- 40-Tell the breeze to change itself into a wall.
- 41-Repeat this command three times.
- 42-You are going to feel something now. Pay attention.
- 43-Your head is getting heavier. And that is good.
- 44-Tell the wall to stay there like a guard.
- 45-Lift up both arms and direct them toward the wall.
- 46-Tell yourself the wall is strong and is blocking everything.
- 47-Tell yourself you are leaving everything that has disturbed you behind the wall.
- 48-Thank the wall and ask the wall to go away.

- 49-Clap your hands twice.
- 50-In your mind, try to remember how did you get here, from the very beginning.
- 51-Now tell yourself you are going back to where you have started...the lake bank you saw first.
- 52-Good. You are at the lake bank now.
- 53-You see, you came back without swimming. Your mind knows what you are doing. He is with you all the way.
- 54-Now tell yourself the lake, the breeze, the wall will always be around you to protect you from other's bad thoughts and vibes.
- 55-Tell yourself nobody can enter or break the wall around you.
- 56-Repeat this 3 times.
- 57-Take a deep breath.
- 58-Open your eyes and stay calm in your chair.
- 59-Right down in a notebook what you have experienced. The more details you put down the better you will feel very very soon.
- 60-Repeat this exercise twice a week, always the same day and same time for one full month.
- 61-After the third exercise, burn your notes.
- 62-After the fourth exercise you are going to feel so good and so strong.
- 63-Bad vibes will never disturb you again.

*** *** ***

212

PART 2: Q&A, AND DISCUSSIONS

Introduction

Section 1: Anunnaki-Ulema Techniques/Lessons.
In this section, I will try to explain in more details, and at length if necessary, some key-passages from each lesson/technique mentioned in this book, that might appear either obscure, or difficult to understand.
I got some help here, thanks to very *a propos* inquiries I received from friends, students and readers who are so eager to practice each technique and get the best out of it.

Section 2: The world of the Anunnaki: Students and readers questions and inquiries. The author's answers and clarifications.
In this section, I will shed some lights on various aspects of the Anunnaki that constitute paramount elements of their nature, and which are not fully understood by Anunnaki enthusiasts and the general public.

Section 3: Subjects of interest:
In this section, we will be addressing very unusual and rarely explained subjects pertaining to the extraordinary faculties of Anunnaki and Ulema, supernatural powers acquired through the study of alien life and the Book of Ramadosh.

*** *** ***

214

Q&A

Section 1: Questions About The Anunnaki-Ulema Techniques

Why The Conduit Is Not Catching Your Messages?

Question 1:

Would you please explain further the passage below, and tell me why my Conduit is not catching all the messages I am sending to my Conduit?

Does this mean that my Conduit is not receiving clear messages from me?

How can I send clear messages to my Conduit?

Passage: "The Conduit will absorb the vibrations and organize them, and from that moment on, the Conduit will take over.

To summarize, by attempting certain activities, you are sending a message to your Conduit.

It will take some time, because at the beginning, your Conduit may not catch the messages, or if it does catch them, may not interpret the messages correctly, because the Conduit is not one hundred percent awake.

With practice, the Conduit becomes familiar with these type of messages, and it begins to give them codes.

Each activity would have its own code."

*** *** ***

Important note to the reader:
Think seriously about this question.
Do not rush to find the answer on the following pages.
Try first to answer the question yourself.
Explore all the possibilities; the pros and the cons.
This would be a fruitful exercise.

Q&A

Answer to Question 1:

- First of all, you have to remember that your mind (Your brain) has nothing to do with your Conduit. Even though, your brain is functioning wonderfully and you are doing great things in your life, not all the cells in your brain have been used.
- There are so many regions in our brain that have not been explored yet by science.
- In those many unexplored regions of the brain, are so many cells yet to be discovered, located and localized. And above all, we need to learn how they function.
- In that mysterious undiscovered region of the brain, the Conduit exists. It could be in the right or left side of your brain, or just adjacent to line dividing the two parts.
- In the Conduit, there are so many cells, each one with a very defined and particular extraordinary faculty/power, that needs to be activated.
- For instance, one cell triggers the faculty of reading others' thoughts, another cell (Or cells) is responsible for the faculty of teleportation, so on.
- If those cells are not activated, you will not be able to do all those wonderful things.
- So, you have to consider the Conduit as a bank where so many cells are deposited. And there are hundreds of thousands of cells deposited in the Conduit.
- Each cell has a precise function and an invisible location.
- This means that the Conduit can do so many things, if cells are activated. It would be impossible in one lifespan to develop and activate all the cells.
- Three or four fully activated cells is more than enough. With four activated cells you can do four great miracles by earth's standards.
- But for the cell to produce this extraordinary power, the cell must be able first to understand what you want to do.

Q&A

- For instance, you cannot tell or command your cell "go ahead and make me fly or let me learn a new language in one hour."
- You should first learn how to send your command to your cell. There is a technique for this.
- Your Ulema teacher knows how to put you on the right track.
- Let's assume you have sent a message (A thought, a wish) to your cell. What's next? Well, the message enters your Conduit. Your conduit acting as a supervisor, and as the main receiver reads your message and directs your message to the appropriate cell.
- Your Conduit knows which cell is activated and designed to comply with your request.
- Instantly, the cell receives the Conduit transfer (Meaning your message.)
- Then what? The cell reads your message.
- If your message was sent correctly, then the cell will accept it and give it a code. So, if in the future you ask again your Conduit to do the same thing you have asked in the past, the cell will execute your request in a fraction of a second.
- In other words, each request is coded, and stored in your cell.
- Only coded messages are stored in your Conduit.
- How would you know if you have or have not sent a message correctly to your Conduit? You will know right away. It is very simple. If you have not been trained, you wouldn't know where and how to start in the first place.
- This is the reason why your Conduit did not catch your message(s). You asked "Does this mean that my Conduit is not receiving clear messages from me? And the answer is yes! Your Conduit received something, a thought, a feeling, a wish, a request, call it whatever you want, but your message was not clear to your Conduit, because you did not send your message according to the rules.

Q&A

- What are these rules?
- They are explained below. But continue to read this first.
- And then you asked: "And how can I send clear messages my Conduit can catch and understand?
- You have to use the "Transmission of Mind" technique. Practice this technique before you send messages to your Conduit. For example, in the past, the SOS (Morse Code) was used by ships, planes, military troops and others. The person who has sent the message (Morse) knew the Code; he/she knew how to tap it. Each word had a code...one dot, two dots, three dots, one dash, two dashes, three dashes, one dit, two dits, one space, two spaces, three spaces, etc. There is a sequence of pulses and marks. And the person who received the message knew how what these dots, and dashes meant. This is how and why he/she was able to read the message or decipher it, if it was a secret message. Your Conduit works exactly in the same way.
- Your Ulema teacher will tell you exactly what dots and sequences to use.
- If your Conduit is hundred percent awake, meaning Open (After training completion), the Conduit will immediately interpret/translate and understand your dots, dashes and sequences.
- Consider those dashes and dots a "Password", a log-in information, a key to open the contact with your Conduit, just like the password you use to open your computer or have access to some websites.
- In the book, you will find several passages referring to the brain waves and mind frequencies, and some techniques used to direct thoughts and mind energies.

*** *** ***

Q&A

The Opening of the Conduit

Question 2:

Is the Conduit something like the Third Eye Lopsang Rampa talked about?
Does it need an operation to open it up?
Rampa said that he went through surgery to open his third eye?

***   ***   ***

Important note to the reader:
Think seriously about this question.
Do not rush to find the answer on the following pages.
Try first to answer the question yourself.
Explore all the possibilities; the pros and the cons.
This would be a fruitful exercise.

***   ***   ***

Q&A

Answer to Question 2:

The Conduit has nothing to do at all with the Third Eye.

It appears from the writings of Lopsang Rampa, that the opening of the Third Eye requires surgery. I am not very familiar with the Third Eye's medical procedures and what takes place during the surgery.

According to the Ulema's teachings, the Conduit opening does not require a surgical operation. It is a state of enlightenment.

And enlightenment does not happen with the use of medical tools.

The Opening of the Conduit is a mental exercise. It requires many things such as introspection, deep concentration, guided meditation, following a specific diet, and above all understanding how the brain emits and receives frequencies and vibes.

In Ulemite's literature, the word Conduit is used instead of brain. But the Conduit is much more powerful than the brain, even though it is located in a miniscule area of the brain.

The Conduit governs and animates the brain and all the cells of the human brain, this is why it is more powerful than the brain. However, the brain can function perfectly without the help of the Conduit. But, the brain on its own, and without the help of the Conduit rarely produces extra-ordinary, supernatural powers.

*** *** ***

Q&A

The Godabaari technique: Moving Objects at Distance

Question 3:

In the Godabaari technique, step 12, you said "In your mind, draw one line from the middle of your left wrist, and another line from the middle of your right wrist, toward the coaster. Visualize the coaster between the two lines."
Does this mean that I will be able to see those two lines with my own eyes, or simply I would be imagining the lines in my head?
Something else I would like to know, how long it would take me to learn this technique, and would I be able to move heavier stuff at distance? How heavy? How much heavier than a coaster? How long does it last?
It is a one time thing?
Is it magic, faith or what?
I am a good Christian and I have a strong faith in the Lord and Jesus. Does this help?

*** *** ***

Important note to the reader:
Think seriously about this question.
Do not rush to find the answer on the following pages.
Try first to answer the question yourself.
Explore all the possibilities; the pros and the cons.
This would be a fruitful exercise.

*** *** ***

Q&A

Answer to Question 3:

On faith: Then, you must be familiar with what Jesus Christ has said about faith? "And He said to them, "Because of the littleness of your faith; for truly I say to you, if you have faith the size of a mustard seed, you will say to this mountain, 'Move from here to there,' and it will move; and nothing will be impossible to you."
Faith is always good, but it has nothing to do with learning and successfully practicing this technique.
The knowledge, the doctrine, the techniques and the teachings of Anunnaki-Ulema are based upon science, para-physical means, and empirical observations. The Ulema do not ask their students and adepts to have a religious faith or any similar faith, because they do not mix religion with their learning/teaching.
The Ulema do neither consider one religion (Or a faith) superior to another religion, nor accept "Faith" as an effective/pragmatic way to discover and learn the truth. So, unfortunately, your faith will not play any role in understanding and mastering the Godabaari technique. "Use your mind, instead", said the Ulema.

Concerning those two lines: Yes, you will be able to see those two lines with your own eyes.
You will not be imagining anything. They are not virtual.
The lines are real.
How long it would take you to learn this technique?
Not very long, if you practice the technique at least three times a week.
Would you be able to move heavier stuff at distance?
Yes! After a consistent practice for at least 6 months.
How heavy?
Heavy enough, but not as big or as heavy as a mountain. There is a limit to everything in life. By the power of his mind, an old Mongolian Ulema was able to lift up a truck, and dump it in a lake.
You have asked: How much heavier than a coaster?

Q&A

And the answer is: Much heavier than a coaster.
Use your own assessment and judgment, short after you have succeeded in moving a slightly heavier object than a coaster.
It is fun!

How long does it last? It is a one time thing?
Once you have learned this technique, it stays with you for ever.

*** *** ***

Q&A

The Gomari "Gumaridu" Technique

Question 4:

In the Gomari "Gumaridu" technique, number 15, you said:
"Start with a linear task, which will anchor you. The best one will
be the trip to the airport, and for this task no Anunnaki-Ulema
powers are used at all. Even though your Conduit is not open,
since you have not been trained by a master, it is still there and it
can calculate what it needs to do, and how to partially and
gradually squeeze the other tasks into the frame of seven hours."

My question is this: Does this mean that my Conduit works
on its own, by itself, and does things outside my control?
If my Conduit knows what to do, such as squeezing the
other tasks into the frame of seven hours, why then my Conduit
has to stop there? Why my Conduit does not go one step further?
Where does the Conduit stop?

*** *** ***

Important note to the reader:
Think seriously about this question.
Do not rush to find the answer on the following pages.
Try first to answer the question yourself.
Explore all the possibilities; the pros and the cons.
This would be a fruitful exercise.

*** *** ***

Answer to Question 4:

Yes, your Conduit has its own mode. As long as your Conduit is not activated, it remains free of your control. Once your Conduit is activated, you become the stimulus and the manager of your Conduit.

Pay attention to the word "Partially". This is very significant.

The Conduit works partially when it is not activated.

And partially means reacting by not acting.

The Conduit functions all the time regardless of your state of awareness, enlightenment or readiness. But it will not give you data and information. Everything the Conduit finds is instantly deposited in its compound.

You will not find what's in there, until the Conduit is fully activated. Consider it for now as a depot of knowledge; a sort of a personal bank account where your daily balance is constantly increasing, however, you are not allowed to have access to your bank account.

So, nothing is lost. Your Conduit collects and stores information all the time, and from various sources, times, and spheres.

*** *** ***

Q&A

Godabaari's projected mental lines toward the coaster

Question 5:

In the Godabaari technique, step 12, you said: "In your mind, draw one line from the middle of your left wrist, and another line from the middle of your right wrist, toward the coaster. Visualize the coaster between the two lines."

Why the wrist is so important? Why this particular place in our body?

Why do we need two lines from both wrists?

*** *** ***

Important note to the reader:
Think seriously about this question.
Do not rush to find the answer on the following pages.
Try first to answer the question yourself.
Explore all the possibilities; the pros and the cons.
This would be a fruitful exercise.

*** *** ***

Q&A

Answer to question 5:

The wrist is so important because it is the base of your hand, where your energy is stored. From the hands emanate the rays of your inner energy, called Rou'am.

The Chinese compare it to Chi; the Japanese to Ki. Here, they are referring to an inner energy which is an internal physical energy. On the surface, and to the inexperienced, the Ki or Chi resembles Rou'am.

But in fact, it is quite different, because Rou'am is not physical at all. If it was physical, it should be enough to use it as a rod or a stick to move the object with, and simplify the whole process.

Bear in mind, that all sorts of energies in the forms of vibrations, frequencies and rays emanate from your body.

In fact, each gland, organ and part of your body has a specific vibration defined by its intensity, colors, emission length and waves strength.

Sometimes, we call it Aura, and some other times, bio-organic radiation. Still, it is not Rou'am.

So Ki, Chi, and Aura are not your Rou'am, simply because they are produced by the composition of your physical body, while the Rou'am is produced by your brain.

You brain has to find a way to eject Rou'am.

It does so, by releasing it from your wrist, channeling it to your fingers' tips, and exiting it from the top of your fingers.

You need two lines to create a visual-spatial equilibrium. As it is necessary in classical arts to create/preserve beauty, symmetry is also and equally essential and necessary in Godabaari technique. On that principle, Taj Mahal was visualized and built. The same thing applies in our technique.

Mental projection of a visual symmetry eliminates chaos in your brain, and particularly in the difficult process of creating balance and harmony for something you can't touch physically.

When you look at the coaster, you just see a coaster.

But you need to frame the coaster into a visual equilibrium. This equilibrium limits the extra dimension of the coaster you don't see.

Q&A

The two lines confine the coaster. The coaster cannot escape the space defined by the two lines you brain has created. And this is how your concentrate your mental energy right on the coaster.

It is this very concentrated mental energy that makes the coaster move in its preliminary phase.

If you use one line only, the coaster will escape, and your mental power has to chase the coaster, instead or trapping it, and controlling the physical place it occupies.

What basically the two lines are doing is emptying the space from under the coaster.

This void destabilizes the coaster, and immediately the two lines take advantage of this, and begin to dispose it, shake it, and finally make it move.

*** *** ***

Q&A

Anunnaki's Miraya and Akashic Records

Question 6:

In the Chapter Gomatirach-Minzari, you said: "Those who are familiar with the concept of the Anunnaki's Miraya would notice a resemblance in the way these tools are used.

However, one should realize that we are not pretending to use the kind of cosmic monitor that is connected, through the Akashic Libraries on Nibiru, to the Akashic Record itself.

It is beyond our scope to even conceive how such a tool had ever been created. Nor are we attempting to recreate the kind of Minzar that is used by the Anunnaki-Ulema, who are enlightened beings whose Conduit has been opened. "

I am not familiar with the Anunnaki's Miraya. What is it?
How does it work?
And what connection it has with the Akashic Records?
Also, I would like to know more about the Anunnaki's libraries.

***   ***   ***

Important note to the reader:
Think seriously about this question.
Do not rush to find the answer on the following pages.
Try first to answer the question yourself.
Explore all the possibilities; the pros and the cons.
This would be a fruitful exercise.

***   ***   ***

Q&A

Answer to question 6:

On Ashtari, the Planet of the Anunnaki (Ne.Be.Ru or Nibiru, to others) each Anunnaki (male and female, young and adult) has a direct access to the Falak Kitbah (Akashic Records) through the Akashic Libraries (Called Shama Kitbah), which are located in every community in Ashtari.

The libraries (Called Makatba or Mat-Kaba) are constructed from materials such as chiselled opaque glass (Called Mir-A't), a substance similar to fibreglass (Called Sha-riit), and a multitude of fibre-plastic-like materials (Called Fisal and Hiraa-Ti); they convey the appearance of ultra-modern, futuristic architecture (By humans' standards), and techno- industrialized edifices.

One enters the libraries through an immense hall (Called Isti-bal), seven hundred to one thousand meters in length, by five hundred meters in width.

The Isti-bal is empty of any furniture, and is lit by huge oval windows that are placed near the top of the ceiling.

The windows (Called Shi-bak) were designed in such a way that the shafts of light that enter through their circular compartments are redirected and projected like solid white laser beams. The effect is spectacular.

At night, quasi identical effect is produced by the projection of concentrated light beams coming from hidden sources of lights located behind (More precisely, inside the frames' structure) the frames (Called Mra) of the windows.

The frames serve as an energy depot.

The energy is transformed into sources of light. The visual effect is stunning. Enormously large and animated metallic billboards (Called La-yiha, pronounced La-ee-haa) are affixed on walls in a parallel alignment, and on the floor, in front of each billboard, there are hundreds of symmetrically rectangular pads (Called Mirkaan).

When visitors enter the library's main hall (Situated just at the front entrance), they approach the billboards, and stand each on a Mirkaan.

Q&A

The pad serves as a scanner and a transportation device, because it has the capacity to read the minds of the visitors, learn what they are searching for, and as soon as it does so, it begins to move, and slides right through the central billboard (Called Kama La-yiha), which is not really solid but is made from blocks of energy, carrying the visitor with it.

Behind the billboard is the main reading room (Called Kama Kira'at) of the Akashic Library.

Under the belly of the pad, there are two separate compartments designed to register what the visitor is looking for, and to direct the visitor to his/her destination; usually, it is a reference section where books in form of cones are located on magnetized shelves.

The Anunnaki's Akashic Library is not a traditional library at all, for it contains no physical books per se, even though, there are plenty of conic publications (Books manufactured as magnetic cylinders and cones.) Instead of searching for books on shelves, as we do on Earth, the visitors find themselves in the presence of an immense white-light blue screen, made of materials unknown to us. The screen is hard to describe; it can be compared to a grid (Called Kadari), with a multitude of matrices and vortices of data.

The visitors communicate with the screen via their Conduit. The screen registers their thoughts and right away finds/records the information the visitors seek. All the visitors have to do is stand still for less than two seconds (In terrestrial terms) in front of the screen, and the data will be displayed in an animated format. The data (Information) is given in codes which are easily understood by the visitors.

The codes are usually divided into sequences; each sequence reflects an aspect of the information.

For example, if you want to know what happened in Alexandria or Phoenicia 3000 B.C., all what you need to do, is to think about either Alexandria or Phoenicia, and one grid will appear, waiting for your command to open it up.

From this precise moment, the visitor's Conduit and the Screen are communicating in the most direct fashion.

The grid opens up and displays three files in sequence.

Q&A

The nearest description of these files would be plasmic-digital, for the lack of the proper word; each file will contain everything that had happened pertaining to that particular date or era in Alexandria or Phoenicia.

Functions of the Conduit, Miraya and retrieving data:

- **1**-The Conduit will sort out all the available information and references (Photos, holographic projections, sounds) available on the subject. On Ashtari, everything is stored in codes.)
- **2**-The Conduit selects and indexes the particular data for the part of the information the visitor is most interested in.
- **3**-Then, the selected information (Complete data in sound and images) is instantly transferred to the cells of the visitor's brain.
- **4**-Because Anunnaki are connected to each other and to their community via the Conduit, the data recently absorbed is sent to others who share similar interest.

This is extremely beneficial, because if the data received from the screen is difficult to understand, other members of the Anunnaki community, will automatically transmit, the explanation needed. This is quite similar to an online technical support on earth, but it is much more efficient since it functions brain-to-brain.

Worth mentioning here, that each Anunnaki community has the same kind of center for these Akashic files.

The complexity of the centers, though, is not the same. Some of the Akashic Libraries include more perplexing and complicated instruments and tools, which are not readily available to other communities.

These tools include the Monitor, which is also called Mirror, or Miraya. Each Miraya is under the direct control of a Sinhar, who serves as custodian and guardian.

- **5**-The screens can expand according to the number of codes that the Anunnaki researcher is using. Seven to ten codes are normal. If a larger number of codes are opened, the screen is fragmented into seven different screens. An amazing phenomenon occurs at this moment – time and space mingle together and become unified into one great continuum. This enables the researcher to grasp all the information in a fraction of a second.
- **6**-An added convenient aspect of the Akashic files is the ability of the researchers to access them in the complete privacy of their homes or offices, since part the files can be teleported there. But since the private screen is not as complicated as the central one in the Library, no multiple screen will open up, only the original one. Yes, Anunnaki do live in homes, and contribute to their societies as we do on Earth.
- **7**-It is important to understand that the data received is not merely visual. There is much more to it than that.
- **8**-By the right side of the screen, where the global data is displayed in files, there are metallic compartments, as thin as parchment paper, which serve as a cosmic audio antennae. These compartments search for, and bring back, any sound that occurred in history, in any era, in any country, and of any magnitude of importance.
- **9**-The compilation includes all sorts of sounds, and voices of people, entities, various civilizations, and living organisms (And life-forms from the past and the future) in the entire cosmos.
- **10**-According to the Anunnaki, every single sound or voice is never lost in the universe. Of course, it may not traverse certain boundaries. For humans, if a sound was produced on earth, such a boundary is the perimeter of the solar system. Each of these antennae-compartments will probe different galaxies and star systems, listening, recording, retrieving, and playing back sounds, voices, and all sorts of frequencies.

Q&A

- **11**-A combined asset of the visual and audio systems is the ability to learn languages that is afforded by the Akashic Library. This applies to any language – past, present or future, and from any part of the universe.
- **12**-The researcher can call up a shining globe of light that will swirl on the screen with enormous speed. As it rotates, the effect blends with an audio transmission that comes from the metallic compartments, and in an instant, any language will sink into the brain cells.
- **13**-On the left side of the main screen, there are several conic compartments that bring still images pertaining to certain important past events. This display informs the researcher that these particular events cannot be altered. In other words, the Anunnaki cannot go back into the past and change it.
- **14**-The Anunnaki are forbidden to change or alter the events, or even just parts or segments of the past events projected on the main screen that came from the conic compartment, if the data (Images; sounds) represents events created by the Anunnaki leaders.
- **15**-This restriction (Altering, changing or erasing past events) which is applicable everywhere on Ashtari functions as a security device.

  For example, a young Anunnaki cannot visit earth sixty five thousand years ago, recreate and enter the genetic laboratory of the Anunnaki in Sumer, Arwad, Ugarit or Phoenicia, and change the DNA and the genetic formula of a human race, especially when the DNA sequence was originally created by an Anunnaki Sinhar (Leader). In other words, a young Anunnaki is not allowed to alter the Akashic Records that contain the primordial events. Alteration such as recreating a new human race in past time will never happen.

  16-However, an Anunnaki leader such as Sinhar Baal Shamroot, Inanna, Ellil or Enki can go back in time and space, and change events, but cannot bring to Earth new human species created according to a new formula that

234

Q&A

contradicts or reverses the primordial prototypes created 100,000 years ago.

- **17**-However, an Anunnaki leader such as Sinhar Baal Shamroot, Inanna or Enki can go back in time and change events, but cannot bring to Earth new human species created according to their new formula and based on the primordial prototypes created 100,000 years ago. Nevertheless, they can transpose their new creation or event alteration, and transport them to another dimension, parallel to the original dimension where the event occurred.
- **18**-This safeguard means that Sinhar Inanna cannot recreate a new race on our earth by the device of sending the current living humans back in time, remolding us, and then bringing us back to the twenty first century as a new species.
- **19**-This is not allowed by the Anunnaki High Council. All she can do is recreate her own experiment in another dimension.
- **20**-Worth mentioning here, that alternation of the fabric of time and space is rigidly and constantly monitored by the Anunnaki High Council via their Miraya; the cosmic mirror and monitor of all living-forms, past, present, and future.
- **21**-The Miraya is a terrific and mind-bending tool. The Anunnaki use it to revisit time and what is beyong time, space, meta-space, and para-space, as well as creating new cosmic calendar.
- **22**-More options are available for research, and one of them is a sort of browsing. Inside the screen, there is a slit where the mind of the Anunnaki can enter as a beam. This will open the Ba'abs, or Stargates, to other worlds that the researcher is not even aware of; they appear randomly as part of the discovery or exploration.
- **23**-In each slit, there is another Akashic file that belongs to another civilization.

235

Q&A

- **24**-Sometimes, these civilizations are more advanced than the Anunnaki themselves, where the researcher can retrieve important information. It is like going back in the future, because everything present, or to occur in the future, has already occurred in a distant past (Timetable) and needed the right time to surface and appear before the current living Anunnaki.

- **25**-There is also the aspect of simply having fun, some of which is not so ethical. Sometimes an Anunnaki will go back in time, let's say 400 C.E., choose a famous historical figure, and at the same time bring over another important person, one thousand years older, simply to see how they would interact.

- **26**-They can easily deceive these personages, since every Anunnaki is an adept at shape changing. Or they can transpose people, move them in time, and see how they will react to the new environment.

- **27**-These games are strictly forbidden, but some low class Anunnaki occasionally try it as a game. Sometimes they interfere with our daily affairs, and temporary loss of memory may be a result of that.

- **28**-Worth reminding the readers, that the Anunnaki no longer interfere in human affairs. They have left planet Earth for good, but they are coming back in 2022.

- **29**-The Miraya is constantly used by the Anunnaki on Ashatari. In addition to its function as a cosmic calendar, the Miraya serves as a galactic monitor. Watching and monitoring other extraterrestrial civilizations are two of the major concerns of the Anunnaki. For the past 10 years (In our terrestrial time), the Anunnaki have been following very closely what was/is happening on other planets and stars, and particularly the experiments of the Greys. Sinhar Ambar Anati known to us as Victoria told us a lot about this. In the Book "Anunnaki Ultimatum: End of Time" (Co-authored by Ilil Arbel and Maximillien de Lafayette), Ambar Anati described at length some of

236

the horrible genetic experiments of the Greys as caught on the Miraya.

Note: Ambar Anati is talking to Sinhar Inannaschamra, her mother-in-law in Ashatari, about the malicious intentions of the Greys. Inannaschamra told her that the Greys constantly conduct genetic experiments on humans, and that the Anunnaki kept on watching their atrocious experiments by using the Miraya (Monitor).

Here are some excerpts from the book: "What do they want from us on earth?"

"There are a few things that they want. First, they want eggs from human women and use them to create hybrids. Let's take a look at this monitor, and I'll show you how they do that. But Victoria, steel yourself. This is pretty horrible, even though I have seen even worse. You will also be able to hear, it is like a television."

The monitor blinked and buzzed, and a small white dot appeared on the screen.

It enlarged itself, moved back and forth, and settled into a window-like view of a huge room, but the view was still rather fuzzy. I heard horrendous screams and froze in my seat, these were sounds I have never heard before.

After a few minutes the view cleared and I saw what seemed to be a hospital room, but it was rounded, not square. Only part of it was revealed, as it was elongated and the far edge was not visible. The walls on the side were moving back and forth, like some kind of a balloon that was being inflated and deflated periodically, with a motion that made me dizzy; they seemed sticky, even gooey.

The room was full of operation tables, of which I could see perhaps forty or fifty, on which were stretched human beings, each attached to the table and unable to move, but obviously not sedated, since they were screaming or moaning.

Everyone was attached to long tubes, into which blood was pouring in huge quantities.

I noticed that some of the blood was turning into a filthy green color, like rotting vegetation. At the time I could not understand what that was, but later that day I found out.

Q&A

This blood was converted to a suitable type for some of the aliens that paid the Grays to collect it, and it was not useful in its raw condition.

People who operated these experiments were small and gray, and they had big bug eyes and pointy faces without any expression. I thought they looked more like insects than like a humanoid species. They wore no clothes, and their skin was shiny and moist, like that of an amphibian on earth. It visibly exuded beads of moisture which they did not bother to wipe away.

Each operating table had complicated machinery that was poised right on top of the person who was strapped to it.

On some of the tables, the machinery was lowered so that needles could be extracted from them automatically, and the needles reached every part of the human bodies, faces, eyes, ears, genitals, stomach. The people screamed as they saw the needles approaching them, some of them fainted.

Many of the people were already dead, I could swear to that. Others were still alive but barely so, and some had arms and legs amputated from their bodies.

It was clear that once the experiment was over, every single person there will die. I don't know how I could continue to look, but somehow I managed. I looked at the ceiling of this slaughter house and saw meat hooks, on which arms and legs and even heads were hanging, like a butcher's warehouse.

On the side of the tables were large glass tanks where some organs were placed, possibly hearts, livers, or lungs, all preserved in liquids.

The workers seemed to be doing their job dispassionately and without any feelings, moving around like ants and making buzzing sounds at each other as they conversed.

They were entirely business-like and devoid of emotion. At least, their huge bug eyes did not convey any emotion to me, neither did their expressionless faces.

I watched until I could no longer tolerate it, and finally covered my eyes and cried out, "Why don't you stop it? Why don't you interfere?"

Sinhar Inannaschamra turned the monitor off. "This event is a record from decades ago, Victoria.

It is not happening now as we look. And even though often we do interfere, we cannot police the entire universe or even the entire earth.

They know how to hide from us. And you must understand, that often the victims cooperate with their abductors."

"Why would they?"

"Basically, through mind control. The Grays have many ways to convince the victims. The Grays can enter the human mind quite easily, and they find what the abductees are feeling and thinking about various subjects. Then, they can either threaten them by various means, or persuade them by a promise of reward."

"Reward? What can they possibly offer?"

"Well, you see, they show the victims images through a monitor, just like this one. They tell them that they can send them through a gate, which is controlled by the monitor, to any number of universes, both physical and non-physical.

That is where the reward come in.

For example, if the abductees had originally reacted well to images of Mary or Jesus, the Grays can promise them the joy of the non-physical dimensions.

They show them images of a place where Mary and Jesus reside, where all the saints or favorite prophets live, and even the abode of God. They promise the abductees that if they cooperate, they could live in this non-physical universe in perpetual happiness with their deities. Many fall for that."

"And if they resist?"

"Then they show them the non-physical alternative, which is Hell. Would you like to see some of it?"

"You can show me Hell?" I asked, amazed.

"No, there is no such thing as Hell... it's a myth that religions often exploited. But I can show you what the Grays show the abductees, pretending it is hell; they are quite devious, you know. You see, some creatures live in different dimensions, where our laws do not apply.

Sometimes, they escape to other dimensions.

These beings have no substance in their new dimensions, and they need some kind of bodies to function.

Q&A

At the same time, the Grays can tap into numerous universes, because they can control their own molecules to make them move and navigate through any dimension. Well, a cosmic trade had been developed.

The Greys supply the substance taken from human abductees, and from the blood of cattle. You must have heard of cattle mutilation, where carcasses of cows are found in the fields, entirely drained of blood? The Grays do it for their customers."

"How do these creatures pay the Grays?"

"By various services, and once they get their substance, they are incredibly powerful in a physical sense.

The old tales of genies who can lift buildings and fly with them through the air were based on these demons; the Grays often have a use for such services.

But let me show you a few of these creatures. Of course, you can only see them when they have already acquired some substance from the Grays."

The monitor hummed again as Sinhar Inannaschamra turned it on. The white dot expanded into its window, which now, for some reason, was larger and took over the entire screen.

All I could see was white fog with swirls floating through it. Sometimes the fog changed from white to gray, then to white again.

I started hearing moans. Not screams, nothing that suggested the kind of physical pain I saw before, but perhaps just as horrible, since they voices where those of hopelessness, despair, and emotional anguish. Every so often I heard a sound that suggested a banshee's wail, or keen, as described in Irish folklore.

"It will take a while for someone to show up," said Sinhar Inannaschamra. "Most of them have no substance, and therefore they are invisible. Others have a shadowy substance.

Then, there are the others...but you will see in a minute. Once they notice they are being watched, they will flock to the area, since they are desperate to get out.

Incidentally, it was never made quite clear to me how they produce sounds without bodies, we are still trying to find out what the mechanics are, but it's not easy, because we would rather not go there in person."

Q&A

"They sound horribly sad," I said.
"This is what makes it so hell-like.

In many cultures, Hell never had any fire and brimstone and tormenting devils, but rather, it was a place of acute loneliness, lack of substance, and alienation from anything that could sustain the individual from a spiritual point of view. Think of the Greek Hades, or the ancient Hebrew Sheol, before the Jews made their Hell more like the Christian one. Look, here comes the first creature. Poor thing, he is a shadow."
I saw a vaguely humanoid shape in deep gray. It seemed to have arms, which it waved in our direction. It seemed fully aware of the monitor.
Then another shadow, then another, all shoving each other and waving desperately at the monitor.
Then something more substantial came into view, and I jumped back as if it could reach me. It seemed to be a severed arm. Cautiously, I came back, and then saw that the arm was attached to a shadow body. I looked at Sinhar Inannaschamra, speechless, and she said, "Yes, here you see one that managed to receive an arm. It wants to complete its body, of course, so that it can get out of this dimension and serve the Grays, but the Grays keep them waiting until they want them." (Source: Anunnaki Ultimatum: End of Time.)

In summary, the Miraya has multiple functions, and remains one of the most important inventions of the Anunnaki.

*** *** ***

Q&A

Gubada-Ari: How to find the healthiest spots and luckiest areas on earth

Question 7:

The Gubada-ri technique included this intro: "There are lines of energy spinning around the world. In this exercise, we will concentrate on the lines that are revealed by the use of the triangle. The energy flows in currents, both negative and positive, mostly underground, traversing the globe. Those who live above the positive lines, will have good health, success, and peace of mind. Those who live above the negative lines, will have bad health. The student might ask, where do I put the triangle? How do I choose the original location? The answer is, you put the triangle wherever you are.
The student might ask, what if I change locations? The answer is, this technique is working within the dictates of the moment. Wherever you are, the triangle follows."
My questions are:
How do I know I live above negative currents?
What should I do to change these bad currents affecting my life?
Are there bad lines everywhere in the world?

*** *** ***

Important note to the reader:
Think seriously about this question.
Do not rush to find the answer on the following pages.
Try first to answer the question yourself.
Explore all the possibilities; the pros and the cons.
This would be a fruitful exercise.

*** *** ***

Q&A

Answer to question 7:

How would you know that you live above negative currents?
You should be the one, the only one (In many instances) to know you are living above negative lines, by assessing your status quo. If you see that you are failing in many of the things you are doing, despite good planning, common sense, hard work and reasonable approach to what you do, then you should realize that something is wrong.
If your health condition is constantly deteriorating with no apparent reasons, or justified symptoms despite intensive health care, a good nutritional system, a good diet, medical attention, regular check ups, and a healthy living, then you should ask yourself why your health is deteriorating. You have here more than one red flag!
Keep watching those unpleasant occurrences very closely, monitor your activities, maintain a meticulous records of what you do on a daily basis, and write down in details what you are going through in relation to dates, days and hours, and especially where usually you move around.
If these mishaps accumulate at an amazing rate without a logical explanation, then use alternative means/analyses to understand the reasons, the mechanism and the continuous avalanches of disastrous events.
Coincidences do happen. But when many bad coincidences don't cease and appear on all fronts, and in all what you do, including health, then you have to do something about it. Some people consult experts in the fields, therapists, experienced consultants, and talk to others who went through similar events. If all these approaches do not work, then you have to realize that you are not in control of these events and mysterious incidents.
You will know when so many things on many fronts and in many areas are getting nasty, worse or threatening.

What should you do to change these bad currents affecting your life?
There is nothing you can do to change these lines because you are not stronger than Mother Nature.

243

Q&A

Consult professionals in the field, physicians and nutrition experts as far as your health is concerned. Business planning consultants and financial advisors when it comes to your business and finances, so on.

But if nothing works, and you know you have tried everything, then one option and only one option is left: Change location, move, live or work somewhere else.

But where?

This is another question (You have not asked, though)!

Try to the find the answer by learn and practicing the Gubada-ri technique. See if it works for you. It could work for you, because it worked for so many people I know.

My advice to you is this:

- **1**-Don't rush to change location.
- **2**-Stay where you are for a while, especially if you own the place where you live or work.
- **3**-Now that you have realized that something quite strange is constantly happening in your life, and you have no means to stop it or a way to explain it, is already a good step.

  So, keep your place for a while, but move temporarily somewhere else, and see if things change to better.

  If they do, and all of a sudden, you start to feel much better, and you have no more problems, then you will know that you were living/working in an area infested by bad vibrations and doomed by negative currents.

  This should work.

*** *** ***

244

Q&A

Gubada-Ari: On the bad and unlucky areas/spots on Earth

Question 8:

From reading the chapter on Gubada-Ari, I got the feeling that there are many bad and unlucky areas on Earth. It is also a sort of a déjà vu experience.

I am talking about my personal experience. Four years ago, I used to live in state X, where I failed in my business and was forced to file for bankruptcy. My daughter became seriously ill, and my wife could not find a job, yet she is Princeton's graduate with a graduate degree and a great resume.

We tried almost everything, everything we could to rescue my business, make my daughter feel better, and my wife to get a job even a temporary job...no matter what we did our situation got worse. We became desperate.

I lost my shop, my daughter's health condition endangered her life, and my wife had a breakdown. In short, we had nothing to live on or for. We left our home and moved to my wife parents home in C....

One month latter, my wife Meg had a job interview and got a wonderful position in a great company. My daughter's health got better and better. Soon after, I managed to get a small loan and I opened a new shop. It was a miracle. And everything is fine now. We were lucky. We made it. But we had to move to another state. Yes, I believe we had back luck because we lived in an area charged with bad vibes...Do you a list of those bad spots?

*** *** ***

245

Q&A

Answer to question 8:

In the past, I ran into big troubles when I pointed at specific locations, where the milieu (Above and underground) was charged with negative currents affecting the health, well-being and businesses of people who lived in those areas.

So, I am not going to reveal anymore the names and locations of those areas. Instead I will speak in general terms.

Indeed, there are areas "allegedly" known (Or to be discovered) for the bad luck and unpleasant events they bring to unfortunate residents.

It was "reported" to me that some of those spots are located somewhere in Brooklyn, District of Columbia, West Virginia, Mississippi, Alabama, Louisiana, Missouri and Baltimore.

*** *** ***

Q&A

The Double and the Baridu Technique

Question 9:

Regarding the Baridu technique... you said that "Once you enter your Double, you will be able to use it in so many beautiful and effective ways as:
  7- A protective shield against danger,
  8- An effective apparatus to protect yourself in hostile and dangerous situations,
  9- A tool to develop your abilities to learn many languages, and enhance your artistic creativity"

My questions are: How a non-physical entity that does not live on Earth can protect me from physical threats?
If this is true, then the President of the United States and the Secretary of State should get rid of their bodyguards and hire a Double? It does not make sense!
Is it really possible to learn a new language just by zooming into our Double?
If this is possible, why then secret agencies and espionage or counter-espionage agencies don't use this technique to teach their agents all the languages in the world?
Why they keep on buying all these foreign languages dictionaries and foreign languages learning lessons on tapes and CDs?

*** *** ***

Important note to the reader:
Think seriously about this question.
Do not rush to find the answer on the following pages.
Try first to answer the question yourself.
Explore all the possibilities; the pros and the cons.
This would be a fruitful exercise.

247

Q&A

Answer to question 9:

Protection against threats and dangers: First of all, you have to remember that people of power, politicians, *et al*, are neither spiritual people, nor adepts of metaphysical studies.

They spend more time campaigning, shaking hands, and giving speeches than developing spiritual and paranormal abilities.

So bodyguards remain a necessity. They should stay around.

Only those who have learned and developed esoteric Ulema techniques can use their Double as a shield. However, a novice or a sincere student who is searching for the ultimate paranormal truth, and who has revealed a high standard of spirituality and goodness will be able to use the Double, once he/she has completed the Ulema studies.

At your stage, your Double is alive and well, and is fully aware of your existence, but YOU are not aware of its existence, because either you do not believe in a Double, or you have not established a rapport with your Double.

Once, a rapport has been established with your Double, your Conduit will throw an invisible protective shield around you. But was is a shield?

Is it a physical barrage?

A protective tool or a device similar to the fibreglass or a metal shield police use in riots?

The answer is no. The shield functions in so many different ways your brain cannot comprehend. However, I will try to explain to you one of the protective measures a shield uses in threatening situations.

The Ulema after years of study and practice, and following the instructions of the Book of Rama-Dosh, became capable of creating a sphere (Or zone) around them that resembles a halo. Some call this halo a "Bubble".

The halo surrounds their physical body.

In the halo, exist molecules and particles charged with high atomic and sub-atomic density (No, not nuclear devices!), i.e. energy. This energy is denser in its composition than any of the molecules and particles that physically create and constitute any physical action or movement against an Ulema's body.

Q&A

Ulema's energy changes constantly and transmutes itself into higher or lower molecules/particles density, according to their surroundings and needs.

Because of the Ulema's denser atomic substance, nothing can penetrate the halo surrounding them. You have to remember, that everything in the universe is composed from molecules and particles. For instance, if you throw a punch at an Ulema, you put in your punch a certain amount of energy and physical effort. The energy and the physical effort are composed from molecules. These molecules are denser in their composition than the molecules floating around the Ulema, and thus cannot penetrate their halo and reach their bodies.

This is why people can't go through walls. Our bodies molecules need "to shrink" and "transmute" themselves into thinner vibrations, to allow us to go through walls.

Secondly, the non-physical entity (Double) you have mentioned is not totally non-physical. It changes.

It materializes and dematerializes.

The Double can project itself as a physical entity.

And it takes on multiple appearances ranging from holographic to multi-dimensional presences.

However, the materialistic apparition does not last very long in a three-dimensional sphere, because its bio-etco-plasma energy is consumed rapidly.

Let's forget for a moment this complicated language, and explore an easier characteristic aspect of the Double, its halo, zone and protective shield. I will try to use a simple language, as much as I can. Disregard everything I have said before, and follow me now step by step.

- **a**-Your Double is extremely intelligent and alert, and it senses things around you. Things currently happening and those en route.
- **b**-Your Double knows right away if what is coming at you is safe or dangerous.
- **c**-If the Double detects a threatening situation, it sends an alert to your Conduit.

Q&A

- **d**-Your Conduit receives the message from your Double. (Note: Sometimes, it is simultaneously, and/or your Open Conduit understands the situation on its own, without the help of your Double.)
- **e**-Your Conduit acts on its own and guides you instantly to a safer position. Call it whatever you want, instinct, an inner feeling, etc...it does not matter what you call it.
- **f**-At the same time, your Conduit emits vibes aimed at the source of the threat to bock it.
- **g**-At this very moment, your Open Conduit and your Double act in unison.
- **h**-In a fraction of a second, the attacker or the negative vibes aimed at you is diverted. Nothing can penetrate the halo around you. If you practice and master the Baridu technique, you will be able to block any threat.

As to your question: "Is it really possible to learn a new language just by zooming into our Double?"

The answer is YES!

However, what you will learn becomes a memory, a sort of a depot of knowledge not activated or accessible by your brain. This happens at the preliminary stage.

Later on, when you revisit your Conduit, you will be able to tap into that depot, work mentally with the language you have just learned, and practice physically by writing down on a paper the words and phraseology from that language.

There is a process to follow that allows you to remember that language and bring it out of your Conduit cell.

*** *** ***

Q&A

Daemat-Afnah

Question 10:

You said the Daemat-Afnah technique keeps us young and makes us look 37 permanently. It is difficult to understand this. I am 54, if I practice this technique for a while, would I look again 37 years old? What would happen to the face I had before? Does it come back?
For how long I would stay 37?

***   ***   ***

Important note to the reader:
Think seriously about this question.
Do not rush to find the answer on the following pages.
Try first to answer the question yourself.
Explore all the possibilities; the pros and the cons.
This would be a fruitful exercise.

***   ***   ***

Q&A

Answer to question 10:

You have to practice the technique for at least one full year. You will not see any improvement or any result before 12 months. I will explain to you what is going to happen step by step.

- For the first 6 months. You will not notice any change on your face.
- At the end of the seventh month, you will begin to feel that some of your facial muscles are getting stronger. A strange and a new sensation you have never felt before in your whole life.
- Your face will look cleaner and firmer.
- Some of the wrinkles under your eyes will disappear. In rare instances, they would not.
- Not all the wrinkles will disappear if you stop practicing.
- At the end of 12 months, you will notice that you eyes have gained vitality. They will look sharper.
- Your eyes will glitter with a sign of good health.
- At the end of 12 months, you will notice that your face's skin is healthier, and almost 90% of your wrinkles (large and small) have diminished.
- The dermatologic results have no side effect.
- A certain incomprehensible inner strength will energize your whole body.
- After 13 months of practice, the face you had when you were 37 starts to reappear gradually. You will not believe what you are seeing.
- This change is usually accompanied by sizeable increase in physical dynamism and mental vitality.
- Your face is younger, almost 100%.
- Only your face gets younger, not your neck, body or any other part of your body.
- Your grey hair will stay grey.
- If you are bold, you will stay bold.

Q&A

- You will keep your new face for a very very long time, as long as you keep a good diet, and you eat well.

*** *** ***

Important note:

> - Bear in mind that the Ulema's teachings, techniques, and/or opinions should not be considered as a professional advice, prescription, or opinion at any level – therapeutic, medical, cosmetic, surgical, health wise, etc.
> - They are of a purely philosophical-esoteric nature.
> - This technique does not substitute for any other medical treatment.
> - This technique is not dangerous or harmful.
> - It could be very beneficial at many levels, even though, it is not proven scientifically.
> - However, many who have practiced this technique were delighted by the results.

Q&A

Bukadari Technique

Question 11:

You said: "People can also send harmful vibrations to your mind, to your body, and to the objects you touch, including tools, materials, equipments you use, such as a computer, a camera, a car, an elevator, a desk, even a can-opener."

Does this mean that people's negative vibrations can screw up my computer? Do they have to be around me, or they could still do it at distance?

Are you talking about sick people, malicious people or all people?

*** *** ***

Important note to the reader:
Think seriously about this question.
Do not rush to find the answer on the following pages.
Try first to answer the question yourself.
Explore all the possibilities; the pros and the cons.
This would be a fruitful exercise.

*** *** ***

Q&A

Answer to question 11:

Most certainly, people's negative vibrations can screw up your computer, and many of your electrical gadgets.
The bitter negativity of some people affects even the battery and starter of your car. You car will not start. Some people have green thumb, others have grey thumbs. Some people emanate healthy and positive vibes that bring comfort and joy to others, and some people diffuse negative vibes that affect the harmony, balance and serenity around them and around others.

You asked: "Do they have to be around me, or they could still do it at distance?" Basically, they have to be at a close proximity. If they are around you, you will feel it.
But to be certain that indeed they are causing you discomfort or disturbing your tools, you must observe what is happening, see if these unusual sensations you are felt when they were around you, and the nuisances or damage to your tool are reoccurring every time they show up or are around.
Now, do not get suspicious and anxious. Coincidences happen all the time. You must remain calm but alert.
If your computer crashes, your telephone does not work anymore, or any of your electric or electronic gadgets is acting weird or stop to function, every time they show up, then you should not be in the same room with them, or you could stay if you have already learned the Bukadari technique and know how to use it.
There are some bizarre situations, where and when you got hit by negatives vibes caused by your own action, and thoughts.
For instance, while you were fixing something or typing on your computer keyboard, and all of a sudden, out of the blue, you think about a person you dislike so much, because he/he caused you some troubles or hurt you in the past, and suddenly the light bulb explodes, or the computer stops to work.
This could happen.

Q&A

Perhaps something wrong with the bulb itself, or there is faulty electrical wiring, maybe your computer was attacked by a virus and just died on you at this peculiar moment.

You will never know and understand what is causing all these strange occurrences, until:

a-You start to take notice,

b-Keep meticulous records of all these events,

c-And find the relation between what you were doing or thinking and what just happened during these particular moments.

In this case, your brain has caused those unpleasant incidents. If your Conduit is open, you will discover right away the cause and source of these strange events. If you Conduit is extremely active, negative vibes or unpleasant incidents will not occur frequently.

Negative vibes are not necessarily produced by sick or malicious people. In many instances, the vibrations emanate from people who really care about you. Unfortunately, they don't know that their unhappy state of mind, fear, anxiety, dissatisfaction from their jobs, bitterness, and their negative attitude toward life are producing such negative and destructive vibes.

Be considerate, polite, and understanding.

Quietly remove yourself from their presence.

Use courtesy and civility.

*** *** ***

Q&A

Arawadi Technique and the Afterlife

Question 12:
Ulema Lambrakis said: "All of us live in two separate dimensions
so close to us. One we know and we call it our physical reality,
the other is the adjacent dimension that surrounds our physical
world."
Is he talking about the after-life dimension?
Can I visit this dimension?
I read in a few books written by Indian gurus that life after death
exists in a dimension adjacent to the one we live in.
Are we talking here about the same dimension?
If not, what is the difference between the two?

*** *** ***

Important note to the reader:
Think seriously about this question.
Do not rush to find the answer on the following pages.
Try first to answer the question yourself.
Explore all the possibilities; the pros and the cons.
This would be a fruitful exercise.

*** *** ***

257

Q&A

Answer to question 12:

The adjacent dimension that surrounds our physical world could mean many things. For example, there is a dimension which is not located in the world of the after-life, because it is accessible to living human beings who wish to visit it.

They are still alive, live a normal life on Earth, and through some techniques can visit that dimension and return safe to Earth.

Their visit could take on many different shapes and forms, and be done via a multitude of means.

It could be psychosomatic, purely mental, visual, holographic, teleported, transposed, spiritual and purely physical.

Essentially, what Ulema Lambrakis was referring to is no more or less than the dimension or zone that exists in a parallel world. Modern quantum physics theorists wrote extensively on this subject, and most particularly on parallel dimensions, multiple universes, future worlds, world from the future and beyond. And these scientists refer to Ulema Lambrakis' dimension.

So, the answer is no. Ulema Lambrakis is not talking about the dimension of the after-life.

You asked: "Can I visit this dimension?

If you are asking about the after-life dimension, I don't think you want to go there yet.

You go there and you will never come back.

Dead people don't come back.

You told me that you have read in a few books written by Indian gurus that life after death exists in a dimension adjacent to the one we live in, and asked: "Are we talking here about the same dimension?"

My answer is no. It is quite different.

As to your final question: "If not, what is the difference between the two?" is this: It would take a whole book to explain all the differences.

Q&A

But I will refer you to the following excerpt on the subject taken from the Book "On the Road to Ultimate Knowledge: The Anunnaki-Ulema Extraterrestrial Tao", I co-wrote with Dr. Ilil Arbel.

First, let me set the stage for you. The scene is between Germain Lumiere, an Ulema from France who has just lost his mother.

It appeared later on, that his mother was an Ulema too, but she has never told him that, for reasons we don't know.

Two days after she passed away in Paris, his mother appeared to him during her funeral, as she has promised him.

The young Ulema asked his mother lots of question about the after-life, and what is she doing there. Herewith, a brief excerpt from their conversation:

From the Book "On the Road to Ultimate Knowledge":
Location: Cemetery of Père-Lachaise, Paris, France.
Time: In the afternoon, during the funeral of Countess....mother of Germain.
Personages:
1-The deceased mother appears as a spirit and talks to her son Germain, while her physical body is in the coffin.
2-Germain in tears talking to his dead mother for the last time.
3-Sylvie: She is Germain's sister.
Excerpt below: Germain is telling us what they talked about at the funeral.

"I returned to Mama, who was looking sadly at Sylvie. It's really too bad I can't talk to her," Mama said to me, "but some day, of course, she will know, like everyone else. Ah, well, let's go to the more secluded areas. We don't want people to think you are talking to yourself."

We wandered around the cemetery. Père-Lachaise, is one of the most beautiful cemeteries in the world, full of trees, impressive statues, and old tombstones. Shady lanes provided privacy, and we could talk freely.

"So tell me about your experience in the Afterlife, Mama," I said.

259

Q&A

"I have not been there very long, you know, but time and space play a different role there, and also, my training allows me to know what it is really like and what will happen next," said Mama. "You will also know, when the time comes."

"Doesn't everyone know?"

"No, many of the dead don't realize that they are dead. They don't seem to see the border between life and afterlife. These people can be very anxious. They sometimes try to get back to Earth, meet their loved ones, and they are very upset when the living cannot see them."

"So what happens to them?"

"The guides, spirits of higher dimensions, help them realize that they are dead. Sometimes, if persons have a real need to go back to Earth to accomplish something, the guides are saddened by their pain, and allow them to go back, manifest, and complete their task. Once they do that, they can come back, much happier and calmer. It only happens once, of course, but after that they are ready to adjust to the afterlife."

"What is it like, over there? Were you scared when you passed on?"

"There is nothing frightening about the afterlife," said Mama. "It is very much like earth, but peaceful, much more beautiful, and there is no strife or violence of any kind. To the departed, who have shed their bodies and are occupying a new body, it is as physical as the earth is to the living. Everyone is healthy, there is no disease, no pain, no violence. There are cities with streets and buildings, gardens and parks, countryside – all seems normal, like a poetic interpretation of life. What you see here is visual projections. You see millions of real people, coming and going in huge waves. There is much to do, since the place you come to first is no more than a quick stop. You only stay here for twenty to thirty days, some times forty days, and then move on."

"Do they know where they are going?"

"It depends. Most people cannot see what is ahead of them, only what is behind them. But they always move on to a higher phase."

"So naturally they are a bit scared of the unknown."

Q&A

"Yes, some of them experience anxiety. That is what the twenty to thirty days period is for, deciding what needs and things to be done. And they are helped by the guides, or by people who chose to stay longer in this place."

"So you can stay there longer?"

"Yes, there are various options, of course. One option is to go to the place you have created when you built your "Minzar" and planned a place of rest and happiness. Many people choose to go there for a while – it is up to them how long they would stay there. Time is not really a very important issue where we are. It seems to me that time has stopped. You can stay there forever if you like it very much."

"The place created with the Minzar must be very appealing to most people, I should say," I said. "It's custom made for your own happiness."

"Yes, and the person already has friends, a place to stay, things to do, anything he or she likes best. It's a good option. But eventually, I would say one should try to evolve into the higher dimensions. You don't know what you miss unless you see it."

"When I built the Minzar, Rabbi Mordechai told me that I could not stay in the place I created for too long, since the energy would dissipate and the living body will call me back. But I suppose it's different when one is dead."

"Yes, since this is now part of the depot of knowledge located in your brain, which was created by the Minzar experience. It is your Spatial Memory, my son."

"So you plan to move on after the thirty days?"

"Yes. It is as it should be, and I want to evolve into the higher dimensions. But as I promised, I will come back for you and be your guide when it is your time to follow me. Think about it as a short, though necessary separation, but temporary all the same. What it all comes down to, Germain, is that there is no death. And the afterlife offers so many opportunities for new growth, new knowledge. There is nothing to fear."

"Will you see Papa? Will I see him when I go there?"

"Of course we will. Do not worry and do not mourn me, Germain."

"I will try not to, Mama. I promise."

261

Q&A

"Well, my son, I will be leaving now. No need to say goodbye. Rather, au revoir." I closed my eyes, not wishing to see her leave, and felt something brush my cheek as if she kissed me. When I opened my eyes, there was no sign of her. She was gone. I went home and helped Sylvie attend to the visitors; I have never felt so numb."

*** *** ***

Subjects of interest

PART 3: SUBJECTS OF INTEREST
Q&A, AND DISCUSSIONS

Introduction

In this section, we will be addressing very unusual and rarely explained subjects pertaining to the extraordinary faculties of Anunnaki and Ulema, supernatural powers acquired through the study of alien life, and of course UFOs.

But first of all, I would like to state one more time, that:
1- I am not an ufologist,
2-I am not a UFO hunter,
3-I am not part of any of the conspiracies theories groups in the West,
4-I do not attend UFO conventions,
5-I do not appear on TV shows,
6-I don't give interviews,
7-And most certainly, I do not advance any theory.
8-I don't take seriously the statements of people who claim to be messengers of extraterrestrials, UFOs' mediums, and channelers.
9-I have never seen a UFO,
10-I do not belong to any UFOs group, nor I will ever be,
11-Psychic, paranormal, supernatural powers, ESP, PSI do exist, however 98% of those who have claimed to have such powers, and whom I have carefully examined their alleged powers were absolutely fake,
12-Alien abductions occur, but almost 97% of reported abduction incidents were not genuine,
13-There is no such thing as being "chosen" by extraterrestrials to deliver a message to humanity,
14-Almost 98% of ufology literature is either distorted or totally fabricated.

263

Subjects of interest

15-Several contacts, secret meetings, quasi treaties, cooperation and collaboration between extraterrestrials from Earth and outer space and official authorities (Governments and governments' agencies) did happen.

I am a linguist and a social-historian, extremely fond of animals, nature, futuristic studies, international law, ancient civilizations, cultures, languages and the arts.
What I have learned about extraterrestrial civilizations, alien life UFOs, parallel dimensions/universes, and spirituality originated in the Kira'at, Dirasat (Readings and lectures) of honorable Ulema, comparative study, and documented findings of scientific and governmental agencies/groups, and my personal rapport with highly educated thinkers, both in the Eastern and Western hemispheres.
I have spent more than a half of a century studying and writing about paranormal and UFOs phenomena.
And I am still searching for the ultimate and absolute truth.
Perhaps, I will never find it.
However, what the Ulema have taught me and showed me have changed the fabric of my life and many of my beliefs in several fields, ranging from science to religion.
Thus, what you are reading in this book is essentially what I have learned from the Ulema, and from most reliable sources.
Some of the ideas and concepts you have read about in this book raise red flags. Others are mocked.
And perhaps few were seriously considered.
But those rare and humble enlightened ones (Who do not sell their services and teachings, who do not give fake séances and ridiculous seminars, and who do not brag about themselves on TV shows) know that the knowledge, information and techniques revealed in this modest book came from authoritative sources.

*** *** ***

The Anunnaki

I. Anunnaki in the Western and Eastern Hemispheres:

Despite the availability of several books, tapes and videos on the Anunnaki, it appears to me, that many researchers, authors and enthusiasts (Sincere or dreamers) don't have yet a clear/precise image and a realistic understanding of the Anunnaki.

In the Western world, the Anunnaki are still a novelty; a sort of a Homeric/Federico Fellini saga, a captivating and misunderstood subject, to say the least.

In the East, and for centuries, the Anunnaki have constituted a major part of the esoteric and metaphysical study of the relation of humans to God or creators who brought the humankind to life. They were studied and explained for centuries by enlightened masters known to us as the Ulema.

The Book of Ramadosh (Rama-Dosh) contains a vast literature on the subject, including an Ana'kh (Anunnaki language) lexicon providing a wealth of information on how this extraterrestrial language was discovered, taught to early humans (First species), and its paramount linguistic influence on Earth's languages and vocabularies, ancient and modern. *

Also, included in the Book are stunning revelations pertaining to the times that constitute the gap between 7,000 B.C. and the creation of the first human race on planet Earth, some 450,000 years ago. Studying the Book of Ramadosh (In English version of course) is a must.

***   ***   ***

* Please refer to my 14 language dictionary: "Thesaurus-Dictionary of Sumerian, Anunnaki, Hittite, Babylonian, Akkadian, Assyrian, Syriac, Phoenician, Aramaic, Anatolian, Mesopotamian, Chaldean, Arabic, and Hebrew". Also to this book: "Anunnaki Dictionary Thesaurus (Available worldwide and directly from amazon.com).

II. Betraying the Ancient Texts:

Some Western authors thought that by translating the ancient Akkadian/Sumerian clay tablets and cylinders, they would or could learn and explain how the Anunnaki have established civilizations, and created the human race on Earth.
On this, my comments are:

- **1**-Many of their translations were not totally correct.
- **2**-Some authors who are nowadays a household name because of their pioneering work in the field (Traditional or alternative), and explosive theories (Real or pure fantasy) attempted to translate ancient Akkadian and Sumerian texts without proper training, and knowledge of the languages of the ancient Near/Middle East; the results were catastrophic.
- **3**-Some very successful authors who wrote several books about the Anunnaki took liberty in interpreting the ancient epics, and passages related to the Anunnaki, without responsibility and accountability.

  Instead of respecting the true essence, original meanings and metaphors of the texts, they fabricated stories and invented myths.

  Unfortunately, millions of their readers in the West who are not well-versed in Akkadian, Sumerian and Old Babylonian were duped, simply because they could not tell the difference between the truth and authors' fabrications (Intentional or accentuated).

  The readers' lack of knowledge of the ancient languages of the Near/Middle East allowed such historic/linguistic atrocity, and prevented them from learning and fully understanding what the ancient Phoenician, Assyrian Akkadian, Sumerian, and Babylonian scribes have said, written, and depicted.

*** *** ***

III. False and outrageous Interpretations:

The Epic of the Creation (Earth and mankind) in the ancient texts do not explain in clear terms how the universe was created, and how the first human races that lived and acted like apes evolved into modern humans.

The style and the texture of the Akkadian/Sumerian texts are metaphoric, poetic, and deeply influenced by the beliefs of the scribes of the ancient times, who wrote the epics and tales of the Anunnaki. Some passages do refer to specific instances, where Anunnaki gods and goddesses manufactured early humans via several processes, including the mixing of clay with the blood of a sacrificed Anunnaki god, various genetic manipulations, and/or by upgrading early human forms.

However, those passages were brief, and inconclusive.

Thus, the vivid imagination of contemporary authors in the West substituted for what was largely lacking or unclear, took over, and created all kinds of scenarios and stories about the origin of Man, the phantasmagoric relations between the Anunnaki gods and the genetically created human races, the fantastic/horrible reptilian races, the malicious Greys, spaceships (UFOs), alien abduction, extraterrestrial visitations, etc., etc... Their work was pure fantasy and alarmingly deceitful and deceiving.

*** *** ***

IV: Lack of Authoritative Sources:

It was fun reading these books, but SF fantasy, and exaggerated imagination of UFOs, ETs, and occult writers have enormously disfigured the veracity about the Anunnaki, disoriented readers, and created unnecessary confusion in the minds of millions. This confusion was very damaging to the truth, because it gave birth to unrealistic hopes, to cults and avalanches of ridiculous new "galactic" religions.

It is a fact, Ufology has become a religion.

And this is very alarming.

Anunnaki

I wonder how come, so many authors in the West (Particularly in the United States) know so much about the Anunnaki?

Who is feeding them with all these nonsense information, data, and reports on the Anunnaki, extraterrestrials, and alien races visiting earth?
Here are some statistics to sink your teeth in:
a-30% of the reports are given by whistleblowers,
b-25% by conspiracies theories advocates, and UFOs' writers,
c-40% by so-called contactees, abductees and experiencers,
d-5% by so-called and self-proclaimed psychics, mediums and chanellers (Channelers).
The truth is, not even 1% million knows anything about the Anunnaki. As to aliens and their "occupations" on earth, I tend to believe that many of the reports, sightings, memoranda and findings are accurate, despite the ridiculous claims of so many that have brought ridicule and mockery to Ufology.
But unfortunately, many of those "reporters" put their spin on these reports and findings.

*** *** **

Consequently, the truth was "lost in the translation", or simply never found.
The real or imaginative multiple worlds of the Anunnaki do not exclusively consist of landing their spaceships in ancient Iraq and Phoenicia, the genetic creation the human race, Anunnaki's interference in daily humans' affairs and Earth governments' operations, and controlling our destiny.
The world of the Anunnaki is more complex, deeper, healthier and more challenging than all of the above.
I thought that by adding this section, we will get closer to the truth, since the information and clarification herewith provided were given by the Ulema, who are the most reliable source(s) on the subject.

Throughout the years, I have met a considerable number of Ulema, both in the Eastern and Western hemispheres, and I became absolutely fascinated by their knowledge and findings.

I have asked them many questions. And tons of answers I got. What you are about to read in this section of the book came directly from the Honorable Ulema.

I am just sharing with you what I have learned from them.

Their opinions and teachings do not necessarily reflect mine. And once again, let me state for the record –as I have done in the past– I am NOT an ufologist or an expert on the paranormal.

I am just like you, an ordinary person seeking the truth, and constantly searching for explanations that please both my mind and my intellectual curiosity.

*** *** ***

Anunnaki

The Anunnaki-Sumeria-Phoenicia-Ulema-Book of Ramadosh Connection

Chronology, Etymology, Human Astro-Genetics/DNA

Author's note:
This is the last time, I will be writing and rewriting about the origin, epistemology, etymology and chronology of the Anunnaki. To learn more on the subject, please refer to my previous books and the Anunnaki Encyclopedia I wrote a few years ago.
However, in this section, I will addressing the very important issue of the relation between the Anunnaki in Sumeria and Phoenicia and the Ulema, and finally the Book of Ramadosh (Rama-Dosh) connection

According to the Ulema (Kira'at and Dirasat) and as mentioned in the Book of Ramadosh (Rama-Dosh), the Anunnaki visited planet Earth some 450,000 to 460,000 years ago.
Through the manipulation of time (In terrestrial terminology) and the curving and bending of the space net of the universe, the Anunnaki were able to traverse the infinity of the cosmos (A multitude of universes and dimensions), and land on Earth. The Book of Ramadosh reveals the Anunnaki's chronology; here it is:

*** *** ***

Anunnaki: Epistemology and Etymology

Variations of their creators' name as well as their own were misinterpreted by the early inhabitants of Arwad (An ancient Ugaritic/Phoenician island, Syria), Sumer, Mesopotamia, Gubla (Byblos, modern Gbeil in Lebanon), Baalbeck (Phoenicia, ancient Lebanon), Babylon, Tyre and Sidon in ancient Phoenicia.

The term "Anunnaki" derived from a multitude of variations of three archaic words:
1-Anoun Elah-IM;
2-A.NUN Il'LOheem;
3-Anu-ELA. Keem.

Limited by a fragmented and not totally correct translation of the ancient Akkadian/Sumerian clay tablets texts, and as mistakenly re-translated in modern languages and particularly in English, "Anunnaki" became what everybody (Almost everybody except the expert linguists) today believes to be, to mean and to represent one of the following:
1-Those who came to earth from the heaven;
2-Those who came from the heavens to earth;

And as time changes, epistemology, new languages and dialects develop and create new meanings and divergent/convergent interpretations of the original definition.
Even though "Anunnaki" is pronounced in the same way to a certain degree in many Near East and Middle East languages, the meaning of "Anunnaki" remains to this day subject to regional interpretations and preferences, according to religious beliefs, local mythology, folklore, and linguistic etymology.

However, one solid fact remains unchallenged: The term or word "Anunnaki" was recorded, understood, pronounced and most certainly interpreted differently throughout the ancient and modern ages in a considerable number of mythologies, religions, epics, countries and civilizations, including the Sumerians, Mesopotamians, Babylonians, Phoenicians, Akkadians, Habiru (Early Hebrews/Judaic tribes), Egyptians, Hyskos, Uraturians, Assyrians (Ashurians), Hittites, and the Assyro-Syrians.
Even, the Bible, the Scriptures and religious texts (Orthodox or Gnostic) in Aramaic, Hebrew, Coptic, Nabatean, Greek, Latin and Anglo-Saxon referred to the Anunnaki very differently, such as the Anakim, Rephaim, Goliim, Elohim, the giants, Nephilim, to name a few.

Anunnaki

The real meaning of the word Anunnaki

Anunnaki is an Ana'kh/Sumerian/Akkadian noun that means many things.
The Anunnaki is an ancient Sumerian/Akkadian term, that has been mistranslated and erroneously interpreted by authors and ufologists.
It is commonly translated as "those who Anu sent from heaven to earth." This is an honest translation, however, not totally correct. The fact is that this translation is rather an interpretation than an epistemological and terminological definition.

Possibly a wrong translation of the word Anunnaki on the part of authors

Literarily, it is composed of three words:
- **1**-Anu (God; leader; king)
- **2**-Na (To send or to follow)
- **3**-Ki (Planet earth)

This is correct to a certain degree, because "Na" is not found in Akkadian or Sumerian, but exclusively in Ana'kh and Ulemite. And few scholars had access to the vocabulary of the Ana'kh.
Consequently, none of them knew, or took into consideration the meaning of "Na" in Ana'kh, because they were not aware of its existence.
Therefore, their cliché interpretation/translation should not be considered as the only and ultimate one.

How the word Anunnaki was used

The word is used in a plural form. The gods together are called Anunnaki, and are represented as ša šamê u erSetim, meaning the Anunnaki of the sky (heaven) and planet earth.

272

Anunnaki

In many instances, the word/term Anunnaki represented two categories of gods; the Anunnaki and the Igigi.

Many contemporary writers and ufologists believe that "The Igigi in that case are the gods of heaven, while the Anunnaki refer to the gods of the netherworld, the empire of the death." Unfortunately, this interpretation is also incorrect.

The different meanings of the word Anunnaki

The Anunnaki were known to many neighboring countries in the Near East, Middle East, by and under different names

The Anunnaki were known to many neighboring countries in the Near East, Middle East, and Anatolia. Consequently, they were understood and called differently. For instance:

- **1**-The early Habiru called them Nephilim, meaning to fall down to earth.
- **2**-Some passages in the Old Testament refer to them as Elohim.
- **3**-In Ashuric (Assyrian-Chaldean), and Syriac-Aramaic, they are called Jabaariyn, meaning the mighty ones.
- **4**-In Aramaic, Chaldean and Hebrew, Gibborim mean the mighty or majestic ones.
- **5**-In literary Arabic, it is Jababira. The early Arabs called them Al Jababira; sometimes Amalika.
- **6**-The Egyptians called them Neteru.
- **7**-The early Phoenicians called them An.Na Kim, meaning the god or heaven who sent them to us or to earth.
- **8**-The early inhabitants of Arwad called then. Anuki, meaning the subjects or followers of Anu.

273

Anunnaki

- **9**-The early Hyskos called them the Anuramkir and Anuramkim, meaning the people of Anu on earth. It is composed of three words: Anu + ram (People) + Ki (Earth). The primitive form of Ki was kir or kiim.
- **10**-The Ulema call them Annakh or Al Annaki, meaning those who came to earth from above.
- **11**-The Anunnaki were also called Anunnaku, and Ananaki.

Considered by Assyriologists and mythologists/alternative anthropologists as a group of Akkadian and Sumerian deities, quite often, the Anunnaki were equated/associated with the Annunna, meaning the fifty great gods. Annuna was written in various forms, such as:
- **a**-A-nun-na,
- **b**-Anu-na,
- **c**-Anuma-ki-ni,
- **d**-Anu-na-ki.

*** *** ***

Various attributes or definitions were given to the Anunnaki

Various attributes or definitions were given to them, such as:
- **a**-Major gods in comparison to the Igigi who were considered minor gods.
- **b**-Those of a royal blood or ancestry.
- **c**-The royal offspring,
- **d**-The great gods of heaven and earth. An means heaven, and ki means earth.
- **e**-The messengers or subjects of god/king Anu.
- **f**-The children of Anu and Ki.

Epistemology and historical terminology of the word Anunnaki

Anunnaki is a Sumerian/Akkadian/Chaldean/Assyrian name. It is composed of:

- **1**-An=Above; sky; heaven; clouds; deity; god;
- **2**-Nak (also Nakh): From; belongs to.

To the early Phoenicians, Arwadians, Adamites and Elamites, Anunnaki meant ruling kings.
But the primordial Phoenician meaning was: Those who gave us life.
This meaning/interpretation is derived for the formation of three ancient Phoenician words:

- **a**-An'kh (Life; god; spirit), so the first part "An" is used,
- **b**-Nunnak (From within),
- **c**- I.

The letter "i" is usually added to the end of a Semitic word or a name to mean one of the following:

- **A**-It belongs to;
- **B**-It came from;
- **C**-My.

Linguistic examples:

For instance, the word Ab means father in many Semitic languages (Assyrian, Sumerian, Aramaic, Arabic, etc.) When we add the letter "i" to Ab, it becomes Abi, which means MY father.
The letter "i" adds a sense of belonging and origin.
Later on in history, non-Semitic people and the neighboring civilizations in the Middle East and the Near East countries, and Anatolia incorporated the letter i, in their vocabularies. However, they attached to i, the letter g. And the new addition became "gi", always meaning: Mine; my, or belongs to.

Anunnaki

For instance, in ancient Turkisk (Osmani language, the language of the Ottoman Empire) words like : Kahwagi or Ahwagi meant the man who makes coffe; it is composed of two words: Kahwa, Ahway, Kahwe (Coffee) + Gi.
The word baltagi is composed from two words: Balta (Ax) + Gi.
It means the man with the ax, or the man who makes axes.

The word Diwangi is composed from two words: Diwan (Forum, an area or an office in a palace, a Majless) + Gi. The meaning becomes: The man who belongs to the forum, to an office of the palatial area. However, and strangely enough, sometimes, a word that is written and spelled exactly the same way in two different languages may not mean the same thing.

For instance, Diwangi in ancient Ousmani language, means the man of the forum or an office in a royal palace. It is quite a respectable word. But in Arabic (Lebanese and Syriac Arabic), it means a charlattan or an impostor.
Not so respectable, as you can see.

*** *** ***

According to Dr. John Heise, Anunnaki is a collective name for the gods of heaven and earth, and in other contexts only for the gods of the netherworld, the empire of the death (In particular beginning in the second half of the second millennium.)
According to several linguists, the word Anunnaki is a loan word (Plural only) from Sumerian a.nun "n-a-k", meaning literarily: semen/descendants of the (Ak) monarch (Nun) and refers to the offspring of the king of heaven An/Anum.

*** *** ***

276

Anunnaki

Anunnaki and Their Time on Earth Chronology

1,250.000 years ago:

The Anunnaki are not the oldest extraterrestrial race, because we don't know at all how many different extraterrestrial races and inhabitable planets and stars exist in the known and unknown universe.

However, we do know from the Book of Ramadosh (Rama-Dosh) and other obscure but reliable sources, that the Anunnaki are the early galactic race (From outer space) to land on planets Mars and Earth, and to established colonies in different regions of our planet, encompassing the lands of Central Africa, Madagascar, Australia, a region of Europe, with a strong concentration in ancient Phoenicia and Iraq.

The early edition of the book of Ramadosh (Mama-Dosh) also refers to the Anunnaki's primordial colonies and their spatial stations on Mars, before their arrival to planet Earth. In one of the Fousool (Chapters) of the Book, the scribes explained the reason and motives of the Anunnaki's expedition to Earth.

In a sharp contrast with a common belief, the Anunnaki did not land on Earth to mine gold.

This theory was ridiculed by some Honorable Ulema.

According to the Ulema, The Anunnaki landed on Earth in order to:

1-Use our planet as bio-aquatic research center,

2-Extract and collect Earth's valuable resources,

3-Conduct genetic experiments.

Note: The extraterrestrial bio-aquatic research center theory surfaced in United States government secret files shared with NSA and NASA. In these files, references were made to currently existing non-terrestrial facilities, habitats, bases, laboratories, and "strange" communities under water on planet Earth; all in the hands of an extraterrestrial race.

277

Anunnaki

The Anunnaki along with the Lyrans (Lyrians, also Lyriyan) and Narim (Nordic extraterrestrial race) are the only humanoid race/extraterrestrial race to resemble modern human beings to a certain degree.

1,250.000 years ago, the Anunnaki Edi-Majla was established.

*** *** ***

450,000-460,000 B.C.:

Anunnaki's first landing in Phoenicia:
The Anunnaki landed in the fields and on the shores of what we call today Lebanon.
The word "Lebanon" is an Anunnaki's adjective meaning "white". Egyptians began to use it in the third Millennium before Christ, and references were made to Lebanon in manifestos and letters pertaining to cedar wood shipments from Lebanese cities to Egypt.
The Greeks called the lands "Phoenicia".
It is derived from the Greek word "Phoenix", meaning purple-red. And purple red was the dye (Ourjouwan) extracted by the Phoenicians from the mollusk shell-fish.
It was used to color linens and fabrics. Purple-red was the royal color of the Anakh (Anunnaki.) The Anunnaki began to build their first colonies on Earth.
They found the cities of: Saydoon, Tyrahk, Kadmosh, Adonakh, Ilayshlim, Markadash.
A-Saydoon became Sidon and Saida;
B-Tyrakh became Tyre and Sour;
C-The Phoenician "Kadmos" is named after Kadmosh;
D-The Phoenician god "Adon" is named after Adonakh. Adon or Adoon became Adoni and Adonai in Hebrew.
E-Ilasyshlim gave birth to the words: El, Al, Eli, Elohim, Ilahi, Illah, Allah (In Anakh, Sumerian, Phoenician, Aramaic, Hebrew and Arabic.)

Anunnaki

F-Markadash became Byblos (named by the Greeks) and Jbeil (named by the Arabs.)

Jbeil is possibly the oldest city in the world.

Archaeologists have uncovered houses of farmers, peasants and fishermen in Jbeil going back to 7,000 B.C. Some of the homes currently occupied by the inhabitants of the region are built on the top of historical foundations and ruins dating back to the days of the early Phoenicians, remnants of the Anunnaki. Archeologists found one-room huts with crushed limestone floors and basins, and stone idol of god El known to the Phoenicians as Baal and El. This makes Jbeil (Gbeil or Byblos) later known as Byblos) the oldest city in the world.

***   ***   ***

449,000 B.C.:

Under the leadership of Enki, the Anunnaki landed on Earth. The Anunnaki established their first colonies on the lands of Phoenicia, Syria and Iraq.

But their first cities and housing facilities were erected near Baalbeck, followed by Eridu. The Anunnaki used a sort of laser beams (anti-gravity tools) to lift and transport enormous stones exceeding 1,500 tones each to build their first labs, landing and launching pads and to strengthen their strongholds.

Their operations extended to regions neighboring Iran, Jordan and Israel.

Years later, they concentrated their operations in Sumer and Africa, where they built enormous cities. However, during their first expedition, the Anunnaki did not relinquish the colonies they established in Phoenicia (Baalbeck and Tyre). The first Anunnaki's expedition included a multitude of scientists, land and space topographers, irrigation experts, engineers, architects, metallurgists, mineralogists, and military men.

The specific objectives and purposes of this expedition were the extraction and processing of rich minerals and aquatic resources from earth's oceans and seas.

Anunnaki

Assessing the natural and enormous resources on earth, the Anunnaki quickly realized that they needed a larger man-power; something they did not anticipate. Thus, it became necessary to bring more Anunnaki to Earth.
Consequently, more landings were en route.

*** *** ***

446,000-445,000 B.C.:

This marks the Anunnaki's second massive landing on Earth. This time, the Anunnaki brought with them, physicians, and geneticists. Their intention was clear: In order to successfully conducting their gold mining operations on a larger scale, the Anunnaki decided the create beings capable of carrying and executing hard labor and continuous physical work. Thus, they began to work on a creation formula using in part their own DNA, blood and other substances extracted from Earth. Their creation of the human race went through several primordial phases:

Phase 1:
The Anunnaki tried to improve on a previous creation of a quasi-human form created by the Igigi.

Phase 2:
The Anunnaki worked on 7 different human forms (world's first half-human-half-animal species.)
Their efforts remained fruitless because these creatures were not equipped with a developed mind, thus communicating with them, and/or explaining to them their duties and tasks was an impossible maneuver.
The Igigi created an inferior race of "working creatures" because the Igigi were not good geneticists. They were experts in weaponry, mineralogy and metallurgy.

Phase 3:
Ninhursag, half-sister of Enki, and the Anunnaki expert in medicine and genetics developed a "creation formula" combining Anunnaki's DNA and terrestrial elements which resulted in the "production" of a human race.

Anunnaki

But this early human race did not meet the expectations of Ninhursag. Although the physical form was improved and the mobility of the body was enormously ameliorated, this newly created race was not intelligent enough to follow the instructions of the Anunnaki.

It will take the Anunnaki few more years to come up with a final "human product" capable of thinking and understanding.

*** *** ***

440.000-430.000 B.C.:

More Anunnaki landed on Earth. And more genetic experiments were conducted on the early human races. The interglacials became warmer, and this change in temperature allowed the Anunnaki's created human races to thrive. The Anunnaki added new mental faculties to their creation.

It was at this time in history that those human races began to acquire additional sensorial and mental capabilities such as "memory" and "sense of collectivity". In the ancient lands of Sumer and Africa, the Anunnaki continued to mine minerals and gold.In the Phoenician waters, the Anunnaki searched for aquatic bacteria such as fungi much needed for the development of certain organs of the Homo Sapiens.

*** *** ***

415,000-416,000 B.C.:

With the arrival of Anu and Enlil on Earth, the gold mining operation shifted to the Central African continent. Enlil was in command of the whole enterprise, and became powerful on Earth ruling the Anunnaki living in the Near East, Middle East and occasionally in Africa. Enlil relinquished his authority in Africa to Enki, and planned on returning to Ashtari (Nibiru). A mutiny exploded in the Sumer lands headed by the grandson of Alalu.

*** *** ***

Anunnaki

400,000 B.C.:

The Anunnaki established seven large settlements in the southern region of Mesopotamia that included:
A-Enormous metallurgical installations and a mining center (Shuruppak);
B-Several space launching and landing pads controlled by centralized center (Sippar);
C-A space travel command center (Nippur).
To establish a peaceful relationship with the Igigi, the Anunnaki gave them a generous portion of Africa's mined gold and other minerals. The Igigi transported the gold and mineral shipments to space stations orbiting the earth, and from there, immense Anunnaki's spacecrafts shipped the loads to Nibiru.

*** *** ***

380,000 B.C.:

A war waged by the Enlilites devastated the region. This was a perfect timing for Alalu's grandson to re-seize power, especially that the Igigi gave him full military support.
These were turbulent days for the Anunnaki.
Marduk's allies, the Igigi, ruled vast estates and irrigated lands in Phoenicia (Modern Lebanon) and Sumer.
Nabu, Marduk's son, summoned these Igigi communities to Marduk's city, Babylon, to build a launch tower from which Marduk could challenge the Enlilites' spaceport on the Sinai.

*** *** ***

350,000 B.C.:

Revolt of the lesser Anunnaki and Igigi.
The mining operations of the Anunnaki expanded on a very large scale. More manpower was needed.

Anunnaki

The Anunnaki requested the help of their leaders both on Earth and Nibiru, but remained in vain. So The Anunnaki and their allies, the Igigi revolted against them. One option was left for the Anunnaki: They asked Enki to create a race to do the heavy physical work. The Anunnaki called this new race "The workers", while the Igigi called them "the slave race".

With genetic manipulations, Ki created the LU.LU slave race. This race was created by combining Anunnaki and Igigi DNA and genes from the Homo-Habilis, who were the most advanced primates living on earth at that time.

*** *** ***

340,000 B.C.:

Ki (Ninmah) and Enki genetically created the Lu.Lu; a slave race. The creation was not totally successful because the Lu.Lu could not reproduce themselves to multiply the population. So Ki (Ninmah) and Enki decided to create a new race, with the assistance of Ninhursag, Enki's wife.

And the new race was called humans.

More precisely, an primordial quasi-human form.

*** *** ***

300,000 B.C.:

During these years, and according to Sumerian records, Nergal was the administrator of the underground mines in Southern Africa from which the concept of Hell in Christianity derives. He was known as Hades in Greek Mythology, the god of the underworld and the god of the dead.

Most of the gods of the 'House of Enlil', lived in Sumer (Sumera), also known as 'Ki-Engi', meaning 'the lands of the Lords on Earth'.Note: Sumer not Sumerian, but Akkadian, referring to the lands of the Enlilites ('Ki-Engi').

*** *** ***

Anunnaki

272,000 B.C.:

Enlil expelled Adam and Eve from the Garden of Eden (Janat Adan, Edin).
Enki interfered to "upgrade" the DNA of Adam and Eve, so both could reproduce. For the first time in the history of humanity, a newly created woman has eggs, intentionally introduced in her body by Enki, so she could bear children. Both Adam and Eve lived 100,000 years and acquired the title of "giants".

*** *** ***

200,000-195,000 B.C.:

In Africa, the human races working for the Anunnaki near Ethiopia's Omo River began to enjoy a limited autonomy. These races were considered by the Anunnaki to be the precursors of the most advanced human races on earth.

Note: The existence of these human races was certified by modern science. According to the National Gographic, the human fossils found 38 years ago in Africa are 65,000 years older than previously thought, a new study says—pushing the dawn of "modern" humans back 35,000 years.
New dating techniques indicate that the fossils are 195,000 years old. The two skulls and some bones were first uncovered on opposite sides of Ethiopia's Omo River in 1,967 by a team led by Richard Leakey.
The fossils, dubbed Omo I and Omo II, were dated at the time as being about 130,000 years old. But even then the researchers themselves questioned the accuracy of the dating technique. The new findings, published in the February 17 issue of the journal Nature, establish Omo I and II as the oldest known fossils of modern humans.
The prior record holders were fossils from Herto, Ethiopia, which dated the emergence of modern humans in Africa to about 160,000 years ago.

284

Anunnaki

"The new dating confirms the place of the Omo fossils as landmark finds in unraveling our origins," said Chris Stringer, director of the Human Origins Group at the Natural History Museum in London.

The 195,000-year-old date coincides with findings from genetic studies on modern human populations. Such studies can be extrapolated to determine when the earliest modern humans lived. The findings also add credibility to the widely accepted "Out of Africa" theory of human origins which holds that modern humans (later versions of Homo Sapiens) first appeared in Africa and then spread out to colonize the rest of the world. Life on planet Earth began to regress during a new glacial period.

*** *** ***

160,000 B.C.:

First recorded court testimony in history; Enoch testified against the "Sons of God" who have committed a major sin, and broke the laws of the Anunnaki by having sexual relationships with the "Daughters of Man" (Daughters of Humans).

*** *** ***

125,000-100,000 B.C.:

This is the last interglacial period, and the weather was as warm as the present climate. The human races were not yet fully integrated into the Anunnaki's society, because they were not yet considered a genetically complete race.

During those years, the Anunnaki began to create the final format (mentally and physically) of humans.

The final format reached its last phase around 65,000-60,000 years ago.

285

Anunnaki

At that time in history, prosperous Anunnaki cities were already established in Sumeria, (Ur), Syria (Ougarit, Island of Arwad, Amrit), part of Jodan (Batra), Baalbeck, Jbeil, Tyre and Sidon in Phoenicia (Modern Lebanon today).

Also during that period, the Anunnaki created the early human women and were called "Women of the Light"; they were the early female-forms on earth.

Contrary to all beliefs, including what Judaism, Christianity and Islam teach us, Eve was not created from the rib of Adam. Men were created from an early female form that was "fertilized" by the leaders and the elite of the Anunnaki.

They lived in quarantined cities, and had both sons and daughters fathered by the Anunnaki.

Early humans who lived during that era called the quarantined city of these women "The City of Mirage", and "The City of Beautiful Illusion," since the most attractive women from earth lived there. And the quasi-humans who were made out of earth were not allowed to interact with these women.

Thousands of years later, the inhabitants of what is today the Arab Peninsula and the lands bordering Persia, the United Arab Emirates, and India, called these women "The Women of Light", and those who were allowed to "mix with them" were called "The Sons of Light".

From this early human race, all humans came to life. The Judeo-Christian God had nothing to do with the creation of the human race. In other words, the God we know, revere, and fear today did not create us. Even the word or term "God" did not exist in the early stages of the existence of the human race on earth.

*** *** ***

75,000 B.C.:

A new Ice Age begins. Handful of remnants of the quasi human races previously created by the Igigi roamed the Earth, later to be totally extinguished. In other parts of the world, variations of the Cro-Magnon man survived for a short period.

286

Anunnaki

70,000 B.C.:

1-Enki genetically created Noah; he was born with a sparkling white skin, and large black eyes.
2-Enlil punished the Sons of God, and killed many. However, a great number escaped to distant lands and to other continents.

*** *** ***

65,000 B.C.:

This era marks the dawn of the modern human race, when and where the final form/format and characteristics of the human body took shape.

In other words, and simply put, today's humans are a carbon copy of their ancestors who lived 65,000 years ago. Grosso modo, this is the beginning of the existence of the human race as we know it today.

Because of its primordial genetic and historic importance, this date inspired an endless number of theorists, spiritual visionaries, channelers, mediums and ufologists to advance (Perhaps to fantasize as well) all sorts of scenarios and theories. Almost 99% of them were not aware of the genetic relation between Anunnaki and early inhabitants of Phoenicia.

*** *** ***

49,000-45,000 B.C.:

Ninhursag and Enki appointed humans of an of Anunnaki origin to rule Shuruppak. More Anunnaki visits to Phoenicia.
The Island of Arwad becomes a very active Anunnaki center.

*** *** ***

Anunnaki

49,000 B.C.:

Massive migrations of humans to Europe, resulting in the early confrontations with the Neanderthals, but managed to cohabit and intermix with them.

*** *** ***

13,000 B.C.:

Enlil hides his plans for the human race.
He confers with geneticists to decide on the fate of humans.

*** *** ***

12,000-10,500 B.C.:

1-The Ice Age comes to an end. Chinese astrologers witnessed an exceptional movement in the skies accompanied by the descent of a celestial race from Sirius.
They called this extraterrestrial race the "Dropa".
2-Enki instructs Ziusudra-Noah to build a submersible ship. The Deluge sweeps over planet Earth.

*** *** ***

7,000 B.C.:

Nibiru passed nearby Earth, and knocked off a considerable part of our planet that later formed our Moon.
Some claim that "The cross pollination of Earth with Nibiru provided the basic elements for the Anunnaki's evolution." These ideas are 9,000 years old and NASA today believes that this could be a very valid theory. NASA is currently searching for what they call Planet X.

Anunnaki

Planet X is believed to be beyond our recognized solar system. (Source: Roc Hatfield).

Here is an excerpt from NASA's report: "The observation of the region of the sky in which it is believed Planet X should now be, based on perturbations observed in the motions of Uranus and Neptune, was determined, and there was no reason to update that determination.

A limited area of that region was photographed, and that will be continued.

A given area is photographed with the twin 20 cm astrograph in New Zealand on two successive nights near the time that area is in opposition, and these plates are blinked in Washington to identify anything that has moved.

The predicted region is in the south, which requires observations from a southern station, and it is in opposition in the April to June period, which means observations have not yet started for the year. Blinking will be done as soon as the plates are received in Washington."

(Sources: In NASA, Washington, Reports of Planetary Astronomy, 1991 p 53; Search for Planet X by Robert Harrington)

NASA's additional reference to Planet X appeared in this report: "The discovery that Pluto's mass is insufficient to explain the discrepancies in the motions of the outer planets has led to the prediction of a tenth planet (planet X) of mass about 1-5 earth masses beyond the orbit of Pluto. Further, the existence of a belt or disk of comets beyond the orbit of Neptune has been proposed in connection with some theories of the origin of the Solar System as a possible source of short-period comets and indirectly as a source of long-period comets. Here it is pointed out that the existence of both planet X and the comet disk at their expected distances may explain not only the observed planetary motions and the origin of comets, but also the recently reported 28-Myr periodicity in terrestrial cratering and in mass extinctions.

The cratering period is associated with the precession of the perihelion of planet X caused by the perturbations of the outer planets." (Sources: Periodic comet showers and planet X, vol. 313, Jan. 3, 1985, p. 36-38; NASA)

*** *** ***

289

Anunnaki

4,750 B.C.:

The first Assyrian temple is erected housing the secret language of the Anunnaki. This year marked the first trip of humans to Nibiru and neighboring stars.
Upon their return to earth, the Sumerian astronomers began to map the universe, and write the illustrative history of their gods and kings; this included an elaborate epic of the Anunnaki depicting them as gods who came to earth from Sirius, Mars and the Pleiades.

*** *** ***

4,000 B.C.:

The word Kassi was a title first used by the Phoenicians and later was adopted by the Babylonians who ruled the Mesopotamian empire. Kassi also appeared as a Phoenician name in Egypt and Cassi was an inspiration for the ruling kings known as Catti in pre-Roman Britain. One minted 'Cas' coins featured the sun-horse and other Phoenician solar symbols.

*** *** ***

3,800 -3,550 B.C.:

3,800 B.C.: The Anunnaki began to urbanize their cities in Eridu and Nippur. The city of Erech is built in honor of Anu.
3,760 B.C.: Kish becomes a great capital. The calendar began at Nippur.
3,550 B.C.: The early Phoenician white Aryan race from the Caucasus Mountains region moved into the Indus Valley of India, and created what is today known as the Hindu religion. They erected a shrine for Inanna.

Anunnaki

3,450 B.C.:

Babylon became the principal spaceship terminal on earth. New launching pads were created.

Marduck revisited the early Anunnaki cities in Phoenicia. Mutiny against Marduck led to his arrest and imprisonment. He was exiled to Egypt, and later locked up inside the Great Pyramid. Followers of the new ruler threw the kingdom in state of chaos and complete disorder.

A group of architects from Phoenicia, Babylon and Hadarmoot built the Tower of Babel. To accomplish this project, they needed a large manpower.

Thus, they began to enslave the population and many inhabitants from neighboring countries. Chaos and confusion reigned over the cities of Sumer.

Many lost their mental faculties and became totally disoriented, and became unable to communicate with each other. This led to mass confusion which resulted in the destruction of the Tower of Babel.

*** *** ***

3,100 B.C.:

This year marks the restoration of law and order in Egypt, and the end of 350 tumultuous years of anarchy. Narmer, (also called Menes), the first Egyptian Pharaoh ascends to the throne in the city of Memphis. Namer came from the north and conquered the south. His conquest united Egypt. Narmer founded Memphis as the first capital of united Egypt. The city of Thebes became the next capital of Egypt. During the reign of King Akhenaten, Amarna became the capital of the kingdom of Egypt.

*** *** ***

Anunnaki

3,000 B.C.- 2,123 B.C.:

3,000 B.C.: The Hayasa-Azzi tribes first inhabit Urartu.

2,900 B.C.: Erech becomes King of Sumer. Inanna rules over the Third Region known as the Indus Valley.

2,650 B.C.: Mutiny in the kingdom of Sumer. The Anunnaki's king, Enlil is disappointed by the behavior of the human race.

2,500 B.C.: Two Assyrian cities Arbel and Nineveh prosper and their trade flourishes in the Near East.

2,371 B.C.: Sargon erects Agade, the new capital of the mighty empire of Akkad.

2,316 B.C.: Sargon's power is unchallenged in Babylon. Marduk fights Inanna. Marduk leaves Mesopotamia.

2,300 B.C.: The power of the Sumerians had declined to such an extent that they could no longer defend themselves against foreign invasion.

2,291 B.C.: Naram-Sin ascends the throne of Akkad. Aided by Inanna, he occupies the Sinai Peninsula, and captures Egypt.

2,255 B.C.: The Anunnaki destroy Agade. Inanna seizes power in Mesopotamia, but her reign would not last long after the defeat of Nippur on the hands of NaramSin. The allied armies of Ninurta and Enlil invade and occupy Akkad and Sumer.

2,220 B.C.: Sumerian civilization reaches its peak. The legendary Ziggurat temple in honor of Ninurta is erected by king Gudea. New laws and ethics code are established by the rulers of Lagash.

2,200 B.C.: Amorites invaded Phoenicia.

2,193 B.C.: Terah, Abraham's father, is born in the city of Nippur to a prominent priestly-royal family.

2,180 B.C.: The kingdom of Egypt is divided; Ra-Marduk subjects remained in the south. Pharaohs retained Lower Egypt.

2,150 B.C.: The Anunnaki left earth for good. They paid a short visit to Phoenicia, and the Island of Arwad.

2,130 B.C.: Inanna's last attempt to regain her throne.

2,123 B.C.: Abraham is born in Nippur.

*** *** ***

Anunnaki

2,100 B.C.:

Discovery of the "ORME" invented by Tubaal Kain (Tubal-Caiin). Only members of the royal family and the first hierarchy of Sumerian priesthood had access to it. In common term, it was called "Man-nah-Iyil", the "Elixir of Eternal Life." But this formula was not successful. Originally created to replace the lost "Orme", the "Man-nah-Iyil", was later used in alchemy.

Centuries later, it will be known to medieval alchemists as the "Philosophical Stone." The French Ulema and alchemist Nicholas Flammel allegedly deciphered a part of its code, and succeeded in transmuting metal into pure gold. Many French historians attribute his sudden wealth to his discovery of the "Philosophical Stone."

*** *** ***

2,096 B.C.-1,363 B.C.:

2,096 B.C.: Ur-Nammu is defeated.
He died from severe injuries on the battlefield. His military commanders are dispersed and his army is totally annihilated. This year marked the departure of Terah to Harran.
2,095 B.C.: Shulgi became the king of Ur.
2,090 B.C.: A major part of the highly advanced Anunnaki technology and science is lost. The human race was not prepared or ready to fully understand how the Anunnaki's advanced tools functioned.
2,080 B.C.: Nabu, the son of Marduk gains major influence in Western Asia.
2,070 B.C.: Marduck, king of mighty Babylonia is the last royal remnant of the Anunnaki on earth. Marduck is worshiped as god.
2,065 B.C.: Enlil is no longer controlling the human race.
2,060 B.C.: Abraham left Ur and headed toward Haran.
2,055 B.C.: Revolt in major Canaanite cities.
The Elamite troops crashed the revolt and restored order.

Anunnaki

2,050 B.C.: Marked the beginning of the decline of the Sumerian civilization. This was caused in part by the departure of the Anunnaki.

2,048 B.C.: Shulgi died. Leading five legions of warriors, AVraham (The early one) captured the lands of Canaan.

2,047 B.C.: Amar-Sin (the biblical Amraphel) becomes king of Ur. AVraham is defeated. He retreats to Egypt, stays there five years, and then returns with more military legions.

2,041 B.C.: Guided by Inanna, Amar-Sin creates a formidable military coalition with the Kings of the East, and attacks the lands of Canaan and Sinai. But AVraham interferes and his blocks Amar-Sin at the main entrance of the "Space port."

Note: Two separate Abrahams existed in history; AVraham was a warrior, the other is the Biblical Patriarch.

2,038 B.C.: Shu-Sin replaces Amar-Sin on throne of Ur.

2,029 B.C.: Ibbi-Sin replaces Shu-Si Marduk gains popularity.

2,024 B.C.: Leading a might army Marduk marches on Sumer, captures the city and declares himself king. Enlil is furious and demands that Marduk and Nabu be punished; Enki sides with Marduk, but his son Nergal sides with Enlil.

2,113 B.C.: Nammmu reigns over Nippur.

Enlil appoints Nannar, lord of Shem. The city of Ur became the capital of the Anunnaki's empire.

1,800 B.C.: The Hyksos invaded Phoenicia.

1,760 B.C.: Hammurabi king of Babylonia conquers Assyria and put an end to the first Assyrian empire.

1,500 B.C., Egypt: The Palace of Pharaoh Thutmosis III.

Many circles of raging fire are said to have hovered over the royal palace while fishes, winged creatures, and other objects rained down from the sky.

1,363 B.C.: Mitanni rules Assyria with an iron hand.

Ashur-Uballit establishes the mighty Assyrian Empire.

*** *** ***

1,362-64 B.C.:

The Phoenicians became the first civilization to capture the sounds of words in writing by inventing the alphabet; a writing system consisting of individual letters. Several letters were taken from the Anakh (Anunnaki) language.

Sumerian cuneiforms (wedge shaped symbols in clay tablets) and Egyptian hieroglyphics (pictographs) were the only known forms of writing before the alphabet as we know. Both scripts, though separately created, used picture writing. Eventually, pictures or signs represented sounds, and finally, the pictures and signs became so simplified that a whole word was written as a single sign. The Phoenicians developed symbols which in time became a real alphabet.

The Phoenician alphabet consisted of twenty-two symbols, all consonants. Each one represented its own sound. The Egyptian symbol for the Ox-head was given the Semitic name aleph, and was sounded as "a." The symbol for house became Beth, and was sounded as "b." It is easy to see how the Phoenician alphabet was used to create other alphabets which followed it. Aleph became the Greek alpha, Beth became beta. In time, these letters became the Roman letters A and B and eventually the English A and B, and so on for the entire alphabet. Once a written language was established, it was inscribed on Egyptian papyrus, a type pf paper made of reeds.

So, closely linked was papyrus with the city of Byblos, (which traded cedar for the paper) that when the writing of the Hebrew prophets were translated into Greek, the city's name was given to the great book - the Bible.

Because the papyrus rotted away in the damp sea air and soil, there are practically very very few Phoenician writings left.

Thus, the literature of the people who influenced the western world has largely vanished. Still, because Egyptian scribes copied the Phoenician letters after hieroglyphics were no longer used, and because artists in Ninevah inscribed them in stone, the alphabet remains with us.

Anunnaki

In their letters to the pharaohs of Egypt, Rib-Addi of Byblos, King Abi-Milki of Tyre, and King Zimrida of Sidon, remnant of the Anunnaki's used Anunnaki alphabet and codes. (Sources: Phoeniciaorg)
Egyptians texts made references to the advanced scientific technology found in the cities of Tyre, Sidon, Byblos, Ushuand, Beirut and Zaraphath.

*** *** ***

1,260 B.C.: -1,080 B.C.:

1,260 B.C.: The Assyrians scribes and inscriptions mention Urartu for the first time.
1,240 B.C.: Babylon is ravaged by the Assyrians.
1,200 B.C.: The Assyrians resist incursions by the Urarturians and the Mushki.
1,155 B.C.: Elam and Assyria attack Babylonia and put an end to the Kassite rule.
1,114 to 1,076 B.C.: This era marked the reign of Tiglath-Pileser the first over Assyria.
1,080 B.C.: Egyptian story of Wen-Amen, mentioned Wereket-El, a Phoenician ships builder who lived in Tanis in the Nile delta. Reference was made to the triangle insignia he placed on his ships. In ancient times, the "triangle" was the logo of the Anunnaki who landed in Phoenicia.

*** *** ***

1,000 B.C.:

Major historical events happened that year:
1-The Phyrgians and the Thracians immigrate to Urartu.
2-The Phoenician city Tyre established colonies throughout the Mediterranean areas and strengthened its commercial ties with the Hyskos (Anunnaki descendants) in Cilicia.

Zinjirli ruled by King Kilamuwa, a remnant of the Anunnaki. King Kilamuwa adopted the Phoenician language that contained Anunnaki's letters and symbols. Anunnaki's and Phoenicians scripts were engraved at the main entrance of the royal palace in Ancient Armenia.

3- Hiram, the Phoenician king of Tyre, became the military ally and business partner of King Solomon. Expedition "Ophir" was carried out by King Solomon and King Hiram. Legend has it that Phoenician ships sailing the Mediterranean were guided by a mysterious light in the form of a crescent hovering over their ships.

4-The Urarturians conquer and overrun the majority of the lands of the mighty empire of Assyria. In exchange for peace, the Phoenicians shared with the Urarturians secret knowledge they have acquired from the Anunnaki; this included maritime compasses and celestial maps and arithmetic formula written in Ana'kh (Anunnaki language.)

At that time in history, the Phoenicians referred to the Anunnaki as Anakh.

5-In Tyre/Sidon cities, the Phoenicians discovered "Ourjouwan"; the famous dye known as the "Tyrian Purple".

Ancient Mesopotamian and Phoenicians tablets mentioned this dye as the "heavenly color" of the Anakh (Anunnaki).

*** *** ***

CONTINUES IN BOOK II

The Anunnaki Ulema Forbidden Knowledge. What Your Government And Your Church Didn't Want You To Know.

INDEX

A

Aagerdi-deh technique, 65
Aamala, 35
Abaari, 75
Abductees who claim to have had sex with Anunnaki, 55
Abductees, general, 54
Abductees: Operations on abductees, 56
Abra (To traverse), 37
Abri, 75
Adam, 48, 49
Adam's apple, 65
Afik-r, 36
Afik-r'-Tanawar, 36
Afterlife, general, 43, 58
Afterlife: Discussion, 257, 258, 259, 260
Afterlife: Life after death, views of the Anunnaki-Ulema, 45, 58
Afterlife: Physical aspect of the afterlife, 59
Afterlife: Physical senses in the afterlife, 44
Afterlife: Punishments in the afterlife, 44
Afterlife: Reunion with loved ones in the afterlife, 44, 45
Afterlife: Reunited with pets in the afterlife, 43
Afterlife: What you see in the afterlife is real to the mind, 44
Agenda: Extraterrestrial agenda, 54
Aging: Halting the process of aging, 133
Akashic Records Hall, 39
Akashic Records, 43, 93
Akashic Records: Discussion, 229, 230, 231, 232, 233, 234
Akkadian, 48, 49
Alabama, 246
Alcoholic beverages, 78, 96
Alexandria, 231
Aliens: Alien babies are retrieved from the containers after 6 months, 55
Aliens: Alien mothers, 55
Aliens: Aliens of lower dimensions, 52
Aliens: Aliens races, 53
Aliens: Aliens-hybrids, 55
Aliens: Evolution of aliens, 50
Aliens: Sex with aliens, 55
Aliens: Summary of aliens' fertilization and reproduction, 55
Allah, 49
Al-Madkhal, 199
Alpha wave, 61
Alphabets: Esoteric letters, 51
Alternate Realities, 91-106
Ana'kh, 41, 43, 49
Anesthesia, 62
Angels, 51
Angels: Fallen angels, 51
Animal fat, 78
Animals, 51

Anše (Magnificent), 37
Anšekadu-ra abra, 37, 39
Anshekadoora-abra, 37
Anti-matter and matter, 43
Anunnaki and Their Time on
    Earth Chronology, (Starting
    1,250.000 years ago), 277
Anunnaki branching out, 37,
    38, 39, 46
Anunnaki can de-fragment
    molecules, 39
Anunnaki entering different
    dimensions, 37
Anunnaki geneticists, 36
Anunnaki going back and forth
    in time and space, 38, 43
Anunnaki Hall of Records, 39
Anunnaki have created us, 36
Anunnaki installed Conduit, 36
Anunnaki no longer condition
    our mind, 37
Anunnaki splits himself/herself
    in two, 38, 46
Anunnaki used clay to
    genetically create the human
    race, 50
Anunnaki, 193
Anunnaki: Anunnaki and God,
    59
Anunnaki: Anunnaki physical
    looks/traits, 54
Anunnaki: Anunnaki schools in
    Ashtari, 40
Anunnaki: Anunnaki sex, 54
Anunnaki: Anunnaki shape-
    shifting, 54
Anunnaki: Anunnaki women,
    54
Anunnaki: Anunnaki's
    characteristics, 53
Anunnaki: Anunnaki's hybrid,
    55

Anunnaki: Anunnaki's long
    robe "Arbiya", 53
Anunnaki: Anunnaki's
    navigation tool, 53
Anunnaki: Discussion, 265,
    266, 267, 268
Anunnaki: Exact copies of the
    person of the Anunnaki, 38,
    39
Anunnaki: General, 38, 39, 41,
    48, 51, 52, 53, 54, 57, 136
Anunnaki: Genetic
    reproduction process of the
    Anunnaki, 54
Anunnaki: Humans are linked
    to the Anunnaki via Fik'r, 57
Anunnaki: Recognizing an
    Anunnaki, 53
Anunnaki's Code Screen, 41
Anunnaki's codes, 42
Anunnaki's Conduit, 40
Anunnaki-Sumeria-Phoenicia-
    Ulema-Book of Ramadosh
    connection, 270, 272, 273,
    274, 275, 276
Anunnaki-Ulema; Glossary of
    terms, 35
An-zalubirach, 60
An-zalubirach: Multiple
    thoughts and images, 40
Arabic, general, 49, 52
Arac-ta, 149
Aramaic, 51
Arawadi technique, 169-173
Arawadi Technique:
    Discussion, 257, 258
Araya (Code), 40, 42
Arbel, Ilil, 72, 77, 107
Arbiya (Anunnaki's long robe),
    53
Ardi, 63
Arwad, 175

Astral body, general, 199, 203
Astral body: Zooming into an
  astral body, 191
Astral dimension,178
Astral memory, 42
Astral projection, 47
Ata Bra Golem Devuk
  Hakhomer VeTigzar Zedim
  Chevel Torfe Yisroel, 71
Aura, 206
Aura, 68
Awareness, 62
Azakar.Ki, 48

B

Baab, 58, 160, 194, 199, 200,
  235
Baaniradu technique, 175-189
Babies: Alien babies are
  retrieved from the containers
  after 6 months, 55
Babylonian, 49
Bahaiim, 51
Balance, 35, 36
Baltimore, 246
Balu, 43
Balu-ram-haba, 43
Baridu technique, 191-200
Baridu Technique: Discussion,
  247, 248, 249, 250
Bases: Underground bases, 52
Bashar (Humans), 36
Beings, 37
Beings: Multi-vibrational
  beings, 37
Beings: Super-beings from the
  future, 51
Beings: Super-beings, 37
Beings: The less developed
  living entities, 37
Beta wave, 61

Bio-organic memory, 42
Bisho-barkadari "Bukadari"
  technique, 201-211
Blueprint: Human blueprint, 57
Body's healing potentials, 61
Brain: Blueprints of the brain
  (Mind), 138
Brain: Brain waves
  synchronization, 60, 62
Brain: Brain's motor, 138
Brain: Cells of the brain, 42
Brain: Development of
  extraterrestrial brain's waves,
  50
Brain: Measuring the brain
  frequencies, 61
Brain: The brain's sixth wave,
  60
Branching out, Anunnaki, 37,
  38, 39, 46
Brooklyn, 246
Brotherhood of the Fish Circle,
  149
Bubble as Fik'r, 57
Budapest, 65
Bukadari technique:
  Discussion, 254, 255, 256

C

Cadari (Plasma-screen), 119
Cadari-Rou'yaa technique, 119-
  125
Cells: Cells of the brain, 42, 57
Centrifugal effect, 42
Chabariduri technique (Remote
  viewing) 127-132
Chakras, 207
Changing the past, 37
Channelers, 51
Chi, 137, 227
Chrononauts, 51

300

Circle Technique, 147-153
Civilizations: Galactic civilizations, 53
Claustrophobia. 53
Clay: Clay used by the Anunnaki to genetically create the human race. 50
Clay: Golem of clay, 71
Cloning: Cloning of extraterrestrials, 50
Code "Araya", 40, 42
Code Screen, 41, 42
Code: Nimera, 41
Codes of the Anunnaki, 42
Communication: Galactic communications, 69
Concentration, 40
Conduit, general, 73, 75, 88, 140, 141, 177, 179, 207, 216, 217, 218, 219, 220
Conduit: Anunnaki's Conduit, 40, 57
Conduit: Conduit, installed by the Anunnaki, 36, 57
Conduit: Data stored in the Conduit, 42, 61, 62
Conduit: Developing the Conduit, 77
Conduit: Light conduit, 55
Conscience, 37
Contact: Contact between the dead and the living, 48
Contact: Contacting our departed ones for a very short time, 68
Copies: Exact copies of the person of the Anunnaki, 38, 39
Copy: Copy of ourselves preserved in the Fourth dimension, 47
Copy: Copy of past event, 39

Copy: Copying extraterrestrials, 50
Copy: Creating a new copy of oneself, 40
Copy: First copy of "You", 57
Corporal form: Acquiring new form, 58
Cosmic Mirror, 43
Cosmos net, 35, 40
Cosmos, general, 35, 39, 41
Cosmos: Several layers of universes, 39
Creator, 51
Crystal glass, 79

D
Dab'Laa, 46
Daemat-Afnah technique, 133-146
Daemat-Afnah technique: Discussion, 251, 252, 253
Da-Ira-Maaref, 147
Da-Irat technique, 147-153
Dar, 74
Dead person: First, the dead person tries to contact relatives and close parents, 47, 48
Dead person: Telepathic messages of the dead, 48
Dead person: The deceased person returns home for a very short period, 47, 48
Dead: Contact between the dead and the living, 48
Dead: Contacting our departed ones for a very short time, 68
Dead: Mind of the dead, 47
Death, general, 43, 57
Death: Beyond death, 59
Death: Life after death, views of

the Anunnaki-Ulema, 45
Death: Manifestation of the dead during a period of less than 40 days, 47
Death: Seven levels/dimensions of life after death, 44
Death: Source of energy after death, 47
Death: Whirling of the soul after death, 69
Delta wave, 62
Dematerialization, 73
Demons, 37
Dimension: Copy of ourselves preserved in the Fourth dimension, 47
Dimension: Entering higher dimension, 59
Dimension: Entering/exiting new or different dimension, 39, 40
Dimension: Ethereal Fourth dimension, 43
Dimension: Etheric dimension, 138
Dimension: Mind entering a new dimension, 47
Dimension: Next dimension, 43
Dimension: Non-physical dimension, 36
Dimension: Physical dimension, 35
Dimension: The Fourth dimension, 36, 69
Dimension: Vibrational dimension, 139
Dimension: Virtual three dimensional reality, 73
Dimensions: Aliens of lower dimensions, 52

Dimensions: Invisible dimensions, 73
Dimensions: Other dimensions, 58
Dimensions: Parallel dimension, 43
Dimensions: Seven levels/dimensions of life after death, 44
Distances, 43
District of Columbia, 246
DNA "Naphsiya", 36, 56
DNA, general, 44, 56, 136, 137, 164
Double, general, 36, 43, 57, 58, 59, 136, 160, 193, 194, 197, 199, 203
Double: Holographic imageries are produced by the Double, 45
Double: Vibes produced by one's double, 73
Double: Zooming into the Double, 43, 191
Dudurisar technique, 155-168
Duplicating oneself by entering a new dimension, 40

E
Ea, 48
Early human beings, 36
Earth, general, 47, 49, 50, 51
Earth: Earth is the lowest organic and human life-form, 37
Earth: Inhabitants of Earth, 48, 49
Ectoplasmic forms, 48
Ectoplasmic substance, 199
Eeh, 48
Eggs: Woman's eggs, 56

302

Eidolon (A phantom), 47
Eido-Rah, 47
Eight Degree, 73
Electroencephalograph, 61
Electro-magnetic beams, 69
Electro-magnetic vibes, 207
Electroplasmic substance, 42
Emotional properties, 57
Employees in the United
    States, 207
Energizing one's mind and
    body, 147
Energy (Internal) "Hara-Kiya",
    36
Enki, 48, 49
Enlightened ones, 43, 63, 147
Enlightenment, 36
Entities: Frightening entities,
    45
Erdi, 49, 51
Erdsetu, 49
Eretz, 49
Ersetu, 49
Esoteric letters, 51
Esoterism, 169
Ethereal Fourth dimension, 43
Ethereal manifestation, 51
Etheric Belt, 178
Etheric dimension, 138
Etheric memory, 178
Events: Anunnaki's registry of
    future events, 35
Events: Foreseeing
    forthcoming events, 40
Events: Future and
    forthcoming events, 35, 43
Evil, 37
Evolution: Evolution of
    extraterrestrials via copying,
    duplicating, and cloning
    themselves, 50
Evolution: Evolution of our

mind, 37
Evolution: Evolution of the
    extraterrestrials, 50
Evolution: Evolution of the
    human race, 50
Evolution: Inter-dimensionally,
    50
Extra, 50
Extra-sensorial faculties, 59
Extraterrestrialogists, 51
Extraterrestrials do not have
    genital organs, 55
Extraterrestrials, 41, 50
Extraterrestrials: Evolution via
    copying, duplicating, and
    cloning themselves, 50
Extraterrestrials:
Extraterrestrial agenda, 54
Extraterrestrials:
    Extraterrestrial technology,
    56
Extraterrestrials:
    Extraterrestrials fertilizing
    their own genes, 50
Extraterrestrials:
    Extraterrestrials with 3
    fingers hands 54
Extraterrestrials: More
    advanced extraterrestrial
    civilizations, 50
Extraterrestrials: Shape-
    shifting, 52
Ez (First creatures), 51
Ezakarerdi, 48
Ezakarfalki, 48, 49
Ezbahaiim-erdi, 48, 51
Ezeridim, 51
Ezra (Manifestation), 51
Ezrai-il, 51

F

303

F "ف", 51
Fadi-ya-ashadi (Non-terrestrial shape-shifting entities), 52
Falak Kitbah, 230
Fallen angels, 51
Fana.Ri, 54
Fik.Ra.Sa, 56, 73
Fik'r, general, 59
Fik'r-Firasa: Reading minds, 56
Fikr: Fikr as substance of energy, 47, 57
Fikrama, 60, 63
First copy of "You", 57
Fisal, 230
Fish Circle Brotherhood, 149
Foreseeing forthcoming events, 40
Foreseeing, general, 41
Formula that created you, 57
Fourth dimension, 36, 69
Frequencies, general, 139
Frequencies: Aliens' thoughts frequencies, 50
Frequencies: Lowering or increasing frequencies, 40, 60
Frequencies: Measuring the brain frequencies, 61
Frightening entities, 45
Future, general, 38, 40
Future: A being from the future, 39, 51
Future: Meta-future, 38

G

Galactic civilizations, 53
Galactic communications, 69
Galactic-organic body, 54
Gen-adi-warkah, 63
Genes: Extraterrestrials fertilizing their own genes, 50

Genesis, 45
Genetic: Genetic codes, 141
Genetic: Genetic creation of mankind, 135
Genetic: genetic labs, 149
Genetic: Genetic operations on abductees, 56
Genetic: Genetic reproduction process of the Anunnaki, 54
Genetic: Underground genetic labs, 52
Geneticists, Anunnaki, 36
Genetics, 51
Genital organs:
Extraterrestrials do not have genital organs, 55
Gensi-uzuru: Apparition of deceased pets, 67
Germain Lumiere, 85, 114
Ghen-ardi-vardeh (Talking to others without using words), 63
Gilgoolem: The cycle of rebirths, 69
Gilgoolim: The non-physical state of a deceased person, 69
Glossary of Anunnaki-Ulema terms. 35
God, 57, 59, 60, 71
Goda, 75
Godabaari technique: Discussion, 221, 222, 223, 226, 227, 228
Godabaari, 75-81
Godumari, 69
Godumu, 69
Goduri, 69
Goirim-dari (A mental catalyst), 73
Goirim-daru (vibes produced

304

by one's double), 73
Golem: An artificially created
   man, 69, 70, 71
Golem: Golem of Prague, 70,
   71, 72
Golibri, 72
Golibu, 72
Golim (A prototype of a created
   presence or entity), 72
Golimu, 73
Gomari (Gumaridu) 83-89
Gomari "Gumaridu" technique:
   Discussion, 224, 225
Gomatirach-Minzari technique,
   91-106
Gomatirach-Minzari:
   Discussion, 229, 230, 231,
232, 233, 234
Gomu Minzar, see Gomatirach-
   Minzari technique
Good deeds, 58
Greys, general, 52, 54
Greys: Greys who live on earth
   and work with scientists, 52
Greys: Greys' claustrophobia.
   53
Greys: Greys' intense crises, 53
Greys: Greys' shape-shifting. 52
Greys: Greys' teleportation, 53
Greys:
   Reproduction/fertilization by
   the Greys, 54
Gubada-Adari technique, 107-
   117
Gubada-Ari: Discussion, 242,
   243, 244, 245, 246
Gudi, 75
Gudi-Ha-abri, 75, 77
Gudinh, 73
Gumaridu, see Gomari

H

H of the Conduit, 73
Haabaari, 73
Haba (Beyond), 43
Habru, 73
Hadiiya, 73
Hag-Addar (Ulema 18th degree
   ritual ceremony), 73
Halida, 74
Hama-dar, 74
Handar: Anunnaki's metal vest,
   53
Hara-Kiya (Internal energy or
   physical strength), 36
Health, 107, 109, 111, 112, 121,
   140
Heaven, 57
Hebraic scholars, 44
Hebrew, general, 43, 49, 51, 63,
   72
Hell, 57
Heth, 152
Higher self, 61
Hiphil, 49
Hiraa-Ti, 230
Holographic images of people,
   animals and places, 44
Holographic images: Produced
   by extraterrestrials, 63
Holographic images: Produced
   by the Double, 45
Holographic projection, 164,
   165
Holographic/parallel
   dimension, 166
How to stay and look 37
   permanently, 135, 141, 143
Human beings: The less
   developed living entities, 37
Human body, 36
Human body: Prototype, 36

Human mind began to evolve, 36

Human race: Final form of the human race, 56

Human: Early human beings, 36

Human: Evolution: Evolution of the human race, 50

Human: Human blueprint, 57

Human: Human eggs, 56

Human: Human prototypes created by the An. Na.Ki., 135

Human: Human sperms, 56

Humans "Bashar", 36

Humans: Departed humans in the next dimension, 43

Humans: Final specimen of humans, 136

Hybrid: Aliens-hybrids, 55

Hybrid: Anunnaki's hybrid, 55

I

Identity: A person without an identity, 39

Identity: Acquiring new identity by entering a new dimension, 40

Ih-tikah'k, 206

Il (Divine), 51

Images: Holographic images of people, animals and places, 44

Images: Mental images, 40

Infidelity, 55

Inner energy, 227

Inner eye, 59

Interdimensional zone, 55

Internal energy or physical strength "Hara-Kiya ", 36

Intra-planetary immigration, 51

Introspection, 40, 61

Invisibility, 74

Invisible dimensions, 73

Islamic scholars, 49

Isti-bal, 230

J

Jewish: Medieval Jewish legends, 70

Jews, 71

K

Kabalah, 70, 72

Kabalistic formulas, 71, 72

Kabbalists, 117

Kadari, 231

Kadu (Ability), 37

Kaf-ra-du, 150

Kama Kira'at, 231

Kama La-yiha, 231

Kaph, 150

Kareit (Kah-Rehyt), 45

Khalek, 59, 138

Khrono, 51

Ki, 227

Ki, 49

Kira, 149

Kira'at (Reading) by Ulema, 36

L

Laboratories: Aliens reproduce in laboratories, 55

Laboratories: Genetic labs, 149

Latin, 50

La-yiha, 230

Lifespan, 36, 38, 135, 136

Light conduit, 55

Logic of numbers, 41

Longevity, 133, 135, 136, 140

Louisiana, 246

Luck, 139

Lyrans, 41

M

Mah-Rit, 149
Makatba, 230
Maktoub, 157
Man: An artificially created man, 69
Manifestation: Ethereal manifestation, 51
Manifestation: Manifestation of the dead during a period of less than 40 days, 47
Manipulating time, 83
Mat-Kaba, 230
Matrix, 66
Matter and anti-matter, 43, 51
Medieval Jewish legends, 79
Mediums, 51
Melkart, 137, 175
Mem, 151
Memory: Astral memory, 42
Memory: Bio-organic memory, 42
Memory: Loss of memory, 42
Memory: Mirrored spatial memory, 46
Memory: Space memory, 42
Memory: String memory, 42
Memory: Time memory, 42
Mental: Goirim-dari, a mental catalyst), 73
Mental: Mental energy, 40
Mental: Mental faculties, 36, 37
Mental: Mental images, 40
Mental: Mental launching pad, 161
Mental: Mental powers, 77
Mental: Mental projection, 47
Mental: Mental vibrations, 63
Messages: Messages as

ectoplasmic forms, 48
Messages: Messages of the dead, 48
Meta-linear, 47
Metaphysical concept (The Soul), 45
Metaphysical-religious context, 59
Metaphysics, 169
Microscopic hair filaments, 52
Military: Underground military research centers, 52
Mind, general, 35, 36, 41, 43
Mind: Blueprints of the brain (Mind), 138
Mind: In the afterlife, the deceased will suffer through the mind, 44
Mind: Mind entering a new dimension, 47
Mind: Mind evolution, 36, 37
Mind: Mind is no longer conditioned by the Anunnaki, 37
Mind: Mind of the deceased, 43, 44, 47
Mind: Multidimensional mind, 36
Mind: Peace of mind, 107, 111, 112
Mind: The Double housing the mind, 45
Mind: The mind as a soul, 45
Mind: Transmission of the mind, 59
Mind: What you see in the afterlife is real to the mind, 44
Minzaar, 69, 93, 95, 96
Mira, 164
Mir-A't, 230
Miraya: Cosmic Mirror, 43, 58,

69, 73, 93, 231

Miraya: Discussion, 229, 231, 232, 233, 234, 241

Mirkaan, 230

Mirror to Alternate Realities, 91

Mishnah, 70

Mississippi, 246

Missouri, 246

Molecule: Molecule as soul, 58

Molecules, general, 44, 46, 57, 58

Molecules: Anunnaki can de-fragment molecules, 39

Molecules: Greys' bodies molecules, 53

Mothers: Alien mothers, 55

Moving objects by mental powers, 78

Mra, 230

Multidimensional holographic images, 44

Multiple universes, 37, 40, 46

Muslims, 49

N

Nafis-Ra, non-physical dimension, 36

Naphsiya "DNA", 36

NASA, 65

NASA's Ames Research Center, 66

Natha", "Nasa", "Al Natha", "Nis-Yan", 49

Ne.Be.Ru, 230

Nerve-signal patterns, 67

Net: Universe net, 42

Nibiru, 38, 39, 41, 57, 230

Nimera: Code, 41

Niphal, 49

Nordics, 41

O

Olam ha-ba, 43

Operations on abductees, 56

Organic-galactic body, 54

Ountha (Oonsa), 48

Outer-space, 50

P

Parallel dimension: It is possible to enter a parallel dimension, 169

Parallel worlds, 42

Past: Changing the past, 37, 157, 158

Past: Most suitable hour to schedule your trip to the past, 160

Peace of mind, 107, 111, 112

Pères du Triangle, 114, 117

Pets: Apparition of deceased pets, 67, 68

Pets: Aura is easily visible to pets, 68

Pets: Messages from dead pets, 68

Pets: Pets communicate with their human friends, 68

Pets: Pets-humans after death contact, 68

Pets: Reunited with pets in the afterlife, 43, 59

Phantom, 47

Phoenicia, 175, 231

Phoenician, 51, 149

Physical senses in the afterlife, 44

Physiognomic resemblance, 41

Planetary: Intra-planetary immigration, 51

Plasma-screen, 119

Pockets: Spatial Pockets, 42
Polyester, 96
Prisoners of war, 64
Prototype of the human body
  by the Anunnaki, 36, 57
Psychosomatic, 77
Psychotelemetry, 73
Punishments in the afterlife, 44
Pveh, 52

Q
Qafra, 150
Qal, 49
Quantum physic, 40, 42, 136,
  169

R
Ra (Godly, heavenly), 37, 149
Rabbi Loeb, 70, 72
Ram (People), 43
Rasha, 151
Reality: Alternate Realities, 91,
  94
Religious trances, 198
Religious-metaphysical
  context, 59
Remote viewing technique,
  127-132
Reptile, 52
Reptilians, general, 53, 54
Reptilians:
Reproduction/fertilization by
  Reptilians, 54
Resh, 151
Reunion in the ethereal Fourth
  dimension, 43, 44
Reunion with loved ones in the
  afterlife, 44, 45
Righteous people, 43
River Moldau, 71
Rou'am, 227

Rou'yaa (Vision), 119
Rouh-Plasma, 57

S
Scanning the body of an
  Anunnaki woman, 54
Screen: Anunnaki's Code
  Screen, 41
Screen: Plasma-screen, 119
Secret words, 52
Sefer Yezira, 71
Semitic, 51
Sensorial properties, 57
Sex: Abductees who claim to
  have had sex with Anunnaki,
  55
Sex; Anunnaki sex, 54
Sexual activity, 78
Shama Kitbah, 230
Shama, 72
Shape-shifting entities, 52
Shape-shifting: Anunnaki
  shape-shifting, 54
Sha-riit, 230
Shem Hameforash, 71, 72
Shi-bak, 230
Simulated Mars rover, 67
Sinhar Ambar Anati, 53
SinharMarduck, 59
Smoking, 78
Soul: Soul as a molecule, 58
Soul: Soul is a metaphysical
  concept, 45, 56
Soul: The mind as a soul, 45
Soul: The soul loses its portion
  in the world to come, 45
Soul: Whirling of the soul after
  death, 69
Space: Anunnaki going back
  and forth in time and space,
  38, 39, 43

309

Space: Bending space, 35, 42
Space: Fabric of space, 42
Space: General, 39, 41, 42
Space: Multiple layers of space, 39
Space: Space net, 42
Spatial memory, 178
Spatial Pockets, 42
Spatial: Mirrored spatial memory, 46
Sperms, 56
Sphere: Vibrational spheres, 37
Spheres: Different spheres, 52
Spiritual excision, 45
Stargate, 200, 235
Star-gate, 58
Stress: Eliminate stress, 147
String: String memory, 42
Subauditory, 66
Subconscience, 45, 208
Substance: Electroplasmic substance, 42
Subvocal Speech, 65, 66
Success, 107, 111, 112
Sumerian, 48, 49
Supernatural powers of the Greys, 53
Supernatural powers, general, 60
Synchronized energetic touch, 179

T

Taddeush, 71
Taharim, 42
Talamouth (A gentle synchronized energetic touch), 179
Tanakh, 45
Tanawar, 36
Tarkiz, 179

Tarquiz: Practices of Tarkiz, 40, 60
Tay Al Ard, 73
Technique: Baaniradu technique, 175-189
Technique: Baridu technique, 191-200
Technique: Bisho-barkadari "Bukadari" technique, 201-211
Technique: Cadari-Rou'yaa technique, 119-125
Technique: Chabariduri technique (Remote viewing) 127-132
Technique: Circle Technique, 147-153
Technique: Daemat-Afnah, 133-146
Technique: Da-Irat technique, 147-153
Technique: Dudurisar technique, 155-168
Technique: Godabaari, 75-81
Technique: Gomari (Gumaridu) 83-89
Technique: Gomatirach-Minzari technique, 91-106
Technique: Gomu Minzar, see Gomatirach-Minzari technique
Technique: Gubada-Adari technique, 107-117
Technique: Gudi-Ha-abri, 75, 77
Technique: Gumaridu, see Gomari
Technique: Remote viewing technique, 127-132
Technology: Extraterrestrial technology, 56
Tehillim, 69
Telekinesis, 40, 60, 73
Telepathic messages of the

dead, 48
Teleportation, general, 40, 60, 73
Teleportation: Greys' teleportation, 53
Terra, 50
Terrain, 50
Terranum, 50
Terrenum, 50
Terrestri, 50
Terrestris, 50
Theta wave, 61
Third Eye, 59
Third Eye. 220
Thoughts frequencies, 50
Time is not linear, 35,
Time, general, 41, 42
Time: Bending time, 42
Time: Fabric of time, 39, 52
Time: Going back in time, 38, 39, 43
Time: Manipulating time, 83
Time: Multiple layers of time, 39
Time: Time memory, 42
Time-sequences. 35
Tobacco, 78
Torah, 45, 52
Tourab (Terrab), 50
Tourba (Terrba), 50
Trances: Religious trances, 198
Transitory stage (Death), 43
Transmission of mind, 218
Triangle of Life, 107-117
Turbah (In Ana'kh), 50
Turkish army, 61

U

Ufologists, 51
Ufology etymology, 50, 51
Ugarit, 175

Ulema 18th degree ritual ceremony, 73
Ulema Albakr, 141
Ulema Albaydani, 54
Ulema Anusherwan Karma Ramali, 157
Ulema Ghandar. 41, 59
Ulema Govinda. 35, 73
Ulema Hanafi, 52
Ulema initiation, 43
Ulema Kira'at, 36, 43, 52, 56, 77, 93, 107, 121, 129, 137, 177, 193, 195, 203, 208
Ulema Marash, 141
Ulema Micah Naphtali Irza, 171
Ulema Mordachai "Mordechai" Ben Zvi, 37, 38, 39, 77, 83, 85, 107, 109, 114
Ulema Openheimer, 39
Ulema Rajani, 35
Ulema Sadiq Al Qaysi, 52, 58, 203
Ulema Seif Eddine Chawkat, 63
Ulema Shimon Naphtali Ben Yacob, 37
Ulema Stambouli. 59
Ulema Stephanos Lambrakis, 169, 257
Ulema use Fik'r to read the mind, 56
Ulema views: Life after death, views of the Anunnaki-Ulema, 45
Ulema W. Li, 36, 59, 153, 203
Unconsciousness, 62
Underground: Underground bases, 52
Underground: Underground environments and habitats, 52
Underground: Underground genetic labs, 52

311

Underground: Underground
military research centers, 52
United States: Employees in
the United States, 207
Universe: Fabric of the
universe, 43
Universe: General, 37, 44
Universe: Universe net, 42
Universes: Future universes, 37
Universes: Many universes, 38
Universes: Multiple universes,
37, 40, 46
Universes: Parallel universes,
37
Universes: Several layers of
universes, 39

V

Vardeh, 63
Vibes produced by one's
double, 73
Vibration: The first vibration,
75
Vibrational levels, 46, 47
Vibrational spheres, 37, 46, 139
Vibrations, general, 139
Vibrations: Lowering or
increasing vibrations, 40
Virtual three dimensional
reality, 73
Vision, 119

W

Warkah, 63
Wave: Brain waves
synchronization, 60, 61
Wave: The brain's sixth wave,
60
Waves: Development of
extraterrestrial brain's waves,
50
West Virginia, 246
Women, 49
World War One, 63
World: Another world, 39, 43
World: Creation your own
world, 93
World: Parallel worlds, 42
World: The world beyond, 42,
45

Z

Zakar, 48, 49
Zetas, 51, 53
Zinnar (Etheric Belt
surrounding our body), 178,
179
Zirufim, special Kabbalistic
formulas, 71, 72
Zooming into a Double, 191
Zooming into an astral body,
191

*** *** ***
CONTINUES IN BOOK II
The Anunnaki Ulema Forbidden Knowledge. What Your
Government And Your Church Didn't Want You To Know.

Made in the USA